# GERMAN
## BILINGUAL
## DICTIONARY

# A Beginner's Guide in Words and Pictures

**By**
## Gladys C. Lipton
*Coordinator of Foreign Language Workshops
and Director of the National F.L.E.S.\* Institute
Department of Modern Language and Linguistics
University of Maryland,
Baltimore, MA*

## Renate Losoncy
*Director, Austrian Society German School
Berwyn, PA*

BARRON'S

With affection to Thomas, Katharina,
the two Barbaras and Maria

All inquiries should be addressed to:
Barron's Educational Series, Inc.
250 Wireless Boulevard
Hauppauge, New York 11788
http://www.barronseduc.com

Library of Congress Catalog Card No. 98-70229


International Standard Book No. 0-7641-0340-7

PRINTED IN THE UNITED STATES OF AMERICA
9 8 7 6 5 4 3

# Table of Contents    Inhaltsverzeichnis

# Introduction

Learning another language can be fun for everybody! This beginner's bilingual *German-English/English-German* dictionary is a book that will be both pleasurable and functional. It will bring many hours of "thumbing-through" enjoyment to all who enjoy looking at pictures, who delight in trying to pronounce new sounds, and who like the discovery of reading words and sentences in German and English. It can be very practical, too, for those who need a rapid course in bilingual language learning for a specific purpose, such as taking a trip to a German- or English-speaking country, conducting international business, and other useful endeavors.

This dictionary will assist in the understanding of written German and English, too, and will provide an aid for the expansion of vocabulary in both languages. It will help in word games, in crossword puzzles, in writing and reading letters in German and English, and in reading signs and instructions. As a pocket dictionary, it will be invaluable in helping travelers obtain information, understand menus, and read magazines and newspapers in the foreign language-speaking country.

This edition reflects advances made in foreign/ second language learning. In particular, the authors have included many of the goals of the national foreign language standards by using words and expressions in the functional contexts of communication, comparison of target language culture(s) through cultural notes and proverbs, etc., and a list of bilingual expressions for measurement to illustrate interdisciplinary connections. This edition contains many contemporary-usage words and expressions.

The pictures in this dictionary will help you clarify word meanings and expand your vocabulary by providing associations of pictures with words and phrases. The sentences will not only illustrate the use of the specific words and expressions, but will also serve as conversational expressions

iv

when communicating in the German-speaking or English-speaking community.

*Beginning German Bilingual Dictionary* incorporates the national foreign language standards. The standards deal with five goal areas: the five C's of Communication, Cultures, Connections, Comparisons, and Communities. Users of this dictionary will find words used in different contexts of communication; there are cultural notes that will help to give dictionary users some insights into the various cultures of speakers of German; the sentences offer connections to everyday activities at home, at work, at school, at play, etc. By looking up words and expressions, dictionary users have an opportunity to compare words and expressions in German and English, as well as the differences in cultures. Finally, by seeing words and expressions in contexts in different aspects of life, dictionary users will find it easy to use German in German-speaking communities around the world.

The German pronunciation key will solve some of the mysteries of foreign language pronunciation. WELCOME TO THE WORLD OF LANGUAGES!

## *Basis of Word Selection*

The selection of words in the German listing is based on a survey of basic words and idiomatic expressions used in beginning language programs in FLES (K-8) and Level I, and simple reading materials. It may also be used at more advanced levels, when appropriate. The words in the English listing have been checked with the first thousand most frequently used words on the *Thorndike-Lorge Frequency List*, as well as with a survey of words and expressions used by young students and words found in juvenile literature. Both listings should be helpful in the development of new curricula, in preparing assessment materials, and in the writing of new textbooks and graded readers to be used on this level.

# How to Use This Dictionary

The dictionary contains approximately 1300 entries in the German-English vocabulary listing and an equal number of English words and expressions in the English-German vocabulary listing. Each German entry consists of the following (whenever possible):

1. *German word*
2. *phonemic transcription**
3. *part of speech*
4. *gender*
5. *English definition(s)*
6. *use of word in German sentence*
7. *English translation of German sentence*

Each English entry consists of the following:

1. *English word*
2. *phonemic transcription*
3. *part of speech*
4. *German definition(s)*
5. *use of word in English sentence*
6. *German translation of English sentence*

In addition, many word entries in both the English and German sections include an illustration.

---

*The *phonemic* alphabet is based on a comparative analysis of English and German sounds; it uses only Roman letters, with minimal modifications. In contrast, the International Phonetic Alphabet is based on a comparison of several languages and uses some arbitrary symbols. It has been the experience of the authors that a *phonemic* alphabet is most helpful to beginners, who need assurance in the pronunciation of a new language. The goal is to provide the beginning language student with an immediate tool for communication. As he or she continues to study and to use the language, greater refinements in vocabulary, structure, and pronunciation will be developed.

## You, the Student

*Beginning German Bilingual Dictionary* will give you pleasure as well as a functional grasp of spoken and written German.

German is easy, especially for someone who already speaks another Germanic language, such as English. Once you recognize three things that are different in German, the rest is easy. First, every noun has a gender: masculine, feminine or neuter. In the plural the gender does not matter. Second, verbs have an ending that matches (agrees with) the subject. Third, some words change when they become a (take a deep breath) direct object, because there are cases.

You can easily understand new, compound words by taking the parts and adding them up. For example, *Handschuh* sounds like a shoe for the hand, which it is: a glove! So *guess* from the context and the parts of the compound word. You know more than you think.

## Special Note

The German spelling, capitalization, and punctuation used in this dictionary correspond to the new *Rechtschreibreform* recently agreed to by all the German-speaking countries.

## Abbreviations Used in This Dictionary

| | |
|---|---|
| *fem.* | *feminine* |
| *masc.* | *masculine* |
| *neut.* | *neuter* |
| *pl.* | *plural* |

# German-English

# (Deutsch-Englisch)

# German Pronunciation Key

A few hints to the beginner on German pronunciation:

**1.** German is easy to pronounce, especially for speakers of a Germanic language such as English.

**2.** With few exceptions, if you see a letter or group of letters that belong together, pronounce everything, including the final "e."

**3.** An umlaut (¨), two dots over a vowel, indicates a sound shift, as though there were an extra "e" right after the vowel with the umlaut: for example, "ü" can also be written as "ue."

**4.** Capital letters in the phonemic symbols indicate the syllable that receives the emphasis. For example, *Gesundheit* is pronounced geh-ZUNT-hit.

## CONSONANTS

| Consonant | Phonemic Symbol | Sounds Like English Word | Example of German Word |
|---|---|---|---|
| b | b | bay | besser |
| c | ts or k | tsar, coffee | Cäsar, café |
| ch | •h• | hook | ich |
| d | d | day | Dame |
| f | f | front | Frau |
| g | g | golf | gut |
| h | h | aha | Hals |
| j | y | young | jung |
| k | k | king | König |
| l | l | elevate | leben |
| m | m | embassy | Mund |
| n | n | entire | Kind |
| p | p | pay | Pastete |
| q | q | queen | Quadrat |
| r | r | air | rot |
| s | s or z or sh or ss | song, zoo, ship, pass | Satz, sieben, Schiff, Straße |
| t | t | take | Turm |
| v | f | father | verboten |
| w | v | move | Wasser |
| x | ck | clicks | Maxime |
| y | y | typical | Yoghurt |
| z | ts | rats | Zeit |

## VOWELS

| Vowel | Phonemic Symbol | Sounds Like English Word | Example of German Word |
|-------|-----------------|--------------------------|------------------------|
| short a | a | hat | hart |
| long a | ah | father | Bahn |
| short e | e | tell | Bett |
| long e | eh | tape | gehen |
| short i | i | will | bitte |
| long i | ee | Egypt | ihn |
| short o | o | for | Ost |
| long o | oh | throw | oben |
| short u | u | full | Butter |
| long u | oo | tooth | Schuh |
| short ä | e | better | Bäcker |
| long ä | eh | fair | Mädchen |
| ö | oe | worst | böse |
| ü | ui | burn | grün |
| au | ow | house | Maus |
| äu | oi | soil | Häuser |
| ei | i | fine | drei |
| eu | oi | boy | feuer |
| ie | ee | here | spielen |

# A

**der Abend** [AH-bent] noun, masc.      **evening**
*Am Abend sehe ich manchmal fern.*
In the evening I sometimes watch television.

---

**das Abenteuer** [AH-ben-toi-er] noun, neut.    **adventure**
*Ich lese gern die Abenteuer vom Gestiefelten Kater*
I like to read the adventures of *Puss in Boots.*

---

**aber** [AH-ber] conjunction      **but, however**
*Ich möchte ins Kino gehen, aber Papa sagt, "nein!"*
I want to go to the movies, but dad says, "no!"

---

**abgemacht** [AP-ge-ma'h't] interjection    **agreed, OK**
*Gehen wir um zwölf Uhr? Abgemacht!*
Shall we leave at twelve o'clock? Agreed.

---

**abnehmen** [AP-neh-men] verb    **to remove, to take off**
*Bitte nimm deinen Hut im Haus ab, Simon.*
Please Simon, remove your hat in the house.

---

**abschreiben** [AP-shri-ben] verb      **to copy**
*Wir müssen die Sätze von der Tafel abschreiben.*
We have to copy the sentences from the blackboard.

---

**absichtlich** [AP-zi'h't-lig] adverb   **intentionally, on purpose**
*Die Katze neckt den Hund absichtlich.*
The cat teases the dog intentionally.

---

**abwesend** [AP-veh-zent] adjective    **absent, not here**
*Georg ist heute abwesend.*
George is absent today.

**acht** [AʹhˊT] adjective                                         **eight**
*Hier sind acht Knöpfe.*
Here are eight buttons.

**achtzehn** [Aʹhˊ-tsehn] adjective                          **eighteen**
*Meine Adresse ist Beethoven Straße achtzehn.*
My address is 18 Beethoven Street.

**achtzig** [Aʹhˊ-tsig] adjective                                **eighty**
*Die Hauptstadt ist fast achtzig Kilometer von hier.*
The capital is almost eighty kilometers from here.

**die Addierung** [a-DEE-rung] noun, fem.              **addition**
*Wir lernen Addierung in der Schule.*
We learn addition in school.

**die Adresse** [a-DRESS-e] noun, fem.                    **address**
*Was ist deine Adresse?*
What is your address?

**der Affe** [AF-e] noun, masc.                                 **monkey**
*Der Affe frisst eine Banane.*
The monkey is eating a banana.

**ähnlich** [ehn-liˊhˊ] adjective                       **similar, alike**
*Die Hunde sehen ähnlich aus.*
The dogs look alike.

**die Aktentasche** [AK-ten-tash-e] noun, fem.       **briefcase**
*Er vergisst seine Aktentasche oft.*
He forgets his briefcase often.

**albern** [AHL-bern] adjective      **silly**
*Dieses Hündchen ist albern.*
This puppy is silly.

---

**alle** [AL-le] pronoun      **everybody**
*Alle sind zu Hause.*
Everybody is at home.

---

**die Allee** [a-LAY] noun, fem.      **boulevard**
*Ich gehe gern auf der Allee spazieren.*
I like to walk on the boulevard.

---

**allein** [a-LIN] adjective      **alone**
*Ich bin allein in der Küche.*
I am alone in the kitchen.

---

**Alles Gute!** [AL-less GOO-te] expression      **Best wishes!**
**Congratulations!**

---

**Alles Gute zum Geburtstag!** expression
     [AL-les GOO-te tsum ge-BURTS-ta`h`]      **Happy birthday!**

---

**das Alphabet** [al-pha-BEHT] noun, neut.      **alphabet**
*Kannst du das Alphabet auf Deutsch sagen?*
Can you say the alphabet in German?

---

**als** [ALS] adverb      **as**
*Er geht zur Party als Wolf verkleidet.*
He is going to the party dressed as the wolf.

---

**alt** [ALT] adjective      **old**
*Hier ist ein altes Buch und dort eine alte Uhr.*
Here is an old book and there an old watch.

**das Alter** [AHL-ter] noun, neut.                          **age**

*Was ist das Alter von dieser Vase?*
What's the age of this vase?

---

**die Ameise** [AH-mi-zeh] noun, fem.                **ant (insect)**

*Die Ameise ist sehr klein.*
The ant is very small.

---

**amerikanisch** [ah-meh-ree-KAHN-isch] adjective   **American**

*Der Fotoapparat ist amerikanisch.*
The camera is American.

---

**die Ampel** [AHM-pel] noun, fem.                **traffic light**

*Man überquert die Straße, wenn die Ampel grün ist.*
You cross the street when the light is green.

---

**die Ananas** [AH-na-nas] noun, fem.               **pineapple**

*Die Ananas ist reif.*
The pineapple is ripe.

---

**ändern** [END-dern] verb                          **to change**

*Er ändert seine Antwort.*
He changes his answer.

---

**anfassen** [AN-fas-sen] verb                        **to touch**

*Fass die Blumen nicht an, Alf!*
Do not touch the flowers, Alf!

---

**der Anführer** [AN-fui-rer] noun, masc.              **leader**

*Nein, du spielst immer den Anführer.*
No, you are always playing the leader.

---

**angeln** [AN-geln] verb        **to fish**
*Wir angeln heute.*
We are fishing today.

---

**angenehm** [AN-ge-ne̲hm] adjective        **pleasant**
*Der Frühling ist eine angenehme Jahreszeit.*
Spring is a pleasant season.

---

**Angst haben vor** expression        **to be afraid of**
    [ANGST ha̲h-ben for]
*Hast du Angst vor dem Löwen?*
Are you afraid of the lion?

---

**ankommen** [AN-kom-en] verb        **to arrive**
*Der Zug kommt um vierzehn Uhr fünfzehn an.*
The train arrives at two fifteen in the afternoon.

---

**anmalen** [AN-ma-len] verb        **to color**
*Wir malen unser Bild mit Farbstiften an.*
We color our picture with crayons.

---

**anrufen** [AN-ro̲o̲-fen] verb        **to call up (telephone)**
*Er ruft seine Freundin an.*
He is calling his girlfriend.

---

**die Ansichtskarte** noun        **(picture) postcard**
    [AN-zi˙h˙ts-KAHR-te]
*Das sind aber schöne Ansichtskarten*
These are pretty postcards.

---

**die Antenne** [an-TEN-ne] noun        **antenna**
    (see **fernsehantenne**)

---

**die Antwort** [ANT-vort] noun                          **answer**
*Er schreibt die Antwort an die Tafel.*
He writes the answer on the blackboard.

---

**antworten** [ANT-vort-ten] verb                        **to answer**
*Das Kind antwortet schnell.*
The child answers quickly.

---

**anwesend** [AN-veh-zend] adjective                     **present**
*Erika ist nicht anwesend.*
Erica is not present.

---

**die Anzahl** [AN-tsahl] noun                    **number, quantity**
*Du hast eine große Anzahl von Büchern.*
You have a great number of books.

---

**sich anziehen** [zi'h' AN-tsee-en] verb          **to get dressed**
*Wir ziehen uns vor dem Frühstück an.*
We get dressed before breakfast.

---

**der Anzug** [AN-tsug] noun, masc.                  **suit (for man)**
**das Kostüm** [kos-tuim] noun, neut.             **suit (for woman)**
*Er trägt einen Anzug, wenn er im Büro arbeitet.*
He wears a suit when he works in the office.

*Annas Kostüme für die Arbeit sind praktisch.*
Anna's suits for work are practical.

---

**der Apfel** [AP-fell] noun, masc.                        **apple**
*Ich esse jeden Tag einen Apfel.*
I eat an apple every day.

---

**die Apotheke** [a-po-TEH-ke] noun, fem.               **pharmacy,**
                                                        **drug store**

*Die Apotheke ist bei der Post.*
The pharmacy is by the post office.

---

**der Appetit** [a-pe-TEET] noun, masc.      **appetite**
*Wir haben keinen Appetit jetzt.*
We have no appetite now.

---

**die Aprikose** [a-pree-KOH-se] noun, fem.      **apricot**
**die Marille** [ma-RILL-e]
*Ist die Aprikose reif?*
Is the apricot ripe?

---

**der April** [ap-REEL] noun, masc.      **April**
*Der April hat dreißig Tage.*
There are thirty days in April.

---

**das Aquarium** [ak-VAH-ree-um] noun, neut.      **aquarium, fish tank**

*Es gibt eine Schildkröte im Aquarium.*
There is a turtle in the aquarium.

---

**arbeiten** [AR-bi-ten] verb      **to work**
  ich arbeite          wir/sie/Sie arbeiten
  du arbeitest        ihr arbeitet
  er/sie/es arbeitet

*Dieser Mann arbeitet in seinem Haus.*
This man works in his home.

---

**die Arbeit** [AR-bit] noun      **work**
*Die Arbeit ist schwer.*
The work is hard.

---

**ärgerlich** [EHR-ger-li·h·] adverb      **angry, displeased**
**böse** [BOE-ze]
*Mutti ist böse, denn ich mache viel Lärm.*
Mom is angry because I make a lot of noise.

---

**arm** [ARM] adjective                        **poor**

*Arme Kinder haben wenig Spielzeug.*
Poor children have few toys.

---

**der Arm** [ARM] noun, masc.                **arm**

*Das Baby hat kräftige Arme.*
The baby has strong arms.

---

**die Armbanduhr** [ARM-bant-<u>oor</u>] noun, fem.   **(wrist) watch**

*Schade, meine Armbanduhr geht nicht.*
What a shame, my watch does not work.

---

**die Armee** [AR-m<u>eh</u>] noun, fem.           **army**

*Die Armee bringt Lebensmittel nach dem Hochwasser.*
The army brings food after the flood.

---

**der Arzt** [ARTST] noun, masc.      **(medical) doctor**
**die Ärztin** [ERTS-tin] noun, fem.

*Die Mutter sagt, "Du bist krank. Ich rufe den Arzt an."*
Mother says, "You are sick. I'm calling the doctor."

---

**der Ast** [AST] noun, masc.             **branch**

*Der Baum hat viele große Äste.*
The tree has many large branches.

---

**der Astronaut** [ast-ro-N<u>OWT</u>] noun, masc.    **astronaut**
**die Astronautin** [ast-ro-N<u>OW</u>-tin] noun, fem.

*Der Astronaut macht eine Reise in einem Raumschiff.*
The astronaut takes a trip in a spaceship.

---

**auch** [<u>ow</u>˙h˙] adverb                              **too, also**
*Wir haben auch einen Volkswagen.*
We also have a Volkswagen.

**auf** [<u>owf</u>] preposition                           **on, on top of**
*Das Buch liegt auf dem Tisch.*
The book is on the table.

**aufpassen** [<u>owf</u>-pas-sen] verb        **to watch out, to be careful**
*Pass auf, die Suppe ist heiß!*
Watch out, the soup is hot!

**aufstehen** [<u>owf</u>- sht<u>eh</u>-en] verb            **to get up**
*Bitte steh auf, Erik, es ist schon spät.*
Please get up, Eric, it is late.

**aufwecken** [<u>owf</u>-vek-en] verb        **to wake (someone up)**
*Der Wecker klingelt und weckt mich auf.*
The alarm rings and wakes me up.

**das Auge** [<u>ow</u>-ge] noun, neut.                     **eye**
*Mein linkes Auge tut weh.*
My left eye hurts.

**der Augenblick** [<u>ow</u>-gen-blik] noun, masc.       **moment**
*Einen Augenblick, bitte!*
Just a moment, please!

**der August** [<u>ow</u>-G<u>OOST</u>] noun, masc.         **August**
*Ist es im August heiß?*
Is it hot in August?

**aus** [<u>ows</u>] preposition                          **out of**
*Die Prinzessin sieht aus dem Fenster.*
The princess looks out the window.

**ausgeben** [OWS-geh-ben] verb     **to spend (money)**
*Er gibt nicht viel Geld aus.*
He does not spend a lot of money.

---

**ausgezeichnet** [OWS-ge-TSI'H'-net] adjective  **excellent, great**
*Der Film ist ausgezeichnet.*
The film is excellent.

---

**ausradieren** [OWS-ra-DEER-en] verb     **to erase**

*Oh, ein Fehler. Ich muss dieses Wort ausradieren.*
Oh, a mistake. I have to erase this word.

---

**sich ausruhen** [si'h' OWS-roo-en] verb     **to rest**
*Fritz ist müde. Er ruht sich jetzt aus.*
Fred is tired. He is resting now.

---

**ausschalten** [OWS-shal-ten] verb     **to turn off**
*Er schaltet das Licht immer aus, wenn er ausgeht.*
He always turns the light off when he goes out.

---

**aussehen** [OWS-seh-en] verb     **to appear, to look like**
*Die Kuh sieht freundlich aus.*
The cow looks friendly.

---

**das Aussehen** [OWS-seh-en] noun     **appearance**

*Der Tiger hat ein wildes Aussehen*
The tiger has a ferocious appearance.

---

**ausziehen** [OWS-ts<u>ee</u>-en] verb       **to take off**
*Wir ziehen unsere Schuhe an der Tür aus.*
We take our shoes off at the door.

**aus ... sein** [<u>ows</u>...<u>zin</u>] expression       **to be made of**
*Dieses Hemd ist aus Baumwolle.*
This shirt is made of cotton.

**das Auto** [<u>ow</u>-to] noun, neut.       **automobile, car**
**der Wagen** [v<u>ah</u>-gen] noun, masc.
*Unser Auto ist alt.*
Our car is old.

**im Auto fahren** expression       **to drive in a car**
    [im <u>ow</u>-to F<u>AH</u>-ren]
**mit dem Auto fahren** expression       **to drive by car**
    [mit d<u>eh</u>m <u>ow</u>-to F<u>AH</u>-ren]
**die Autobahn** noun, fem.       **expressway, turnpike**
    [<u>ow</u>-to-b<u>ah</u>n]

## B

**das Baby** [B<u>EH</u>-bee] noun, neut.       **baby**

*Maria spielt mit dem Baby.*
Maria plays with the baby.

**der Bäcker** [BEK-er] noun, masc.       **baker**
**die Bäckerin** [BEK-er-in] noun, fem.
*Der Bäcker macht Brot.*
The baker makes bread.

**die Bäckerei** [bek-er-ɪ] noun      **bakery**

*Der Bäcker ist in der Bäckerei.*
The baker is in the bakery.

---

**das Bad, das Badezimmer** noun, neut.      **bath, bathroom**
    [BAHD, BAHD-e-tsim-er]

*Wo ist das Badezimmer?*
Where is the bathroom?

---

**der Badeanzug** [BAHD-e AN-tsoog] noun, masc.    **bathing suit**
**die Badehose** [BAHD-eh HOH-ze] noun, fem.      **swim trunks**

*Ich trage einen Badeanzug am Strand.*
I wear a bathing suit at the beach.

---

**baden** [BAH-den] verb      **to bathe**

*Mutti badet das Baby.*
Mama is bathing the baby.

---

**der Bahnhof, der Hauptbahnhof** noun, masc.    **train station,**
    [BAHN-hof, HOWPT-bahn-hof]      **main train station**

*Der Zug hält nur im Bahnhof.*
The train stops only in the station.

---

**bald** [BALT] adverb      **in a little while, soon**

*Die Post kommt bald.*
The mail will come soon.

---

**der Ball** [BAL] noun, masc.      **ball**

*Der Fussball ist schwarz und weiß.*
The soccer ball is black and white.

---

**der Ballon** [bal-LOHN] noun, masc.      **balloon**

*Der Ballon ist nicht schwer.*
The balloon is not heavy.

16

**Ball spielen** [BAL shp<u>ee</u>-len] expression     **to play ball**

*Lass uns Basketball spielen!*
Let's play basketball.

---

**die Banane** [ba-N<u>AH</u>-ne] noun, fem.     **banana**

*Der Affe frisst eine Banane.*
The monkey is eating a banana.

---

**das Band** [BANT] noun, neut.     **ribbon**

*Sie trägt ein schönes Band im Haar.*
She is wearing a pretty ribbon in her hair.

---

**die Bank** [BANK] noun, fem.     **bench**

*Lass uns doch eine Bank im Park finden.*
Let's find a bench in the park.

---

**die Bank** [BANK] noun, fem.     **bank**

*Ich muss Geld wechseln. Wo ist die Bank?*
I have to change money. Where is the bank?

---

**der Bär** [B<u>EHR</u>] noun, masc.     **bear**

*Der Bär spielt im Wasser.*
The bear is playing in the water.

---

**der Bart** [BART] noun, masc.     **beard**

*Der Präsident hat keinen Bart.*
The president does not have a beard.

---

**der Baseball** noun, masc.     **baseball**

*Spielen wir doch Baseball!*
Let's play baseball.

---

**der Basketball** noun, masc.     **basketball**

*Kannst du Basketball spielen?*
Do you know how to play basketball?

---

**der Bauer** [BOW-er] noun, masc.                    **farmer**
**die Bäuerin** [BOI-er-in] noun, fem.

*Der Bauer melkt die Kuh.*
The farmer milks the cow.

---

**der Bauernhof** [BOW-ern-hof] noun, masc.          **farm**

*Gibt es hauptsächlich Gemüse
oder Tiere auf diesem Bauernhof?*
Are there mostly vegetables or animals on this farm?

---

**der Baum** [BOWM] noun, masc.                      **tree**

*Wir sitzen unter einem Baum.*
We are sitting under a tree.

---

**die Baumwolle** [BOWM-vol-le] noun                 **cotton**
*Das Kleid ist aus Baumwolle.*
The dress is made of cotton.

---

**beängstigend** [be-ENG-sti-gend] adjective      **frightening**

*Schlangen können beängstigend sein.*
Snakes can be frightening.

---

18

**beantworten** [be-ANT-vor-ten] verb      **to reply,**
**to answer (a question)**

*Das kleine Mädchen beantwortet die Frage.*
The little girl answers the question.

---

**bedeuten** [be-DOI-ten] verb        **to mean**

*Was bedeutet dieses Wort?*
What does this word mean?

---

**das Beefsteak** noun        **beefsteak**

*Ich möchte Beefsteak, bitte.*
I would like beefsteak, please.

---

**sich beeilen** [si'h' be-I-len] verb      **to hurry**

*Sie beeilen sich, denn sie sind verspätet.*
They hurry because they are late.

---

**beginnen** [be-GIN-nen] verb        **to begin**

*Der deutsche Film beginnt jetzt.*
The German film is beginning now.

---

**behalten** [be-HAL-ten] verb        **to keep**

*Ich möchte den Hund behalten.*
I want to keep the dog.

---

**bei** [BI] preposition        **by, near**

*Bremen ist bei der Nordsee.*
Bremen is near the North Sea.

---

**das Bein** [BIN] noun        **leg**

*Vögel haben zwei Beine, Katzen und Hunde haben vier Pfoten.*
Birds have two legs, cats and dogs have four paws.

---

19

**beißen** [BIS-sen] verb                          **to bite**
*Dieser Hund beißt nicht.*
This dog does not bite.

**bekommen** [be-KOM-en] verb          **to receive, to get**
*Ich bekomme einen Brief von meinen Großeltern.*
I receive a letter from my grandparents.

**sich benehmen** [si`h` be-NEH-men] verb        **to behave**
*Die Kinder benehmen sich sehr gut.*
The children are behaving very well.

**benutzen** [be-NOO-tsen] verb                    **to use**
*Sie benutzen den Bus oft.*
They use the bus often.

**das Benzin** [ben-TSEEN] noun                  **gasoline**
*Mutti sagt, "Wir haben nicht genug Benzin."*
Mama says, "We don't have enough gasoline."

**bequem** [be-kvehm] adjective              **comfortable**
*Das Sofa ist bequem.*
The sofa is comfortable.

**bereit** [be-RIT] adverb                            **ready**
*Bist du bereit? Wir sind spät dran.*
Are you ready? We are late.

**der Berg** [BERG] noun, masc.                 **mountain**
*Die Berge in der Mitte Europas sind die Alpen.*
The mountains in central Europe are the Alps.

**berühmt** [be-RUIMT] adjective                  **famous**
*Die deutsche Schauspielerin ist berühmt.*
The German actress is famous.

**beschäftigt** [be-SHEF-teegt] adjective     **occupied, busy**

*Walters ist beschäftigt jetzt. Er staubsaugt.*
Walter is occupied now. He is vacuuming.

**der Besen** [BEH-zen] noun, masc.         **broom**

*Wir kehren den Fußboden mit dem Besen.*
We sweep the floor with a broom.

**besetzt** [be-ZETST] adjective     **occupied, busy**

*Schade, Annas Telefon ist jetzt besetzt.*
Too bad, Anna's telephone is busy now.

**besonders** [be-ZON-ders] adverb     **especially**

*Ich liebe Eis, besonders Zitrone.*
I love ice cream, especially lemon.

**besser** [BES-sehr] adjective     **better**

*Ich finde, dass die Kirschen besser als die Trauben sind.*
I think that the cherries are better than the grapes.

**bestellen** [be-SHTEL-len] verb     **to order**

*Im Restaurant bestellen wir endlich das Essen.*
At the restaurant we finally order dinner.

**bestrafen** [be-SHTRAH-fen] verb     **to punish**

*Wenn ich sehr schlimm bin, bestrafen mich die Eltern.*
When I am very naughty, my parents punish me.

**besuchen** [be-ZOO-'h'en] verb     **to visit, to attend**

*Meine Familie besucht unsere Großeltern oft.*
My family visits our grandparents often.

**betrügen** [be-TRUI-gen] verb          **to cheat, to deceive**

*Im Film betrügt der Dieb die Polizistin.*
In the film, the robber deceives the policewoman.

---

**das Bett** [BET] noun, neut.                          **bed**

*Die Katze ist auf meinem Bett.*
The cat is on my bed.

---

**die Bettdecke** [BET-de-ke] noun, fem.   **blanket, bed covers**

*Die Bettdecke ist sehr warm.*
The blanket is very warm.

---

**zu Bett gehen** [tsu BET geh-en] expression     **to go to bed**

*Sie ist müde und geht jetzt zu Bett.*
She is tired and going to bed now.

---

**bewachen** [be-VA'h'-en] verb                     **to guard**

*Der Hund bewacht das Geschäft.*
The dog guards the store.

---

**bewegen** [be-VEH-gen] verb          **to move (something)**

*Er bewegt die Finger schnell, wenn er Klavier spielt.*
He moves his fingers quickly when he plays the piano.

---

**bezahlen** [be-TSAH-len] verb                        **to pay**

*Vati bezahlt das Fleisch beim Metzger.*
Dad pays for the meat at the butcher's.

---

**die Bibliothek** [bib-<u>lee</u>-oh-TEHK] noun, fem.     **library**

*Es gibt so viele Bücher in der Bibliothek.*
There are so many books in the library.

**die Biene** [BEE-ne] noun, fem.     **bee**

*Die Biene ist gefährlich.*
The bee is dangerous.

**das Biest** [<u>BEE</u>ST] noun, neut.     **beast, pest**

*Mücken sind überall Biester.*
Mosquitoes are pests everywhere.

**das Bild** [BILT] noun, neut.     **picture**

*Erstklässler malen oft Bilder.*
First graders often color pictures.

**billig** [BIL-li·h·] adjective     **cheap, inexpensive**

*Orangen sind heute billig.*
Oranges are cheap today.

**die Birne** [B<u>EE</u>R-ne] noun, fem.     **pear**

*Maria isst eine Birne zum Nachtisch.*
Mary eats a pear for dessert.

**bis** [BIS] adverb     **until**

*Er arbeitet bis sechs Uhr abends.*
He works until six o'clock in the evening.

**Bis bald!** [bis BALT] expression     **Until soon! See you soon!**

**ein Bisschen** [BISS-'h'en] noun, neut.     **a little bit, a small amount**

*Möchtest du etwas Nachtisch? Ja, ein Bisschen, bitte.*
Would you like some dessert? Yes, a little, please.

---

**Bitte!** [BIT-te] interjection              **You're welcome!**
**Bitte schön! Bitte sehr!**                  **You're very welcome!**
[BIT-te sho͟en, BIT-te zehr]

*Ich sage "Danke" und die andere Person sagt, "Bitte!"*
I say "Thank you" and the other person says, "You're welcome."

**Bitte? Wie bitte?** expression              **How's that?**
[BIT-te, VEE bit-te]                          **Beg your pardon?**

---

**bitten um** [BIT-ten u͟m] expression     **to ask for, to request**

*Das Mädchen bittet um ihr Taschengeld.*
The girl asks for her allowance.

---

**das Blatt** [BLAT] noun, neut.                          **leaf**

*Es gibt im Herbst viele Blätter auf dem Boden.*
There are many leaves on the ground in autumn.

---

**blau** [BLO͟W] adjective                                **blue**

*Der Alpensee ist blau.*
The Alpine lake is blue.

---

**bleiben** [BLI͟-ben] verb                      **to stay, remain**

*Wir bleiben zehn Tage bei der Großmutter.*
We will stay for ten days at Grandmother's house.

---

**der Bleistift** [BLI͟-shtift] noun, masc.              **pencil**

*Wir schreiben die Aufgabe mit einem Bleistift.*
We write the assignment with a pencil.

---

**blind** [BLINT] adjective            **blind**

*Beethoven war nicht blind, sondern taub.*
Beethoven was not blind, but deaf.

---

**blinde Kuh spielen** expression    **to play blind man's bluff**
    [BLIN-de KOO SHPEE-len]

*Lass uns doch blinde Kuh spielen!*
Let's play blind man's bluff.

---

**das Blitzen** [BLIT-tsen] noun, neut.       **lightning**

*Ich habe Angst vor Blitzen.*
I am afraid of lightning.

---

**blond** [BLONT] adjective           **blond**

*Sie ist blond. Sie hat blonde Haare.*
She is blond. She has blond hair.

---

**die Blume** [BLOO-me] noun, fem.       **flower**

*Viele Blumen wachsen im Garten.*
There are many flowers growing in the garden.

*Es gibt viele Blumen im Garten.*
There are many flowers in the garden.

---

**der Blumenstrauß** noun, masc.       **bouquet**
    [BLOO-men SHTROWS]

*"Hier ist ein Blumenstrauß, Gretchen," sagt er.*
"Here is a bouquet of flowers, Margie," he says.

---

**das Blut** [BLOOT] noun, neut.       **blood**

*Mein Fuß tut weh. Sieh nur das Blut!*
My foot hurts. Look at the blood.

---

**das Bockspringen** [BOK-shprin-gen] noun, neut.    **leapfrog**

*Kinder lieben Bockspringen.*
Children love leapfrog.

---

**der Boden** [BOH-den] noun, masc.    **floor, ground**

*Der Boden ist zu hart zum Pflanzen.*
The ground is too hard for planting.

---

**die Bonbons** [BON-bons] noun, pl.    **candy, sweets**

*Erik mag Bonbons.*
Eric likes candy.

---

**das Boot** [BOHT] noun, neut.    **boat**

*Ich sehe ein Boot im Wasser.*
I see a boat in the water.

---

**borgen** [BOR-gen] verb    **to borrow**

*Ich borge einen Bleistift vom Lehrer.*
I'll borrow a pencil from the teacher.

---

**böse** [BOE-ze] adjective    **angry**

*Mutti ist böse, denn ich mache viel Lärm.*
Mom is angry because I make a lot of noise.

---

**brauchen** [BROW-'h'en] verb    **to need, to use**

*Ein Astronaut braucht Sauerstoff.*
An astronaut needs oxygen.

---

**braun** [BROWN] adjective    **brown**

*Sie hat braune Augen.*
She has brown eyes.

---

**Bravo!** [BRAH-vo] interjection    **Hurray! Bravo!**

**brechen** [BRE-ʹhʹen] verb **to break**

*Pass auf! Brich das Glas nicht, Anne!*
Be careful! Don't break the glass, Anne.

**breit** [BRĪT] adjective **wide, broad**

*Der Tisch ist breit.*
The table is wide.

---

**der Brief** [BREEF] noun, masc. **letter**

*Ich stecke den Brief in den Umschlag.*
I put the letter in the envelope.

---

**der Briefkasten** [BREEF-kas-ten] noun, masc. **mailbox**

*Ich werfe den Brief in den Briefkasten.*
I am putting the letter in the mailbox.

---

**die Briefmarke** [BREEF-mar-ke] noun, fem. **stamp**

*Liechtenstein hat schöne Briefmarken.*
Liechtenstein has beautiful stamps.

---

**der Briefträger** [BREEF-treh-ger] noun, masc. **mail carrier,**
**die Briefträgerin** [BREEF-treh-ger-in] noun, fem. **letter carrier**

*Der Briefträger bringt Briefe und Pakete.*
The mail carrier brings letters and packages.

---

**die Brille** [BRIL-le] noun, fem. **(pair of) glasses**

*Ich suche meine Brille.*
I am looking for my glasses.

---

**bringen** [BRIN-gen] verb **to bring**

*Ich bringe Brote für das Picknick.*
I am bringing sandwiches for the picnic.

**die Brosche** [BRO-she] noun, fem.                **pin, brooch**

*Helenes Broche ist von ihrer Großmutter.*
Helene's brooch is from her grandmother.

---

**das Brot** [BROT] noun, neut.                    **bread**

*Das Brot ist frisch.*
The loaf of bread is fresh.

---

**das Brötchen** [BROET-'h'en] noun, neut.         **(kaiser) roll**
**die Semmel** [ZEM-mel] noun, fem.

*Susanne isst frische Brötchen zum Frühstück.*
Susan eats fresh rolls for breakfast.

---

**die Brücke** [BRUIK-e] noun, fem.                **bridge**

*Die Adenauer Brücke führt in Bonn über den Rhein.*
The Adenauer Bridge crosses the Rhine in Bonn.

---

**der Bruder** [BROO-der] noun, masc.              **brother**

*Wie viele Brüder hat Georg?*
How many brothers does George have?

---

**der Bub** [BUP] noun, masc.                      **boy**
**der Junge** [YOON-ge] noun, masc.

*Der Junge spielt mit seinen Geschwistern.*
The boy is playing with his siblings.

---

**das Buch** [BU'h'] noun, neut.                   **book**

*Wir suchen deutsche Bücher.*
We are looking for German books.

---

**bügeln** [BUI-geln] verb                         **to iron**
**das Bügeleisen** [BUI-gell-I-zen] noun, neut.    **iron**

*Das Bügeleisen ist kaputt. Er kann seine Hemden nicht
bügeln.*
The iron is not working. He cannot iron his shirts.

---

**die Burg** [BURG] noun, fem.                                    **castle**

*Die Burg ist auf einem Berg.*
The castle is on a hill.

**der Bürgersteig** [BUIR-ger-shtig] noun, masc.          **sidewalk**

*Die Kinder spielen auf dem Bürgersteig.*
The children are playing on the sidewalk.

**das Büro** [bui-ROH] noun, neut.                              **office**

*Das ist das Büro einer großen Firma.*
This is the office of a large company.

**die Bürste** [BUIR-steh] noun, fem.                          **brush**

*Die Haarbürste ist größer als die Zahnbürste.*
The hairbrush is bigger than the toothbrush.

**bürsten** [BUIR-sten] verb                              **to brush**

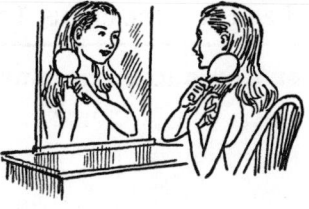

*Das Mädchen bürstet ihre Haare.*
The girl is brushing her hair.

**der Bus** [BUS] noun, masc.                                      **bus**

*Die Kinder fahren mit dem Bus.*
The children go by bus.

**die Butter** [BU-ter] noun, fem.                              **butter**

*Die Butter, bitte!*
Pass the butter, please!

## C

**das Café** [KA-feh] noun, neut.        **coffeehouse, café**

*Das Café ist gleich um die Ecke.*
The café is just around the corner.

---

**die CD** [TSEH-DEH] noun, fem.        **compact disc**
**der CD-Spieler** [TSEH-DEH shpee-ler] noun, masc.    **CD player**

*Ich habe zwei CDs, aber keinen CD-Spieler.*
I have two CDs, but no CD player.

---

**Ciao!** [CHOW] interjection        **hello, goodbye**

*Wenn ich meine Freunde sehe, sage ich "Ciao"!*
When I see my friends, I say "hello!"

---

**der Clown** [KLOWN] noun, masc.        **clown**

*Wenn ich im Zirkus bin, begrüße ich den Clown.*
When I'm at the circus, I say hello to the clown.

---

**der Computer** [komp-YOU-ter] noun, masc.        **computer**

*Hast du einen Computer?*
Do you have a computer?

## D

**das Dach** [DA·h·] noun, neut.        **roof**

*Ich sehe die Stadt vom Dach unseres Hauses.*
I see the city from the roof of our house.

---

**die Dame** [D<u>AH</u>-me] noun, fem.        **lady**
*Wer ist denn diese Dame?*
Who is this lady?

---

**der Dampfer** [DAMP-fer] noun, masc.      **steamship, ocean liner**
*Dieser Dampfer überquert den Atlantischen Ozean.*
This ocean liner crosses the Atlantic Ocean.

---

**der Damm** [DAM] noun, fem.      **avenue, boulevard**
*Ich gehe auf dem Kurfürstendamm gern spazieren.*
I like to walk on Kurfürstendamm Boulevard.

---

**Danke! Vielen Dank!** expression      **Thank you!**
[DANK-e, V<u>EEL</u>-en DANK]      **Thank you very much!**

---

**dann** [DAN] adverb      **then**
*Ich stehe auf, dann frühstücke ich.*
I get up, then I eat breakfast.

---

**Darf ich...?** [DARF i·h·...] expression      **May I...?**
*Darf ich mitkommen?*
May I come along?

---

**das** [DAS] pronoun      **that, this**
*Das ist sicher eine Überraschung!*
That is certainly a surprise!

---

**Das ist schade!** expression      **That's too bad!**
[DAS ist SH<u>AH</u>-de]

---

**das Datum** [D<u>AH</u>-tum] noun, neut.      **date**
*Was ist das Datum heute?*
What is the date today?

**die Decke** [DEK-e] noun, fem.        **cover, blanket**

*Die Decke ist sehr warm.*
The blanket is very warm.

---

**die Decke** [DEK-e] noun, fem.        **ceiling**

*Die Decke des Ballsaals ist interessant.*
The ceiling of the ballroom is interesting.

---

**denken** [DEN-ken] verb        **to think, to believe**

*Sie denkt, dass sie die Aufgabe versteht.*
She thinks that she understands the assignment.

---

**denn** [DEN] conjunction        **because**

*Ich gehe nicht zum Schwimmbad, denn ich habe keinen Badeanzug.*
I am not going to the pool, because I don't have a bathing suit.

---

**dein** [DIN] adjective        **your (informal sing.)**

*Ist das deine Katze, Anna?*
Is this your cat, Anna?

---

**der** [DER] article, masc.        **the**
**die** [DEE] fem. & pl.
**das** [DAS] neut.

*Die Kinder sind schon hungrig.*
The children are hungry already.

---

**deutsch** [DOI-TSH] adjective        **German**

*Das sind deutsche Kinder.*
These are German children.

---

**(das) Deutschland** [DOITSH-lant] noun, neut.    **Germany,**
**die Bundesrepublik Deutschland**    **Federal Republic of**
                                               **Germany**

**der Dezember** [de-TSEM-ber] noun, masc.          **December**

*Es schneit im Dezember.*
It snows in December.

---

**dick** [DIK] adjective                            **fat, thick**

*Das Baby ist nicht dick.*
The baby is not fat.

---

**der Dieb** [DEEP] noun, masc.                     **thief, robber**

*Man sucht den Dieb überall.*
They are looking for the thief everywhere.

---

**der Dienstag** [DEENS-tahg] noun, masc.           **Tuesday**

*Am Dienstag habe ich frei.*
Tuesday is my day off.

---

**dieser** [DEE-zer] adjective, masc.               **this**
**dieses** [DEE-zes] neut.
**diese** [DEE-ze] fem. & pl.

*Ich kaufe dieses Hemd, aber nicht diese Hosen.*
I will buy this shirt, but not these pants.

---

**dir** [DEER] pronoun                              **to you**

*Ich gebe dir die Antwort, Anna.*
I will give you the answer, Anna.

---

**dirigieren** [dir-i-GEER-en] verb    **to conduct (an orchestra)**

*Der Musiklehrer dirigiert das Schülerorchester.*
The music teacher conducts the pupils' orchestra.

---

**der Dollar** [DOL-lar] noun, masc.                          **dollar**

*Das Schließfach im Bahnhof kostet einen Dollar.*
The locker in the train station costs one dollar.

---

**der Domino** [DO-mee-no] noun, masc.                      **dominos**

*Meine Tante spielt Domino gut.*
My aunt plays dominos well.

---

**der Donner** [DO-ner] noun, masc.                           **thunder**

*Der Donner kommt nach dem Blitz.*
The thunder comes after the lightning.

---

**der Donnerstag** [DON-ners-tahg] noun, masc.           **Thursday**

*Am Donnerstag habe ich meinen Deutschunterricht.*
On Thursday I have my German lesson.

---

**das Dorf** [DORF] noun, neut.                               **village**

*Viele Touristen kommen in dieses Dorf.*
Many tourists come to this village.

---

**dort** [DORT] adverb                                           **there**

*Der Hammer liegt dort.*
The hammer is lying there.

---

**dort drüben** [dort DRU-ben] expression                 **over there**

*Das ist mein Vater dort drüben.*
That's my father over there.

---

**dran sein** [DRAN zin] expression          **(take a) turn, be next**

| | |
|---|---|
| ich bin dran | wir/sie/Sie sind dran |
| du bist dran | ihr seid dran |
| er/sie/es ist dran | |

*Ich bin dran.*
It is my turn.

---

**draußen** [DR<u>OWS</u>-sen] adverb                    **outside**

*Die Tiere müssen draußen bleiben.*
The animals must stay outside.

---

**der Drachen** [DRA-ʼhˑen] noun, masc.              **kite**

*Es ist windig. Spielen wir doch mit unserem Drachen.*
It is windy. Let's play with our kite.

---

**drehen** [DR<u>EH</u>-en] verb                          **to turn**

*Ich drehe das Bild zu mir.*
I turn the picture to me.

---

**drei** [DR<u>I</u>] adjective                            **three**

*Es sind drei Gläser auf dem Tisch, nicht wahr?*
There are three glasses on the table, aren't there?

---

**dreißig** [DR<u>I</u>-sig] adjective                    **thirty**

*Es ist schon zehn Uhr dreißig.*
It is already ten thirty.

---

**dreizehn** [DR<u>I</u>-ts<u>eh</u>n] adjective              **thirteen**

*Sie hat dreizehn Bücher im Rucksack.*
She has thirteen books in her backpack.

---

**du** [DU] pronoun                          **you (informal, sing.)**

*Hast du ein Telefon, Anna?*
Do you have a telephone, Anna?

---

**dumm** [DUM] adjective                               **stupid**

*Der Fuchs ist kein dummes Tier.*
The fox is not a stupid animal.

---

**dunkel** [DUN-kel] adjective                          **dark**

*Der Himmel ist dunkel vor einem Sturm.*
The sky is dark before a storm.

---

**dünn** [D<u>U</u>N] adjective                                     **thin**

*Der kleine Junge ist dünn.*
The little boy is thin.

---

**durch** [DUR͑h͑] preposition                               **through**

*Der Bär geht durch den Wald.*
The bear is walking through the forest.

---

**dürfen** [D<u>U</u>R-fen] verb                   **to be permitted, may**

| ich/er/sie/es darf | wir/sie/Sie dürfen |
| du darfst | ihr dürft |

*Ich darf ins Konzert gehen.*
I may go to the concert.

---

**Durst haben** [DURST HAH-ben] expression          **to be thirsty**

*Das Pferd hat Durst.*
The horse is thirsty.

---

**das Duzend** [DU-tsent] noun, neut.                        **dozen**

*Ein Dutzend ist zwölf Stück.*
A dozen is twelve pieces.

---

**E**

---

**die Ecke** [E-ke] noun, fem.                              **corner**

*Überqueren wir die Straße an der Ecke.*
Let's cross the street at the corner.

---

**Es ist mir egal.** expression          **It's all the same to me.**
   [es IST meer e-G<u>AH</u>L]

---

**das Ei** [I] noun, neut.                                     **egg**

*Er isst ein Ei zum Frühstück.*
He eats an egg for breakfast.

---

**eigen** [I-gen] adjective                                         **own**

*Ich habe mein eigenes Zimmer.*
I have my own room.

---

**der Eimer** [I-mer] noun, masc.                                  **bucket, pail**

*Der Bauer füllt den Eimer mit Milch.*
The farmer fills the pail with milk.

---

**ein (masc., neut.)** [IN] adjective, article                     **a, an**
**eine (fem.)** [I-ne]

*Ein Affe ist im Baum.*
A monkey is in the tree.

*Ich trage eine Krawatte.*
I am wearing a tie.

---

**Kein Eingang!** [KIN IN-gang] expression         **No entrance!**

---

**einkaufen** [IN-kow-fen] verb                                    **to shop**

| | |
|---|---|
| ich kaufe ein | wir/sie/Sie kaufen ein |
| du kaufst ein | ihr kauft ein |
| er/sie es kauft ein | |

*Meine Eltern kaufen mittwochs ein.*
My parents shop on Wednesdays.

---

**einkaufen gehen** [IN-kow-fen GEH-en] verb   **to go shopping**

*Alle gehen für Kleidung einkaufen.*
They all go shopping for clothes.

---

**einladen** [IN-lah-den] verb                  **to invite**

ich lade ein           wir/sie/Sie laden ein
du lädst ein           ihr ladet ein
er/sie/es lädt ein

*Der Mann lädt seinen Enkel in den Zoo ein.*
The man invites his grandson to the zoo.

---

**einmal** [IN-mahl] adverb             **once, one time**

---

**eins** [INS] adjective                      **one**

*Das Kind zählt: eins, zwei, drei.*
The child counts: one, two, three.

---

**einschenken** [IN-shenk-en] verb          **to pour**

*Papa schenkt den Kindern Milch ein.*
Daddy pours the children milk.

---

**einsteigen** [IN-shti-gen] verb    **to get into, enter (a vehicle)**

*Großvater steigt zuerst ins Auto ein.*
Grandfather gets into the car first.

---

**eintreten** [IN-tre-ten] verb         **to enter (a place)**

*Sie tritt in das Haus ein.*
She goes into the house.

---

**einverstanden** [IN-fer-SHATN-den] interjection     **agreed**

*Gehen wir um zwölf Uhr? Einverstanden!*
Shall we leave at twelve o'clock? Agreed.

---

**das Eis** [IS] noun, neut.                 **ice cream**

*Isst du Eis im Winter? Nein, nie!*
Do you eat ice cream in the winter? No, never!

---

**das Eisen** [I-zen] noun, neut.               **iron**

*Der Nagel ist aus Eisen.*
The nail is made of iron.

---

**der Elefant** [eh-leh-FANT] noun, masc.          **elephant**

*Der Elefant hat zwei grosse Ohren.*
The elephant has two large ears.

---

**elektrisch** [eh-LEK-trish] adjective          **electrical**

*Toll! Dort ist ein elektrisches Auto!*
Wow! There is an electric car!

**die electrische Eisenbahn** noun, fem.          **electric train**
    [eh-LEK-trish-e I-zen-bahn]

**der Elektroherd** noun, masc.          **electric stove**
    [eh-LEK-troh-hert]

**der Elektrorasenmäher** noun, masc.   **electric lawn mower**
    [eh-LEK-troh-RAZ-en-meh-er]

**der Elektroingenieur** noun, masc.          **electrical engineer**
    [eh-LEK-troh-en-je-NUIR]

---

**elf** [ELF] adjective          **eleven**

*Der Student trägt elf Bücher.*
The university student carries eleven books.

---

**die Eltern** [EL-tern] noun, pl.          **parents**

*Meine Eltern gehen morgens zur Arbeit.*
My parents go to work every morning.

---

**das Ende** [EN-de] noun, neut.          **end**

*Das Ende des Buches ist traurig.*
The end of the book is sad.

---

**endlich** [ENT-liˑhˑ] adverb　　　　　　**finally**

*Das Wetter ist endlich gut.*
The weather is finally good.

---

**eng** [ENG] adjective　　　　　　**tight, narrow**

*Dieser Mantel ist zu eng für mich.*
This coat is too tight for me.

---

**der Enkel** [EN-kel] noun, masc.　　　　**grandson**
**die Enkelin** [EN-kel-in] noun, fem.　**granddaughter**
**die Enkelkinder** [EN-kel-kin-der] noun, pl.　**grandchildren**

*Die Großeltern lieben ihre Enkelkinder.*
The grandparents love their grandchildren.

---

**die Ente** [EN-te] noun, fem.　　　　　**duck**

*Es gibt viele Enten auf dem See.*
There are many ducks in the lake.

---

**Entschuldigung!** interjection　**Excuse me! Beg your pardon!**
　　　　[ent-SHOOL-di-gung]

*Entschuldigung, wie viel Uhr ist es?*
Excuse me, what time is it?

---

**er** [EHR] pronoun　　　　　　　　　**he**

*Er liest gut.*
He reads well.

---

**die Erbsen** [EHRB-sen] noun, pl.　　　**peas**

*Die Kinder haben Erbsen gern.*
The children like peas.

---

**der Erdapfel, die Kartoffel** noun, masc.　**potato**
　　　　[EHRD-ap-fell, kar-TOF-fell]

*Peter kocht Kartoffeln.*
Peter is cooking potatoes.

---

**die Erdbeere** [EHRD-beh-re] noun, fem.          **strawberry**

*Es gibt Erdbeeren zum Nachtisch.*
There are strawberries for dessert.

---

**die Erde** [EHR-de] noun, fem.          **earth, ground**
*Wenn die Astronautin im Weltall ist, sieht sie die Erde.*
When the astronaut (fem.) is in space, she sees the earth.

---

**der Erdgeschoß** [EHRD-ge-shoss] noun, masc.   **ground floor**
*Ich wohne im Erdgeschoß.*
I live on the ground floor.

---

**die Erdnuss** [EHRD-nuss] noun, fem.          **peanut**
*Der Elefant hat Erdnüsse gern.*
The elephant likes peanuts.

---

**erfolgreich sein** expression          **to be successful**
 [er-FOLG-riˈhˈ-zin]
*Sie ist erfolgreich bei den Prüfungen.*
She is successful with the exams.

---

**sich erinnern an** expression          **to remember**
 [z-iˈhˈer-IN-ern an]
*Ich erinnere mich nicht an seinen Namen.*
I don't remember his name.

---

**erkältet sein** [er-KEL-tet zin] expression   **to have a cold**
*Ich huste und niesse, wenn ich erkältet bin.*
I cough and sneeze when I have a cold.

---

**erklären** [er-KLEH-ren] verb  **to explain**

*Sie erklärt Adam die Karte.*
She explains the map to Adam.

---

**die Erlaubnis** [er-LOWB-nis] noun, fem.  **permission**

*Wir haben Erlaubnis in der Garage zu parken.*
We have permission to park in the garage.

---

**ernst** [EHRNST] adjective  **serious**

*Es gibt einen ernsten Film im Kino.*
There is a serious film at the movies.

---

**erst** [EHRST] adjective  **first**

*Das Frühstück ist die erste Mahlzeit des Tages.*
Breakfast is the first meal of the day.

---

**erzählen** [ER-TSEH-len] verb  **to tell (a story)**

*Der Babysitter erzählt uns ein Märchen.*
The babysitter is telling us a fairy tale.

---

**es** [ES] pronoun  **it**

*Ich mag das Hemd. Ich nehme es!*
I like the shirt. I'll take it!

---

**der Esel** [EH-zel] noun, masc.  **donkey**

*Der Esel will nicht gehen.*
The donkey does not want to walk.

---

**essen** [ES-sen] verb  **to eat**

| | |
|---|---|
| ich esse | wir/sie/Sie essen |
| du/er/sie/es isst | ihr esst |

*Linda isst ein Käsebrot.*
Linda is eating an open-faced cheese sandwich.

---

**die Etage** [e-TA-zhe] noun, fem.      **floor (of building)**

*Ich wohne auf der dritten Etage.*
I live on the third floor.

---

**etwas** [ET-vas] pronoun      **something**

*Gibt es etwas zu essen?*
Is there something to eat?

---

**die Eule** [OI-le] noun, fem.      **owl**

*Man hört die Eule in der Nacht.*
One hears the owl in the night.

---

**euch** [OI-'h'] pronoun      **you, to you (pl.)**

*Ich sehe euch nicht, Sabastian und Fritz.*
Sebastian and Fred, I do not see you.

*Ich erzähle euch die Geschichte, Sebastian und Fritz.*
Sebastian and Fred, I am telling you the story.

---

## F

**die Fabrik** [fa-BRIK] noun, fem.      **factory**

*Die Fabrik ist bei unserer Wohnung.*
The factory is near our apartment.

---

**fahren** [FAH-ren] verb      **ride, drive**

| | |
|---|---|
| ich fahre | wir/sie/Sie fahren |
| du fährst | ihr fahrt |
| sie/er/es fährt | |

*Fahren wir doch nach München.*
Let's drive to Munich.

**der Fahrer** [FAHR-er] noun, masc.                    **driver**
**die Fahrerin** [FAHR-er-in] noun, fem.

*Der Fahrer hält, wenn die Ampel rot ist.*
The driver stops when the light is red.

---

**fair** [FAIR] adjective                    **fair, just**

*Aber ich bin dran. Das ist nicht fair.*
But it's my turn. It isn't fair.

---

**fallen** [FAL-len] verb                    **to fall**

*Blätter fallen vom Baum, wenn es windig ist.*
Leaves fall from the tree when it is windy.

---

**der Fallschirm** [FAL-shirm] noun, masc.                    **parachute**

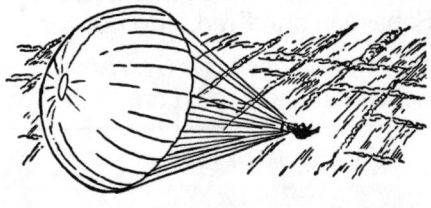

*Der Fallschirm ist offen.*
The parachute is open.

---

**die Familie** [fa-MEEL-ye] noun, fem.                    **family**

*Es gibt sieben Leute in meiner Familie.*
There are seven people in my family.

---

**fangen** [FAN-gen] verb                    **to catch**

*Hurrah! Anna fängt den Ball.*
Hurray! Anna catches the ball.

---

**Fantastisch! (Toll! Super!)** interjection                    **Great!**
[fan-TAHS-tish] (see **ausgezeichnet**)

---

**die Farbe** [FAR-be] noun, fem.       **color**
*Meine Lieblingsfarbe ist blau.*
My favorite color is blue.

---

**der Farbstift** [FARB-shtift] noun, masc.       **crayon**
*Angela hat neue Farbstifte.*
Angela has new crayons.

---

**fast** [FAST] adverb       **almost**
*Es ist fast zehn Uhr.*
It is almost ten o'clock.

---

**faul** [FOWL] adjective       **lazy**
*Schüler sind faul, wenn es warm ist.*
School kids are lazy when it is warm.

---

**der Februar** [FEH-broo-ar] noun, masc.       **February**
*Der Februar hat meistens achtundzwanzig Tage.*
February usually has twenty-eight days.

---

**die Fee** [FEH] noun, fem.       **fairy**
*Wie heißt denn die Fee im Märchen?*
What's the fairy's name in the fairy tale?

---

**der Fehler** [FEHL-er] noun, masc.       **mistake, error**
*Marta macht selten Fehler.*
Martha seldom makes mistakes.

---

**der Feiertag** [FI-er-tahg] noun, masc.       **holiday**
*Wann ist der Nationalfeiertag der Schweiz?*
When is the national holiday of Switzerland?

---

**das Feld** [FELD] noun, neut.                    **field**

*Die Schafe sind auf dem Feld.*
The sheep are in the field.

---

**das Fenster** [FEN-ster] noun, neut.            **window**

*Unser Hund sieht gern aus dem Fenster.*
Our dog likes to look out of the window.

**das Ladenfenster** noun, neut.            **shop window**
        [LAH-den-fen-ster]

---

**die Ferien** [FAIR-ee-en] noun, pl.        **(school) vacation**

*Was machst du in den Schulferien?*
What are you doing during the summer vacation?

---

**die Fernsehantenne** noun, fem.            **TV antenna**
        [FEHRN-seh-an-TEN-e]

---

**fernsehen** [FEHRN-seh-en] verb            **to watch TV**

  ich sehe fern                    wir/sie/Sie sehen fern
  du siehst fern                   ihr seht fern
  er/sie/es sieht fern

*Mein Bruder und ich sehen gern fern.*
My brother and I like to watch TV.

---

**der Fernseher** [FEHRN-seh-er] noun, masc.      **TV set**

*Unser Fernseher ist kaputt.*
Our television is broken.

---

**das Fest** [FEST] noun, neut.      **party, celebration**

*Ist das Fest am Samstag?*
Is the party on Saturday?

---

**feucht** [FOI'h'T] adjective      **moist**

*Mein Badeanzug ist noch feucht.*
My bathing suit is still damp.

---

**das Feuer** [FOI-er] noun, neut.      **fire**

*Es gibt ein Feuer im Wald.*
There is a fire in the forest.

---

**der Feuerwehrmann** noun, masc.      **fireman, fire fighter**
     [FOI-er-vehr-MAN]

*Der Feuerwehrmann ist kräftig.*
The fireman is strong.

---

**der Feuerwehrwagen** noun, masc.      **fire truck**
     [FOI-er-vehr-VAH-gen]

---

**das Fieber** [FEE-ber] noun, neut.      **fever**

*Wenn ich Fieber habe, bleibe ich zu Hause.*
When I have a fever, I stay home.

---

**der Film** [FILM] noun, masc.                    **movie, film**

*Läuft ein guter Film im Kino?*
Are they playing a good film at the movies?

*Ich muss einen Film für meine Kamera kaufen.*
I need to buy film for my camera.

**finden** [FIN-den] verb                              **to find**

*Ich finde Muscheln gern.*
I like to find shells.

**der Finger** [FEN-gair] noun, masc.                   **finger**

*Ich habe fünf Finger an jeder Hand.*
I have five fingers on each hand.

**der Fingernagel** [FIN-ger-nah-gel] noun, masc.    **fingernail**

*Ich schäme mich. Meine Fingernägel sind schmutzig.*
I am ashamed. My fingernails are dirty.

**die Firma** [FEER-ma] noun, fem.              **company, firm**

*Die Firma Bayer befindet sich hier.*
The Bayer Company is located here.

**der Fisch** [FISH] noun, masc.                         **fish**

*Es gibt viele Fische in diesem See.*
There are many fish in this lake.

**flach** [FLA'h'] adjective                             **flat**

*Ihr Dach ist flach.*
Their roof is flat.

**die Flagge** [FLAG-geh] noun, fem.                    **flag**

*Was sind die Farben der schweizer Flagge? Rot und weiß.*
What are the colors of the Swiss flag? Red and white.

**die Flasche** [FLA-sheh] noun, fem.                    **bottle**

*Pass auf! Die Flasche ist aus Glas.*
Be careful! The bottle is made of glass.

**der Flecken** [FLEK-en] noun, masc.                    **spot, stain**

*Es gibt einen Flecken auf dem Teppich.*
There is a spot on the rug.

**das Fleisch** [FLISH] noun, neut.                    **meat**

*Wir kaufen Fleisch beim Metzger.*
We buy meat at the butcher shop.

**der Fleischer (der Metzger)** noun, masc.                    **butcher**
[FLI-sher]

*Der Fleischer verkauft Fleisch.*
The butcher sells meat.

**die Fleischerei (die Metzgerei)** noun, fem.    **butcher shop**
[FLI-she-ri]

*Man kauft Fleisch und Würste in der Metzgerei.*
You go to the butcher shop to buy meat and sausage.

**die Fliege** [FL<u>EE</u>-ge] noun, fem.                **(house) fly**

*Da sind Fliegen in der Küche!*
There are flies in the kitchen!

---

**fliegen** [FL<u>EE</u>-gen] verb                              **to fly**
*Der Junge fliegt zum ersten Mal im Flugzeug.*
The boy flies in the airplane for the first time.

---

**der Flugbegleiter** noun, masc.        **flight attendant**
     [FLUG-be-gl<u>i</u>-ter]
**die Flugbegleiterin** [FLUG-be-gl<u>i</u>-ter-in] noun, fem.

*Meine Nachbarin ist Flugbegleiterin bei Lufthansa.*
My neighbor (fem.) is a flight attendant with Lufthansa.

---

**der Flügel** [FL<u>UI</u>-gel] noun, masc.                       **wing**
*Ein Vogel hat zwei Flügel.*
A bird has two wings.

---

**der Flughafen** [FLUG-h<u>ah</u>-fen] noun, masc.        **airport**

*Mein Onkel arbeitet am Flughafen.*
My uncle works at the airport.

---

**das Flugzeug** [FLUG-ts<u>oig</u>] noun, neut.            **airplane**
*Der Pilot fliegt das Flugzeug.*
The pilot flies the airplane.

---

**der Fluss** [FLUSS] noun, masc.            **river**
*Viele Brücken überqueren diesen Fluss.*
Many bridges cross this river.

---

**folgen** [FOL-gen] verb          **to follow, to obey**
*Wenn ich mich gut benehme, folge ich meinen Eltern.*
When I am well behaved, I obey my parents.

---

**das Foto** [FOH-to] noun, neut.         **photograph**
*Das ist ein Foto von dir. Hast du es gern?*
This is a photo of you. Do you like it?

---

**fortsetzen** [FORT-zet-tsen] verb         **to continue**
*Setzen wir das Spiel jetzt fort.*
Let's continue the game now.

---

**die Frage** [FRAH-ge] noun, fem.         **question**
*Die Schüler haben viele Fragen.*
The pupils have many questions.

---

**fragen** [FRAH-gen] verb         **to ask, to question**
*Sie fragt, "Was ist denn das Datum heute?"*
She asks, "What is today's date?"

---

**Frankreich** [FRANK-ri̱h˙] noun         **France**
*Wo ist die Karte von Frankreich?*
Where is the map of France?

---

**französisch** [fran-TSOEZ-ish] adjective         **French**
*Ich lese ein französisches Buch.*
I am reading a French book.

---

**die Frau** [FROW] noun, fem.         **wife, woman, Mrs., Ms.**
*Frieda möchte, daß man sie Frau Braun nennt.*
Frieda wants to be called Ms. Braun.

*Frau Albert ist unsere Lehrerin.*
Mrs. Albert is our teacher.

---

**das Fräulein** [FROI-lin] noun, neut.       **Miss**
*Sie möchte, dass man sie Fräulein
Schmidt nennt.*
She wants to be called Miss Schmidt.

---

**der Freitag** [FRI-tahg] noun, masc.       **Friday**
*Manche Leute essen Fisch am Freitag.*
Some people eat fish on Friday.

---

**der Fremde** [FREM-de] noun, masc.       **stranger**
**die Fremde** noun, fem.
**die Fremden** [FREM-den] noun, pl.
*Wer ist denn die Frau? Sie ist eine Fremde.*
Who is the woman? She is a stranger.

---

**der Freund** [FROIND] noun, masc.       **friend, boyfriend**
**die Freundin** [FROIN-din] noun, fem.       **friend, girlfriend**
*Ich bin dein Freund.*
I am your friend.

---

**frisch** [FRISH] adjective       **fresh**
*Das Brot ist frisch.*
The bread is fresh.

---

**froh** (see **glücklich**) [FROH] adjective       **happy, pleased**
**fröhlich** [FROE-li·h·] adjective       **happy, joyful**
*Sie ist fröhlich an ihrem Geburtstag.*
She is happy on her birthday.

**der Frosch** [FROSH] noun, masc.        **frog**

*Der Frosch springt ins Wasser.*
The frog jumps into the water.

**der Fuchs** [FUKS] noun, masc.        **fox**

*Der Fuchs rennt sehr schnell.*
The fox runs very fast.

**früh** [FRUI] adverb        **early**

*Der Hahn steht früh auf.*
The rooster gets up early.

**der Frühling** [FRUI-ling] noun, masc.        **spring**

*Man sieht viele Blumen im Frühling.*
You see a lot of flowers in the spring.

**das Frühstück** [FRUI-shtuik] noun, neut.        **breakfast**

*Ist das Frühstück die größte Mahlzeit?*
Is breakfast the biggest meal?

**sich (wohl) fühlen** expression        **to feel (good)**
    [zi`h` VOHL FUI-len]

*Ich fühle mich nicht wohl heute.*
I do not feel well today.

**füllen** [FÜ-len] verb       **to fill**

*Susi füllt den Kopierer mit Papier.*
Susi fills the copier with paper.

---

**fünf** [FÜNF] adjective       **five**

*Sie hat fünf Geschwister.*
She has five siblings.

---

**fünfzehn** [FÜNF-tsehn] adjective       **fifteen**

*Es gibt fünfzehn Kinder auf der Straße.*
There are fifteen children in the street.

---

**fünfzig** [FÜNF-tsig] adjective       **fifty**

*Die Flagge der Vereinigten Staaten hat fünfzig Sterne.*
The flag of the United States has fifty stars.

---

**funktionieren** [funk-tsyoh-NEER-en] verb   **to work, function**

*Funktioniert der Kühlschrank gut?*
Does the refrigerator work well?

---

**für** [FÜR] preposition       **for**

*Diese Geschenke sind für die Kinder.*
These gifts are for the children.

---

**der Fuß** [FUS] noun, masc.       **foot**
**zu Fuß gehen** [tsu FUS geh-en] expression    **to go on foot,**
                                     **to walk**

*Wir gehen zu Fuß zum Museum.*
We are going to the museum on foot.

---

**das Fußballspiel** [FUS-bal-shpeel] noun, neut.    **soccer game**

*Hier ist unsere Fußballmannschaft.*
Here is our soccer team.

**der Fußboden** [FUS-b<u>oh</u>-den] noun, masc.    **floor (of a room)**

*Der Fußboden ist aus Holz.*
The floor is made of wood.

---

## G

**die Gabel** [G<u>AH</u>-bel] noun, fem.             **fork**

*Ich esse mit Messer und Gabel.*
I eat with a knife and fork.

---

**ganz** [GANTS] adjective             **whole**

*Natürlich möchte ich den ganzen Kuchen essen.*
Of course, I would like to eat the whole cake.

---

**die Garage** [ga-R<u>AH</u>-zhe] noun, fem.      **garage**

*Das Auto ist in der Garage.*
The car is in the garage.

---

**der Garten** [GAR-ten] noun, masc.        **garden**

*Tomaten wachsen im Garten.*
Tomatoes grow in the garden.

---

**das Gas** [G<u>AHS</u>] noun, neut.             **gas**
**der Gasherd** [G<u>AHS</u>-hert] noun, masc.    **gas stove**

*Ihr habt einen Gasherd! Wir haben einen Elektroherd.*
You have a gas stove! We have an electric stove.

---

**das Gebäude** [geh-B<u>OI</u>-de] noun, neut.     **building**

*Die Gebäude in der Stadt sind sehr groß.*
The buildings in the city are very tall.

---

**geben** [GEH-ben] verb             **to give**

| | |
|---|---|
| ich gebe | wir/sie/Sie geben |
| du gibst | ihr gebt |
| er/sie/es gibt | |

*Er gibt mir die Kamera.*
He gives me the camera.

---

**ist geboren** [ge-BOHR-en] expression     **was born**

*Meine Mutter ist in der Schweiz geboren. (Sie lebt.)*
My mother was born in Switzerland. (She is living.)

**wurde geboren** [VOOR-de ge-BOHR-en] expression    **was born**

*Beethoven wurde in Bonn geboren. (Er ist jetzt tot.)*
Beethoven was born in Bonn. (He is dead now.)

---

**der Geburtstag** [ge-BURTS-tahg] noun, masc.     **birthday**

*Komm zu mir. Mein Geburtstag ist am Samstag.*
Come to my house. My birthday is on Saturday.

---

**gefährlich** [ge-FEHR-li´h´] adjective      **dangerous**

*Es ist gefährlich, mit Streichhölzern zu spielen.*
It is dangerous to play with matches.

---

**gefleckt** [ge-FLEKT] adjective         **spotted**

*Dort ist der gefleckte Hund.*
There is the spotted dog.

---

**das Geheimnis** [ge-HIM-nis] noun, neut.      **secret**

*Sag mir doch das Geheimnis!*
Tell me the secret.

---

**gegen** [GEH-gen] preposition         **against**

*Uwe stellt den Spiegel gegen die Wand.*
Uwe puts the mirror against the wall.

---

**gehen** [GEH-en] verb                          **to go, to walk**

*Wohin gehst du, Sabina? Ich gehe nach Hause.*
Where are you going, Sabina? I am going home.

**Gehen wir doch!** [GEH-en veer DO'h'] expression    **Let's go!**
**zu Bett gehen** [tsu BET GEH-en] expression    **to go to bed**

*Sie ist müde und geht jetzt zu Bett.*
Sie is tired and is going to bed now.

**zur Arbeit gehen** expression                  **to go to work**
    [tsur AR-bit GEH-en]

*Wann geht sie zur Arbeit?*
When is she going to work?

---

**die Geige** [GI-ge] noun, fem.                 **violin, fiddle**

*Die Geige liegt auf dem Klavier.*
The violin is on the piano.

---

**gelb** [GELP] adjective                         **yellow**

*Eine Zitrone ist gelb oder grün.*
A lemon is yellow or green.

---

**das Geld** [GELT] noun, neut.                  **money**

*Wie viel Geld hat er?*
How much money does he have?

---

**das Gemüse** [ge-MUI-se] noun, neut.           **vegetable**

*Rotkraut ist ein Gemüse.*
Red cabbage is a vegetable.

---

**der Gemüsehändler** (see **Lebensmittelhändler**)    **grocer**
    [ge-MUI-se HEND-ler] noun, masc.

---

**genug** [ge-NU'h'] adverb                      **enough**

*Haben Sie genug Kartoffeln, Herr Moritz?*
Do you have enough potatoes, Mr. Moritz?

---

**die Geographie** [geh-oh-gra-FEE] noun, fem.      **geography**
*Mein Lieblingsfach ist Geographie.*
My favorite subject is geography.

---

**das Gepäck** [ge-PEK] noun, neut.      **baggage**
*Das Gepäck ist fertig für die Reise.*
The baggage is ready for the trip.

---

**das Geschäft** [ge-SHEFT] noun, neut.      **shop, store**
*Schließen alle Geschäfte um sechs Uhr abends?*
Do all the shops close at six in the evening?

---

**das Geschenk** [ge-SHENK] noun, neut.      **gift, present**
*Ein Geschenk für mich? Danke!*
A gift for me? Thank you!

---

**gern haben** [GERN HAH-ben] verb      **to like**

ich habe gern                    wir/sie/Sie haben gern
du hast gern                     ihr habt gern
er/sie/es hat gern

*Mutti hat ihre Geburtstagsgeschenke gern.*
Mom likes her birthday gifts.

---

**die Geschichte** [ge-SHI'h-te] noun, fem.      **story, tale, history**
*Der Lehrer liest den Kindern eine Geschichte vor.*
The teacher is reading the children a story.

---

**das Geschirr** [ge-SHEER] noun, neut.      **dishes**
*Ich spüle das Geschirr.*
I am washing the dishes.

---

**das Gesicht** [ge-ZI'h'T] noun, neut.      **face**
*Sie wäscht ihr Gesicht.*
She is washing her face.

---

**gestern** [GES-t<u>eh</u>rn] adverb                                    **yesterday**
*Heute ist Mittwoch, gestern war Dienstag.*
Today is Wednesday, yesterday was Tuesday.

---

**die Gesundheit** [ge-ZUNT-h<u>i</u>t] noun, fem.                       **health**
*Zigaretten schaden der Gesundheit.*
Cigarettes harm your health.

**Gesundheit!** interjection              **Bless you! Stay healthy!**
      [ge-ZUNT-h<u>i</u>t]

---

**gesund und munter** expression                      **safe and sound**
      [ge-ZUNT unt MUN-ter]
*Das Kind kommt gesund und munter nach Hause.*
The child comes home safe and sound.

---

**das Gewehr** [ge-V<u>EHR</u>] noun, neut.                      **gun, weapon**
      (see **die Waffe**)

---

**gewinnen** [ge-VIN-en] verb                                    **to win**
*Markus gewinnt das Schachspiel.*
Mark wins the game of chess.

---

**es gibt** [es GIBT] expression                      **there is, there are**
*Gibt es einen Mantel für mich?*
Is there a coat for me?

---

**gießen** [G<u>EE</u>S-sen] verb                      **to pour, to water**
*Margarete gießt die Blumen.*
Margaret waters the plants.

---

**die Gitarre** [gi-T<u>AH</u>-re] noun, fem.                      **guitar**
*Ich kann Gitarre spielen.*
I can play the guitar.

**das Glas** [GLAS] noun, neut.            **glass**

*Ich stelle das Glas sorgfältig auf den Tisch.*
I put the glass on the table carefully.

**aus Glas** [<u>ows</u> GLAS] expression       **of glass**

---

**das Glatteis** [GLAT-is] noun, neut.    **ice (on pavement)**

*Es gibt Glatteis auf der Autobahn.*
There is ice on the highway.

---

**glauben** [GL<u>OW</u>-ben] verb      **to believe, to think**

*Sie glaubt, dass sie ins Konzert gehen kann.*
She thinks that she can go to the concert.

*Wir glauben Herrn Blau. Ja, wir glauben ihm.*
We believe Mr. Blau. Yes, we believe him.

---

**gleich (sofort)** [GLI̯h·] adverb    **right away, immediately**

*Wenn der Papa mich ruft, gehe ich sofort.*
When Daddy calls me, I go immediately.

---

**gleich** [GLI̯h·] adjective            **same**

*Meine Freundin und ich tragen das gleiche Kleid.*
My girlfriend and I are wearing the same dress.

---

**die Glocke** [GLO-ke] noun, fem.          **bell**

*Diese Glocke läutet um zwölf Uhr mittags.*
This bell rings at twelve o'clock noon.

---

**das Glück** [GL<u>UI</u>K] noun, neut.    **luck, good fortune**

**Viel Glück!** expression         **Good luck!**

*Vor der Prüfung sagt die Lehrerin, "Viel Glück"!*
Before the examination, the teacher (fem.) says,
"Good luck!"

---

**glücklich** [GLU̲ɪK-liˑhˑ] adjective        **happy**

**glücklich sein** [GLU̲ɪK-liˑhˑ zi̲n]
  expression               **to be happy,**
                     **to be fortunate**

*Ich bin glücklich, dass der Frühling endlich da ist.*
I am happy that spring is finally here.

---

**das Gold** [GOLT] noun, neut.          **gold**

*Johann Sutter findet Gold in Kalifornien.*
John Sutter finds gold in California.

**aus Gold** [o̲ws GOLT] expression     **(made) of gold**

*Ich möchte eine Armbanduhr aus Gold.*
I would like a watch made of gold.

**der Goldfisch** [GOLT-fish] noun, masc.    **goldfish**

---

**die Grapefruit** noun, fem.        **grapefruit**
  see **die Pampelmuse**

---

**der Grashüpfer** [GRAS-hu̲i̲p-fer]
  noun, masc.             **grasshopper**

*Das Kind will den Grashüpfer fangen.*
The child wants to catch the grasshopper.

---

**grau** [GRO̲W] adjective          **gray**

*Die Maus ist grau.*
The mouse is gray.

---

**groß** [GROS] adjective       **big, large, tall**

*Der Elefant ist sehr groß.*
The elephant is very big.

---

**die Größe** [GRŒ-se] noun, fem.                    **size**

*Im Geschäft fragt man, "Welche Größe haben Sie?"*
In the store they ask, "What is your size?"

---

**die Großeltern** [GROS-el-tern] noun, pl.          **grandparents**

**die Großmutter** [GROS-mut-ter]                    **grandmother**
    noun, fem.

**der Großvater** [GROS-fa-ter] noun, masc.          **grandfather**

*Die Großeltern lieben ihre Enkelkinder.*
The grandparents love their grandchildren.

---

**größer** [GRŒS-er] adjective                    **bigger, taller**

*Mein Bleistift ist größer als dein Bleistift.*
My pencil is bigger than your pencil.

---

**grün** [GRÜN] adjective                    **green**

*Dieser Apfel ist grün, nicht rot.*
This apple is green not red.

---

**grüne Bohnen** [grün-e BOHN-en]                    **string beans**
    expression

*Die grünen Bohnen sind reif zum Pflücken.*
The string beans are ready to be picked.

---

**der Grund** [GRUNT] noun, masc.                    **ground**
    see **der Boden**

---

**das Gummi** [GUM-mee] noun, neut.                    **rubber**

*Die Stiefel sind aus Gummi, nicht aus Leder.*
The boots are made of rubber, not of leather.

---

**(die) Gummibärchen** [GUM-mee BEHR-ˈhˈen]
    noun, pl.                    **Gummi Bears (a sweet)**

---

**der Gürtel** [GUIR-tel] noun, masc.  **belt**
*Toll! Du hast einen neuen Gürtel.*
Great! You've got a new belt.

---

**gut** [GOOT] adjective  **good**
*Es ist ein interessantes Buch; es ist ein gutes Buch.*
It is an interesting book; it is a good book.

---

**gutaussehend** [GOOT-ows-ZEH-end]  **good looking,**
  adjective  **handsome**
*Der Schauspieler ist gutaussehend und die Schauspielerin ist hübsch.*
That actor is handsome, the actress is beautiful.

---

**gutgelaunt** [GOOT-geh-lownt] adjective  **cheerful**
*Meine Schwester ist immer gutgelaunt.*
My sister is always cheerful.

---

**Gut gemacht!** [GOOT ge-MA`h`T] expression  **Well done!**

---

**gut, na gut** [GOOT, nah GOOT]  **good, fine, I understand,**
  interjection  **O.K.**
*Lass uns draußen spielen. Gut!*
Let's play outside! O.K!

---

**Guten Abend!** [GOO-ten AH-bent]  **Good evening!**
  expression

**Guten Appetit!** [GOO-ten A-peh-TEET]
  expression  **Bon appetit! Enjoy your meal!**

**Guten Morgen!** [GOO-ten MOR-gen]  **Good morning!**
  expression

**Guten Tag!** [GOO-ten TAG] expression  **Good day! Hello!**

**Gute Nacht!** [GOO-te NA`h`T]  **Good night! (going to bed)**
  expression

---

# H

**die Haare** [H<u>AH</u>-re] noun, pl.                              **hair**

*Die Kinder haben lange Haare.*
The children have long hair.

**die Haarbürste** [H<u>AH</u>R-b<u>ui</u>r-ste] noun, fem.       **hair brush**

---

**haben** [H<u>AH</u>-ben] verb                                   **to have**

| | |
|---|---|
| ich habe | wir/sie/Sie haben |
| du hast | ihr habt |
| er/sie/es hat | |

*Sie hat einen Frosch.*
She has a frog.

---

**der Hahn** [H<u>AHN</u>] noun, masc.                            **rooster**

*Der Hahn kräht früh.*
The rooster crows early.

---

**eine halbe Stunde** [<u>I</u>-ne HAL-be SHTUN-de]          **half an hour**
    expression

*Ich warte schon eine halbe Stunde auf dich!*
I have been waiting for you for half an hour already!

---

**die Hälfte** [HELF-te] noun, fem.                              **half**

*Bitte gib mir die Hälfte der Banane, Helene!*
Please give me half of the banana, Helene!

---

**Hallo!** [HA-l<u>oh</u>] expression                            **Hello!**

*Wenn ich meine Freunde sehe, sage ich "Hallo"!*
When I see my friends, I say "hello!"

---

**der Hals** [HALS] noun, masc.  **throat, neck**

*Hast du Halsschmerzen?*
Do you have a sore throat?

*Meine Großmutter sagt, "Mein Hals tut weh."*
My grandmother says, "My neck hurts."

---

**aus vollem Halse** [ows FOL-lem HALS-e]  **top of one's voice**
  expression

---

**halten** [HAL-ten] verb  **to stop, to hold**

  ich halte  wir/sie/Sie halten
  du hältst  ihr haltet
  er/sie/es hält

*Die Autos halten bei Rot.*
The cars stop at the red light.

---

**der Hammer** [HAM-mer] noun, masc.  **hammer**

*Alfred benutzt den Hammer jetzt, Frieda.*
Alfred is using the hammer now, Frieda.

---

**die Hand** [HANT] noun, fem.  **hand**

*Meine Hände sind schmutzig.*
My hands are dirty.

---

**(die) Hände schütteln** [HEND-de SHUI-teln]  **to shake hands**
  expression

*Die Gäste schütteln die Hände zum Abschied.*
The guests shake hands goodbye.

---

**die linke Hand** [dee LINK-e HANT]  **the left hand**
  expression

**die rechte Hand** [dee re'h'-te HANT]  **the right hand**
  expression

---

**der Handschuh** [HANT-shoo] noun, masc.      **glove**

*Sie trägt warme Handschuhe.*
She is wearing warm gloves.

---

**die Handtasche** [HANT-tash-e] noun, fem.    **handbag, purse**

*Die Handtasche liegt auf dem Sessel.*
The handbag is on the armchair.

---

**das Handtuch** [HANT-tuˈhˈ] noun, neut.      **towel**

*Dieses Handtuch ist sehr weich.*
This towel is very soft.

---

**hart** [HART] adjective      **hard**

*Der Stuhl ist hart.*
The chair is hard.

---

**der Hase** [HAH-ze] noun, masc.      **hare, rabbit**

*Der kleine Hase rennt und hüpft.*
The little rabbit runs and hops.

    see **das Kaninchen** [ka-NEEN-ˈhˈen]      **rabbit, bunny**
    noun, neut.

---

**hässlich** [HESS-liˈhˈ] adjective      **ugly**

*Ich mag diesen Hut nicht; er ist hässlich.*
I don't like this hat; it's ugly.

---

**hassen** [HAS-sen] verb      **to hate**

*Die Katze hasst Wasser.*
The cat hates water.

**die Hauptstadt** [H<u>OW</u>PT-shtat] noun, fem.     **capital (city)**

*Wie heißt die Hauptstadt der Vereinigten Staaten?*
What is the capital of the United States?

---

**das Haus** [H<u>OW</u>S] noun, neut.                     **house**

*Hier ist das Haus meines Onkels.*
Here is my uncle's house.

---

**die Hausaufgabe** [H<u>OW</u>S-<u>owf</u>-<u>gah</u>-be]       **homework**
        noun, neut.

*Wir machen unsere Hausaufgaben zusammen.*
We are doing our homework together.

---

**nach Hause gehen** [na˙h˙ H<u>OW</u>-ze <u>geh</u>-en]     **to go home**
        expression

*Ich gehe um vier Uhr nachmittags nach Hause.*
I go home at four o'clock in the afternoon.

---

**zu Hause sein** [tsu H<u>OW</u>-ze z<u>i</u>n] verb       **to be at home**

*Wo ist denn deine Schwester? Sie ist zu Hause.*
Where is your sister? She is at home.

---

**das Haustier** [H<u>OW</u>S-T<u>ee</u>R] noun, neut.            **pet**

*Unser Haustier, ein Meerschweinchen, ist sehr laut.*
Our pet, a guinea pig, is very loud.

---

**die Haut** [H<u>OW</u>T] noun, fem.                        **skin**

*Zu viel Sonne verbrennt die Haut.*
Too much sun burns your skin.

---

**das Heft** [HEFT] noun, neut.                        **notebook**

*Sie schreibt ihre Aufgaben in einem Heft.*
She writes her homework in a notebook.

---

---

**heiraten** [HI-rah-ten] verb        **to marry**

*Der Prinz heiratet die Prinzessin.*
The prince marries the princess.

---

**heiß** [HISS] adjective        **hot**

**Es ist heiß.** [ehs est HISS] expression        **It is hot.**

*Mir ist heiß im Sommer!*
I am hot in the summer!

---

**heißen** [HIS-sen] verb        **to be called, to be named**

| | |
|---|---|
| ich heiße | wir/sie/Sie heißen |
| du/er/sie/es heißt | ihr heißt |

*Er heißt Frank.*
He is called Frank.

---

**helfen** [HEL-fen] verb        **to help**

| | |
|---|---|
| ich helfe | wir/sie/Sie helfen |
| du hilfst | ihr helft |
| er/sie/es hilft | |

*Johanna hilft dem Mann.*
Joanna helps the man.

---

**hell** [HELL] adjective        **light, bright**

*Das ist eine helle Farbe.*
This is a light color.

---

**das Hemd** [HEMT] noun, neut.        **shirt**

*Er braucht ein sauberes Hemd.*
He needs a clean shirt.

---

**der Herbst** [HERBST] noun, masc.        **autumn, fall**

*Was hast du lieber, Frühling oder Herbst?*
Do you prefer spring or fall?

---

**der Herd** [HERT] noun, masc.               **stove**

*Der Herd ist gefährlich für kleine Kinder.*
The stove is dangerous for small children.

---

**der Herr** [HER] noun, masc.      **gentleman, mister, Mr.**

*Herr Meier ist am Telefon.*
Mr. Meier is on the telephone.

---

**das Herz** [HERTS] noun, neut.              **heart**

*Ich sehe die Herzen auf der Spielkarte!*
I see the hearts on the playing card!

---

**Herzlichen Glückwunsch zum Geburtstag!**
      [HEHRTS-le'h'en GLUIK-vunsh tsum geh-BURTS-tahg]
      expression

                                         **Happy birthday!**

---

**das Heu** [HOI] noun, neut.                    **hay**

*Das Pferd frisst Heu.*
The horse eats hay.

---

**heute** [HOI-te] adverb                    **today**

*Heute ist der vierte Oktober.*
Today is October fourth.

---

**hier** [HEER] adverb                 **here, present**

*Hier spricht man Deutsch.*
German is spoken here.

---

**Hilfe!** [HIL-fe] expression                  **Help!**

---

**der Himmel** [HIM-mel] noun, masc.          **sky, heaven**

*Wie viele Sterne gibt es im Himmel?*
How many stars are there in the sky?

---

**Himmel und Erde spielen**          **to play hopscotch**
    expression

*Lass uns Himmel und Erde spielen!*
Let's play hopscotch!

---

**hinter** [HIN-ter] preposition                **behind**

*Die Katze ist hinter dem Sofa.*
The cat is behind the sofa.

---

**hoch** [ho'h'] adjective                          **high**

| | |
|---|---|
| *hoher Berg* | high mountain |
| *hohes Gebäude* | high building |
| *hohe Kirche* | high church |

*Der österreichische Dachstein, eine Alp, ist sehr hoch.*
The Austrian Dachstein, an Alp, is very high.

---

**der Hochzeitstag**          **wedding day, anniversary**
    [HO'h'-tsits TAG] noun, masc.

*Heute ist der Hochzeitstag meiner Eltern.*
Today is my parents' wedding anniversary.

---

**hoffen** [HOF-en] verb                        **to hope**

*Er hofft, dass er einen Brief bekommt.*
He hopes that he will get a letter.

---

**höflich** [HOEF-li'h'] adjective  **polite**
*Mein Bruder ist immer höflich.*
My brother is always polite.

---

**holen** [HOH-len] verb  **to fetch, to get**
*Die Schüler holen die Bücher.*
The pupils are getting the books.

---

**das Holz** [HOLTS] noun, neut.  **wood**
*Der schöne Fußboden ist aus Holz.*
The beautiful floor is made of wood.

---

**hören** [HOER-en] verb  **to hear**
*Ich höre die Musik.*
I hear the music.

---

**die Hose** [HOH-seh] noun, fem.  **pants**

*Die Hose des Jungen ist zu lang.*
The boy's pants are too long.

---

**das Hospital** [hos-pit-TAHL] noun, neut.  **hospital**
    see **das Krankenhaus**
*Die Krankenschwester arbeitet im Krankenhaus.*
The nurse works at the hospital.

---

**das Hotel** [HOH-tel] noun, neut.  **hotel**
*Wie heißt dieses Hotel?*
What is the name of this hotel?

---

**hübsch** [H<u>UI</u>PSH] adjective      **beautiful, handsome**

*Schneewittchens Stiefmutter, die Königin, ist hübsch,
aber grausam.*
Snow White's stepmother, the queen, is beautiful but cruel.

**der Hubschrauber**             **helicopter**
     [HUP-shr<u>ow</u>-ber] noun, masc.

*Was ist es denn? Ein Hubschrauber.*
What is it? A helicopter.

**das Huhn** [H<u>OO</u>N] noun, neut.      **chicken**

*Was hast lieber, Huhn oder Fisch?*
What do you prefer, chicken or fish?

**der Hund** [HUNT] noun, masc.      **dog**

**das Hündchen** [H<u>UI</u>NT-'h'en] noun, neut.      **puppy**

*Das Hündchen sucht seine Mutter.*
The puppy looks for its mother.

**hundert** [HUN-dert] adjective      **one hundred**

*Es gibt ein hundert Leute am Strand.*
There are one hundred people at the beach.

**hungrig sein** [HUN-grig Z<u>I</u>N] expression      **to be hungry**

*Wir sind hungrig.*
We are hungry.

**Hurra!** [hoo-R<u>AH</u>] interjection      **Hurray!**

**husten** [HOO-sten] verb         **to cough**

*Ich huste, wenn ich erkältet bin.*
I cough when I have a cold.

---

**der Hut** [HOOT] noun, masc.         **hat**

*Der Schneemann trägt einen Hut.*
The snowman is wearing a hat.

---

## I

**ich** [i'h'] pronoun         **I**

*Ich spreche mit meinen Freunden.*
I am speaking with my friends.

---

**Ich bin es!** [i'h' bin ess] expression      **It's me!**

---

**die Idee** [ee-DEH] noun, fem.        **idea**

*Sie hat immer gute Ideen.*
She always has good ideas.

---

**ihm** [EEM] pronoun        **to him, to it**

*Ich will ihm dieses Buch geben.*
I want to give this book to him.

---

**ihn** [EEN] pronoun         **him**

*Ich sehe ihn später in der Bibliothek.*
I will see him later in the library.

---

**ihnen** [ee-nen] pronoun                       **to them**
**Ihnen** [ee-nen] pronoun                 **to you (formal)**

*Ich gebe ihnen eine Speisekarte.*
I give (to) them a menu.

---

**ihr** [eer] pronoun                   **you (informal, pl.)**

*Kommt ihr, Sebastian und Fritz?*
Are you coming, Sebastian and Fred?

---

**Ihr** [EER] adjective                       **your (formal)**

*Ist das Ihr Wagen, Herr und Frau Barker?*
Is this your car, Mr. and Mrs. Barker?

---

**ihr** [EER] pronoun                       **her, to her**

*Ich kenne sie schon seit einem Jahr.*
I know her for a year already.

*Ich gebe ihr meine Adresse.*
I give my address to her.

---

**ihre** [EE-RE] adjective                       **their**

*Die Mädchen ziehen ihre Schlitten.*
The girls are pulling their sleds.

---

**ihr seid** [EER zit] expression       **you are (informal, pl.)**

*Ihr seid Amerikaner?*
You are Americans?

---

**immer** [IM-mer] adverb                       **always**

*Die Blätter verändern immer im Herbst die Farbe.*
The leaves always change color in the fall.

---

**impfen** [IMP-fen] verb                    **to vaccinate**

*Der Arzt impft das Kind.*
The doctor vaccinates the child.

---

**in** [IN] preposition                    **(to go) in, to**
*Sie gehen in die Schule.*
They go to the school.

---

**in** [IN] preposition                    **(be) in**
*Sie sind jetzt in der Schule.*
They are now in the school.

---

**der Ingenieur** [in-zhen-NEER] noun, masc.     **engineer**
**die Ingenieurin** [in-zhen-NEER-in] noun, fem.
*Die Ingenieurin reist viel.*
The engineer (fem.) travels a lot.

---

**die Insel** [IN-sel] noun, fem.                    **island**

*So eine schöne Insel!*
What a beautiful island!

---

**das Insekt** [in-SEKT] noun, neut.                **insect**
*Eine Biene ist ein Insekt.*
A bee is an insect.

---

**intelligent** [in-tel-ee-GENT] adjective          **intelligent**
*Meine Tante ist sehr intelligent.*
My aunt is very intelligent.

---

**interessant** [in-ter-eh-SANT] adjective          **interesting**
*Die Nachrichten von heute sind interessant.*
Today's news is interesting.

**ist** [IST] verb                      **(he/she/it) is**
     see **sein**

**sich irren**                    **to be wrong,**
     [si'h' EER-ren] verb     **to make a mistake**
*Sie irrt sich. Wir haben die Antwort.*
She is wrong. We have the answer.

# J

**ja** [YAH] adverb                        **yes**
*Möchten die Kinder Bonbons? Ja, natürlich.*
Do the children want some candy? Yes, of course.

**die Jacke** [YA-ke] noun, fem.          **jacket**
*Mein Großvater trägt eine Hose und eine Jacke.*
My grandfather wears pants and a jacket.

**der Jäger** [YEH-ger] noun, masc.        **hunter**
**die Jägerin** [YEH-ger-in] noun, fem.     **huntress**
*Der Jäger geht in den Wald.*
The hunter goes into the forest.

**das Jahr** [YAHR] noun, neut.             **year**
*Es gibt zweiundfünfzig Wochen in einem Jahr.*
There are fifty-two weeks in a year.

**die Jahreszeit** [YAHR-es-TSIT] noun, fem.   **season**
*Welche Jahreszeit hast du am liebsten?*
Which season do you like best?

**der Januar** [YAHN-oo-ahr] noun, masc.   **January**
*Wie viele Tage gibt es im Januar?*
How many days are there in January?

**die Jeans** [JEANS] noun, pl.          **jeans**

*Meine Jeans sind in der Wäsche.*
My jeans are in the wash.

**jeder, jede, jedes**          **each, every**
     [YEH-der, YEH-de, YEH-des] adjective

**jeder Mann** (masc.)
**jede Frau** (fem.)
**jedes Kind** (neut.)

*Jeder Tourist hat eine Karte.*
Each tourist has a map.

**jemand** [YEH-mant] pronoun      **somebody, someone**

*Jemand ist im Restaurant.*
Somebody is in the restaurant.

**jung** [YUNG] adjective          **young**

*Das Hündchen ist jung.*
The puppy is young.

**der Junge, der Bub** [YUNG-e, BUP] noun, masc.     **boy**

*Der Junge spielt mit seinen Geschwistern.*
The boy is playing with his siblings.

**der Juli** [YOO-lee] noun, masc.          **July**

*Im Juli gibt es mehrere Feiertage.*
In July there are several holidays.

**der Juni** [YOO-nee] noun, masc.          **June**

*Mein Geburtstag ist im Juni.*
My birthday is in June.

# K

**der Kaffee** [KAH-feh] noun, masc.      **coffee**

*Mutti trinkt ihren Kaffee schwarz.*
Mom drinks her coffee black.

---

**der Kalender** [ka-LEND-der] noun, masc.      **calendar**

*Der Kalender hängt an der Wand.*
The calendar is hanging on the wall.

---

**kalt** [KALT] adjective      **cold**

*Er hat kaltes Wasser gern.*
He likes cold water.

---

**Es ist kalt.** [ess ist KALT] expression      **It is cold.**
**Mir ist kalt.** expression      **I am cold.**

*Mir ist so kalt heute. Ich brauche eine Jacke.*
I am so cold today. I need a jacket.

---

**die Kamera** [KAHM-er-a] noun, fem.      **camera**

*Sieh mal meine Kamera an! Sie ist neu.*
Look at my camera. It is new.

---

**der Kamin** [ka-MEEN] noun, masc.      **fireplace, chimney**

*Es gibt ein Feuer im Kamin.*
There is a fire in the fireplace.

---

**der Kamm** [KAM] noun, masc.      **comb**

*Wo ist denn mein Kamm?*
Where is my comb?

---

**kämmen** [KEM-en] verb        **to comb**

*Ich kämme meine Haare oft.*
I comb my hair often.

---

**das Känguru** [ken-goo-roo] noun, neut.        **kangaroo**

*Das Känguru ist ein sonderbares Tier.*
The kangaroo is an unusual animal.

---

**das Kaninchen**        **rabbit, bunny**
    [ka-NEEN-'h·en] noun, neut.

*Das kleine Kaninchen rennt und hüpft.*
The little rabbit runs and hops.

---

**die Karotte, die Möhre** [ka-ROHT-te] noun, fem.        **carrot**

*Kaninchen fressen Karotten.*
Rabbits eat carrots.

---

**die Karte** [KAHR-te] noun, fem.        **map, ticket**

*Hast du eine Karte von den Alpen?*
Do you have a map of the Alps?

*Ich möchte eine Karte kaufen.*
I would like to buy a ticket.

**die Landkarte** [LANT-kahr-te] noun, fem.        **map**

---

**Karten spielen**        **to play cards**
    [KAHR-ten SHPEE-len] expression

*Spielt er Karten?*
Does he play cards?

---

**die Kartoffel, Erdapfel**        **potato**
    [kar-TOF-fel, EHRD-ap-fell] noun, fem.

*Peter kocht Kartoffeln.*
Peter is cooking potatoes.

---

**das Karusell** [k<u>ah</u>-ru-SEL] noun, neut.          **merry-go-round**

*Wir reiten die Pferde auf dem Karussell.*
We ride the horses on the merry-go-round.

---

**der Käse** [KEH-se] noun, masc.                          **cheese**

*Ich möchte etwas Käse, bitte.*
I would like some cheese, please.

---

**der Kassettenrekorder**                        **tape recorder**
          [ka-SET-ten-re-KOR-der] noun, masc.

*Der Lehrer benutzt einen Kassettenrekorder im
Unterricht.*
The teacher uses a tape recorder in class.

---

**das Kätzchen** [KETS-ˈhˈen] noun, neut.                  **kitten**

*Das Kätzchen schläft viel.*
The kitten sleeps a lot.

---

**die Katze** [KATS-e] noun, fem.                              **cat**

*Die Katze spielt mit dem Mädchen.*
The cat is playing with the girl.

---

**kaufen** [K<u>OW</u>-fen] verb                              **to buy**

*Ich möchte eine Orange kaufen.*
I would like to buy an orange.

---

**kein** [KIN] adjective, masc, & neut.          **not a, not an,**
**keine** [KIN-e] fem. & pl.                    **not any, no**

*Das ist keine Katze, es ist ein Hund.*
This is not a cat, it is a dog.

*Sie haben keine Haustiere.*
They have no pets.

---

**der Keller** [KEL-er] noun, masc.          **basement, cellar**

*Der Keller ist trocken.*
The basement is dry.

---

**der Kellner** [KEL-ner] noun, masc.          **waiter**
**die Kellnerin** [KEL-ner-in] noun, fem.       **waitress**

*Der Kellner bringt die Speisekarte.*
The waiter brings the menu.

---

**kennen** [ken-nen] verb        **to know, be acquainted**
                                    **with** (person, place)

*Ich kenne seinen Onkel.*
I know his uncle.

*Sie kennen die Stadt Zürich gut.*
They know the city of Zurich well.

---

**das Kilometer** [kil-o-MEH-ter] noun, neut.     **kilometer**

*Wir wohnen zehn Kilometer (sechs Meilen) vom See entfernt.*
We live ten kilometers (six miles) from the lake.

---

**das Kind** [KINT] noun, neut.                  **child**

*Die Kinder spielen auf dem Spielplatz.*
The children are playing on the playground.

---

**der Kinderspielplatz**                  **playground**
     [KIN-der-SHPEEL-plahts] noun, masc.

*Die Rutschbahn ist auf dem Spielplatz.*
The slide is on the playground.

---

**der Kinderwagen**                                 **baby carriage**
   [KIN-der-VAH-gen] noun, masc.

*Das Baby ist im Kinderwagen.*
The baby is in the carriage.

---

**das Kinn** [KIN] noun, neut.                              **chin**

*Hier ist das Kinn der Puppe.*
Here is the doll's chin.

---

**ins Kino gehen**                          **to go to the movies**
   [ins KEE-no geh-en] expression

*Lass uns am Freitagabend ins Kino gehen.*
Let's go to the movies on Friday night.

---

**die Kirche** [KIR-'h˙e] noun, fem.                      **church**

*Die Kirche ist dort drüben an der Ecke.*
The church is over there on the corner.

---

**die Kirsche** [KIR-she] noun, fem.                      **cherry**

*Pflücken wir doch die Kirschen.*
Let us pick the cherries.

---

**das Kissen** [KIS-sen] noun, neut.                      **pillow**

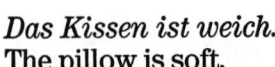

*Das Kissen ist weich.*
The pillow is soft.

---

**klagen** [KLAH-gen] verb                          **to complain**

*Er klagt wieder.*
He is complaining again.

---

**klar** [KLAHR] adjective                                               **clear**
*Das Wasser ist klar.*
The water is clear.

---

**die Klasse** [KLAS-se] noun, fem.                    **class (the students)**
*Meine Klasse hat achtundzwanzig Schüler.*
My class has twenty-eight students.

---

**das Klassenzimmer**                                            **classroom**
　　　[KLAS-sen-TSIM-mer] noun, neut.
*Wo ist das Chemieklassenzimmer?*
Where is the chemistry classroom?

---

**das Klavier** [KLA-VEER] noun, neut.                              **piano**
*Ihr habt ein Klavier? Wer spielt denn?*
You have a piano? Who plays?

---

**kleben** [KLEH-ben] verb                                  **to paste, glue**
*Er klebt das Bild in sein Album.*
He is pasting the picture in his album.

---

**das Kleid** [KLIT] noun, neut.                                    **dress**
*Johannas Kleid ist aus Seide.*
Joanna's dress is made of silk.

---

**die Kleider** [KLI-der] noun, plural               **clothing, clothes**
*Meine Kleider sind im Karton.*
My clothes are in the box.

---

**die Kleiderbürste**                                        **clothes brush**
　　　[KLI-der-BUIRS-teh] noun, fem.

---

**klein** [KLIN] adjective                                    **small, little**
*Unser Haus ist klein.*
Our house is small.

---

**das Kleingeld** [KLIN-gelt] noun, neut.     **change (money)**

*Moment, er bringt mein Kleingeld.*
Wait, he is bringing my change.

**klettern** [KLET-tern] verb     **to climb**

*Das Kätzchen klettert in den Baum.*
The kitten climbs the tree.

**klopfen** [KLOP-fen] verb     **to knock**

*Der Gast klopft an die Tür.*
The guest knocks at the door.

**klug** [KLOOG] adjective     **clever**

*Die Katze ist ein kluges Tier.*
The cat is a clever animal.

**das Knie** [KNEE] noun, neut.     **knee**

*Tut dein Knie weh? Schade!*
Do you have a sore knee? That is too bad!

**der Knopf** [KNOPF] noun, masc.     **button**

*Dieser Mantel hat nur drei Knöpfe.*
This coat has only three buttons.

**kochen** [KO'h'-en] verb     **to cook**

*Er kocht oft.*
He cooks often.

**der Kochherd, der Herd**     **stove**
      [KO'h'-hert, HERT] noun, masc.

*Der Herd ist gefährlich für kleine Kinder.*
The stove is dangerous for small children.

**der Koffer** [KOF-fer] noun, masc.     **suitcase**

*Sie trägt einen Koffer.*
She is carrying a suitcase.

**der Kofferraum**                                      **trunk (of car)**
   [KOF-fer-r<u>ow</u>m] noun, masc.

*Das Gepäck ist im Kofferraum.*
The baggage is in the trunk.

---

**der Kohl** [K<u>OH</u>L] noun, masc.                                      **cabbage**
**das Kraut** [KR<u>OW</u>T] noun, neut.

*Was hast du lieber Kraut oder Karotten?*
Do you prefer cabbage or carrots?

---

**komisch** [K<u>OH</u>-mish] adjective                                      **strange**

*Das Wetter ist komisch diesen Sommer, kühl und
regnerisch.*
The weather is strange this summer, cool and rainy.

---

**kommen** [KOM-men] verb                                      **to come**

*Meine Eltern kommen bald.*
My parents are coming soon.

---

**die Konditorei**                                      **café, coffeehouse**
   [kon-dee-tor-R<u>I</u>] noun, fem.

*Die Konditorei ist gleich um die Ecke.*
The café is just around the coner.

---

**können** [K<u>OE</u>N-nen] verb                                      **be able to, can**

   ich/er/sie/es kann     wir/sie/Sie können
   du kannst              ihr könnt

*Ich kann das Puzzle nicht machen. Es ist zu schwer.*
I can't do the puzzle. It is too difficult.

---

**der Kopfsalat** [KOPF-za-L<u>AH</u>T] noun, masc.                                      **lettuce**

*Mutti macht den Salat mit Kopfsalat.*
Mom makes the salad with lettuce.

---

**der König** [KOEN-i˙h˙] noun, masc.  **king**
**die Königin** [KOEN-ig-in] noun, fem.  **queen**

*Gibt es einen König in den Vereinigten Staaten? Nein!*
Is there a king in the United States? No!

**der Kopf** [KOPF] noun, masc.  **head**

*Der Kopf der Puppe braucht Haare.*
The doll's head needs hair.

**der Korb** [KORP] noun, masc.  **basket**

*Es gibt drei Äpfel im Korb.*
There are three apples in the basket.

**kosten** [KOS-ten] verb  **to cost**

*Wie viel kostet dieses Wörterbuch?*
How much does this dictionary cost?

**das Kostüm** [kos-TUIM] noun, neut.  **suit (for a woman)**
    see **der Anzug** [AHN-tsoog]  **suit (for a man)**
    noun, masc.

*Annas Kostüme für die Arbeit sind praktisch.*
Anna's work suits are practical.

**das Kotelett** [ko-te-LET] noun, neut.  **cutlet**

*Das Kotelett ist lecker.*
The cutlet is delicious.

**der Krach** [KRA˙h˙] noun, masc.  **noise**

*Der Donner macht einen lauten Krach.*
Thunder makes a loud noise.

**kräftig** [KREF-ti'h'] adjective          **strong**

*Der Fußballspieler ist kräftig.*
The soccer player is strong.

**krank** [KRANK] adjective          **sick, ill**

*Der Junge ist krank.*
The boy is sick.

**das Krankenhaus** [KRANK-en-h<u>ow</u>s] noun, neut.      **hospital**

*Die Krankenschwester arbeitet im Krankenhaus.*
The nurse works at the hospital.

**die Krankenschwester**             **nurse**
    [KRANK-en-SHVES-ter] noun, fem.

*Meine Nachbarin ist Krankenschwester.*
My neighbor (fem.) is a nurse.

*Das ist eine Krankenschwester.*
This is a nurse.

**der Krankenwagen**           **ambulance**
    [KRANK-en-V<u>AH</u>-gen] noun, masc.

*Der Krankenwagen ist am Krankenhaus.*
The ambulance is at the hospital.

**das Kraut** [KR<u>OW</u>T] noun, neut.        **cabbage**

*Was hast du lieber Kraut oder Karotten?*
Do you prefer cabbage or carrots?

**die Krawatte** [kra-VAT-te] noun, fem.                    **tie, cravat**

*Ich kann meine Kravatte binden.*
I can tie my tie.

---

**die Kreide** [KRI-de] noun, fem.                                    **chalk**

*Die Lehrerin sucht die Kreide.*
The teacher (fem.) looks for the chalk.

---

**der Kreis** [KRIS] noun, masc.                                    **circle**

*Sie bilden einen Kreis, um Handball zu spielen.*
They form a circle to play handball.

---

**der Kreisel** [KRI-zel] noun, masc.                                    **top**

*Ein Kreisel ist ein Spielzeug.*
A top is a toy.

---

**der Krieg** [KREEG] noun, masc.                                    **war**

*Mein Onkel ist Soldat im Krieg.*
My uncle is a soldier in the war.

---

**die Küche** [KUI'h'-e] noun, fem.                                    **kitchen**

*Die Küche ist sehr klein.*
The kitchen is very small.

---

**der Kuchen** [KU-'h'en] noun, masc.                                    **cake**

*Mutti bäckt mir einen Kuchen. Er ist so schön.*
Mom makes me a cake. It is so pretty.

---

**die Kuh** [KOO] noun, fem.                                    **cow**

*Die Kuh ist auf dem Feld.*
The cow is in the field.

---

**kühl** [KUIL] adjective                       **cool**

*Es ist kühl abends.*
It is cool in the evenings.

---

**der Kühlschrank** [KUIL-shrank] noun, masc.    **refrigerator**

*Der Kühlschrank ist in der Küche.*
The refrigerator is in the kitchen.

---

**der Kuli** [KOO-lee]
**der Kugelschreiber**                **ballpoint pen**
    [KOO-gel-SHRI-ber] noun, masc.

*Darf ich deinen Kuli borgen?*
May I borrow your ballpoint pen?

---

**sich kümmern um**        **to look after, to care for**
    [si`h` KUIM-ern] expression

| | |
|---|---|
| ich kümmre mich um | wir/sie/Sie kümmern sich um |
| du kümmerst dich um | ihr kümmert euch um |
| er/sie/es kümmert sich um | |

*Die Katze kümmert sich um ihre Kätzchen.*
The cat looks after her kittens.

---

**der Künstler** [KUINST-ler] noun, masc.       **artist**
**die Künstlerin** [KUINST-ler-in] noun, fem.

*Meine Mutter ist Künstlerin.*
My mother is an artist.

---

**der Kürbis** [KUIR-bis] noun, masc.         **pumpkin**

*Wo ist der große Kürbis?*
Where is the large pumpkin?

---

**kurz** [KURTS] adjective                **short**

*Ein Lineal ist kurz, das andere ist lang.*
One ruler is short, the other is long.

---

**die Kusine** [ku-ZEE-ne] noun, fem.        **cousin**

*Mein Vetter Paul ist elf Jahre alt und meine Kusine
Maria ist siebzehn.*
My cousin Paul is eleven years old and my cousin Mary
is seventeen.

---

**der Kuss** [KUSS] noun, masc.        **kiss**

*Ich gebe meinem kleinen Bruder einen Kuss.*
I give my little brother a kiss.

---

**küssen** [KUIS-sen] verb        **to kiss**

*Der Vater küsst das Kind.*
The father is kissing the child.

---

## L

**lächeln** [LE'h'-eln] verb        **to smile**

*Das Baby lächelt, wenn es einen Hund sieht.*
The baby smiles when he sees a dog.

---

**lachen** [LA-'h'en] verb        **to laugh**

*Sie lacht, wenn sie die Clowns sieht.*
She laughs when she sees the clowns.

---

**das Ladenfenster**        **store window**
    [LAH-den-FEN-ster] noun, neut.

---

**das Lager, das Sommerlager**        **camp, summer camp**
    [LAH-ger, ZOHM-mer-LAH-ger] noun, neut.

---

**die Lampe** [LAM-pe] noun, fem.        **lamp**

*Die Lampe ist im Wohnzimmer.*
The lamp is in the living room.

---

**sich langweilen** [ZI'h' LANG-vi-len] verb     **to be bored**
*Ich langweile mich nie.*
I am never bored.

---

**das Land** [LANT] noun, neut.     **country**
*Kanada ist ein Land.*
Canada is a country.

---

**aufs Land gehen**     **to go to the country**
     [aufs LANT geh-en] expession
*Lasst uns am Wochenende auf's Land gehen.*
Let's go to the country on the weekend.

---

**lang** [LANG] adjective     **long**
*Ihr Mantel ist lang.*
Her coat is long.

---

**langsam** [LANG-zam] adverb     **slowly**
*Die Schildkröte geht langsam.*
The turtle walks slowly.

---

**das Lamm** [LAM] noun, neut.     **lamb, young sheep**
     see **das Schaf**
**das Lammkotelett**     **lamb chop**
     [LAM-ko-te-LET] noun, neut.

---

**der Lastwagen** [LAST-vah-gen] noun, masc.     **truck**

*Der Lastwagen liefert Gemüse.*
The truck is carrying vegetables.

---

**laufen** [L_OW_-fen] verb            **to run**

ich laufe         wir/sie/Sie laufen
du läufst         ihr lauft
er/sie/es läuft

*Läuft sie auf dem Schulhof?*
Is she running on the playground?

---

**laut** [L_OWT_] adjective            **loud**

*Der Ballon platzt. Der Knall ist laut.*
The balloon breaks. The bang is loud.

---

**läuten** [L_OI_-ten] verb            **to ring**

*Das Telefon läutet oft.*
The telephone rings often.

---

**leben** [L_EH_-ben] verb            **to live**

*Leben wilde Tiere in diesem Wald?*
Do wild animals live in this forest?

---

**das Lebensmittelgeschäft**          **grocery store**
     [L_EH_-bens-mit-tel-ge-S_HEFT_] noun, neut.

*Man kauft Zucker im Lebensmittelgeschäft.*
One buys sugar in the grocery store.

---

**der Lebensmittelhändler (Gemüsehändler)**      **grocer**
     [L_EH_-bens-mit-el-H_END_-ler] noun, masc.

*Der Lebensmittelhändler verkauft Obst, Gemüse,*
*und so weiter.*
The grocer sells fruits, vegetables, and so on.

---

**lecker** [LEK-er] adjective                 **yummy, delicious**

*Die Trauben sind lecker.*
The grapes are delicious.

**das Leder** [LEH-der] noun, neut.          **leather**
**aus Leder** expression             **(made of) leather**

*Die Jacke meines Bruders ist aus Leder.*
My brother's jacket is made of leather.

**leer** [LEHR] adjective                    **empty**

*Diese Flasche ist leer.*
This bottle is empty.

**legen** [LEH-gen] verb          **to lay, to put (down)**

*Legt bitte das Besteck auf den Tisch.*
Please put the silverware on the table.

**der Lehrer** [LEH-rehr] noun, masc.        **teacher**
**die Lehrerin** [LEH-rehr-in] noun, fem.

*Wo ist denn unser Musiklehrer?*
Where is our music teacher?

**leicht** [LIHT] adjective                **light, easy**

*Der Karton ist leicht. Er ist nicht schwer.*
The box is light. It is not heavy.

**leihen** [LI-en] verb                   **to lend**

*Ich leihe dir einen Bleistift.*
I'll lend you a pencil.

**leiten** [LI-ten] verb                  **to lead**

*Sie leitet die Gruppe auf einer Wanderung.*
She leads the group on a hike.

**der Leopard** [le-oh-PARD] noun, masc.      **leopard**

*Der Leopard ist im Wald.*
The leopard is in the forest.

---

**lernen** [LER-nen] verb      **to learn, to study**
                                     **(for school test)**

*Wir lernen zusammen für den Test.*
We are studying together for the test.

---

**lesen** [LEHZ-en] verb      **to read**

  ich lese            wir/sie/Sie lesen
  du/er/sie/es liest    ihr lest

*Wir lesen in der Bibliothek.*
We read in the library.

---

**letzt** [LETST] adjective      **last**

  der/die/das letzte (masc., fem., neut.)
  die letzten (pl.)

*Das ist die letzte Briefmarke.*
This is the last stamp.

---

**die Leute** [LOI-te] noun, pl.      **people**

*Viele Leute sind im Geschäft.*
Many people are in the store.

---

**das Licht** [LI'h'T] noun, neut.      **light**

*Der Mond gibt nicht viel Licht.*
The moon does not give much light.

---

**lieb** [LEEP] adjective      **dear**
**liebe** (fem.)
**lieber** (masc.)
**liebes** (neut.)

*Mein Brief beginnt, "Liebe Mama und lieber Vati."*
My letter begins, "Dear Mom and Dad."

---

**lieben** [LEE-ben] verb         **to love**
*Ich liebe meine Katze.*
I love my cat.

---

**lieber haben**        **to prefer (to have)**
    [LEEB-er HAH-ben] expression
*Hast du den Herbst oder den Winter lieber?*
Do you prefer fall or winter?

---

**Lieblings-** [LEEB-lings] adjective    **favorite**
*Das ist mein Lieblingslied und mein Lieblingssänger.*
This is my favorite song and my favorite singer.

---

**das Lied** [LEET] noun, neut.       **song**
*Welches Lied hast du am liebsten?*
Which song do you like best?

---

**das Lineal** [lin-ne-AHL] noun, neut.    **ruler**
*Mein Lineal ist kaputt.*
My ruler is broken.

---

**die linke Hand**       **the left hand**
    [dee LIN-ke HANT] expression

---

**links** [LINKS] adverb        **left**
*Die Bäckerei ist links.*
The bakery is on the left.

---

**Auf der linken Seite!**    **On the left side!**
    [owf dair LENK-en ZI-teh] expression

---

**die Lippe** [LIP-pe] noun, fem.       **lip**
*Der Lehrer legt seinen Finger auf die Lippen.*
The teacher puts his finger to his lips.

---

**das Loch** [LO·h·] noun, neut.                              **hole**

*Ich habe ein Loch in meiner Socke.*
I have a hole in my sock.

---

**der Löffel** [LOEF-el] noun, masc.                         **spoon**

*Ich habe keinen Löffel.*
I don't have a spoon.

---

**der Lolli** [LOL-lee] noun, masc.                          **lollipop**

*Das Geburtstagskind bringt Lollis für die Klasse.*
The birthday child brings lollipops for the class.

---

**der Löwe** [LOE-ve] noun, masc.                              **lion**
**die Löwin** [LOE-vin] noun, fem.                         **lioness**

*Ein Löwe kann grausam sein.*
A lion can be ferocious.

---

**per Luftpost** [pair-LUFT-post] expression              **by airmail**

*Mein Brief geht per Luftpost.*
My letter is going by airmail.

---

**lügen** [LUI-gen] verb                                      **to lie**

*Ich lüge nicht.*
I do not lie.

---

**der Lunch** [dair LUNCH] noun, masc.                         **lunch**

*Wir essen unseren Lunch schnell.*
We eat our lunch quickly.

**lustig** [LU-stig] adjective                    **amusing, funny**
*Der Bär ist lustig.*
The bear is amusing.

## M

**machen** [MA-ʻhʻen] verb                    **to make, to do**
*Meistens macht er seine Aufgaben nach dem Abendessen.*
Usually he does his homework after dinner.

**Es macht nichts!**                          **It doesn't matter!**
   [es MAʻhʻT niʻhʻts] expression
*Du hast kein Geld? Komm sowieso, es macht nichts.*
You have no money? Come anyway, it doesn't matter.

**das Mädchen** [MEHD-ʻhʻen] noun, neut.        **girl, maiden**
*Das Mädchen trägt neue Schuhe.*
The girl is wearing new shoes.

**der Magen** [MAH-gen] noun, masc.               **stomach**
*Georg hat Magenschmerzen.*
George has a stomachache.

**die Mahlzeit** [MAHL-tsit] noun, fem.               **meal**
*Welche Mahlzeit hast du lieber.*
Which meal do you prefer?

**der Mai** [MI] noun, masc.                            **May**
*Der Mai hat einunddreißig Tage.*
May has thirty-one days.

**der Mais** [MIZ] noun, masc.                          **corn**
*Dieser Mais ist lecker.*
This corn is tasty.

**malen** [MAH-len] verb                                    **to paint**

*Seine Schwester ist Künstlerin. Sie malt gut.*
His sister is an artist. She paints well.

---

**die Mama, Mutti**                              **mama, mom**
        [MAH-mah, MUT-tee] noun, fem.

*Mama, hier sind deine Schlüssel.*
Mom, here are your keys.

---

**manchmal** [MAN'h'-mahl] adverb                    **sometimes**

*Manchmal singe ich in der Küche.*
Sometimes I sing in the kitchen.

---

**man** [MAN] pronoun                    **one, a person (subject)**

*Man muss in die Schule gehen.*
One must go to school.

---

**der Mann** [MAN] noun, masc.                    **man, husband**

*Der Mann sitzt im Park.*
The man is sitting in the park.

*Der Mann meiner Tante ist mein Onkel.*
My aunt's husband is my uncle.

---

**die Mannschaft** [MAN-shaft] noun, fem.                    **team**

*Wir spielen alle in einer Mannschaft.*
We all play on the same team.

---

**der Mantel** [MANN-tel] noun, masc.                    **coat**

*Er zieht seinen Mantel an.*
He is putting on his coat.

---

**das Märchen** [MEH-'h'en] noun, neut.        **fairy tale, story**

*Der Lehrer liest den Kindern eine Geschichte vor.*
*Es ist ein Märchen.*
The teacher is reading the children a story. It is a fairy tale.

---

**die Marille (die Aprikose)**         **apricot**
     [ma-REEL-e] noun, fem.

*Ist die Aprikose reif?*
Is the apricot ripe?

---

**der Markt** [MARKT] noun, masc.         **market**

*Man findet frisches Gemüse auf dem Markt.*
You find fresh vegetables at the market.

---

**die Marmelade**         **marmelade, jam**
     [mar-me-LAH-de] noun, fem.

*Er mag Erdbeermarmelade.*
He likes strawberry jam.

---

**der März** [MERTS] noun, masc.         **March**

*Der März kommt zwischen Februar und April.*
March is the month between February and April.

---

**die Maschine** [ma-SHEEN-e] noun, fem.       **machine**

*Der Staubsauger ist eine praktische Maschine.*
The vacuum cleaner is a useful machine.

---

**die Mauer** [MOW-er] noun, fem.         **wall**

*Die Berliner Mauer ist keine Grenze mehr.*
The Berlin Wall is no longer a border.

---

**die Maus** [MOWS] noun, fem.         **mouse**

*Es gibt Mäuse auf diesem Feld.*
There are mice in this field.

---

**der Mechaniker** [meˈhˉ-AHN-i-ker] noun, masc.   **mechanic**
**die Mechanikerin** [meˈhˉ-AHN-i-ker-in] noun, fem.

*Sie wird Automechanikerin.*
She is becoming an automobile mechanic.

---

**die Medizin** [me-dee-TSEEN] noun, fem.     **medicine**
*Die Medizin hilft dem kranken Kind.*
The medicine helps the sick child.

**das Meer** [MEHR] noun, neut.     **sea, ocean**

*Ich sehe das Meer gern.*
I like looking at the sea.

**mehr** [MEHR] adverb     **more**
*Mehr Salat, bitte!*
More salad, please.

**mehrere** [MEHR-er-re] adjective     **several**
*Es gibt mehrere Autos auf der Straße.*
There are several cars on the road.

**die Meile** [MI-le] noun, fem.     **mile**
*Meine Kusine Erika wohnt eine Meile von hier.*
My cousin Erika lives one mile from here.

**mein** [MIN] adjective     **my**
*Mein Bruder ist gutaussehend.*
My brother is handsome.

*Meine Schwester ist intelligent.*
My sister is intelligent.

*Meine Nachbaren sind freundlich.*
My neighbors are friendly.

**das Messer** [MESS-er] noun, neut.     **knife**
*Ich schneide das Brot mit dem Messer.*
I cut the bread with the knife.

**der Metzger** [METS-ger] noun, masc.         **butcher**

*Der Metzger verkauft Fleisch.*
The butcher sells meat.

---

**die Metzgerei** [mets-ger-I] noun, fem.     **butcher shop**

*Man kauft Fleisch und Würste in der Metzgerei.*
You go to the butcher shop to buy meat and sausage.

---

**mich** [MI'h'] pronoun                        **me**

*Meine Mutter ruft mich.*
My mother calls me.

---

**die Milch** [MIL'h'] noun, fem.                **milk**

*Ich trinke Milch und Vati trinkt Kaffee mit Milch.*
I drink milk and Daddy drinks coffee with milk.

---

**die Million** [mil-yohn] noun, fem.        **million**

*Wie viele CDs hast du, Anke? Eine Million!*
How many CDs do you have, Anke? A million!

---

**die Minute** [min-oo-te] noun, fem.        **minute**

*Wie viele Minuten hat eine Stunde?*
How many minutes are there in an hour?

---

**mir** [MEER] pronoun                       **to me**

*Sie gibt mir das Brot.*
She gives (to) me the bread.

---

**mischen** [MISH-en] verb                              **to mix**

*Anne mischt die Zutaten für das Brot.*
Anne is mixing the ingredients for the bread.

---

**mit** [MIT] preposition                               **with**

*Ich esse mit meiner Familie.*
I eat with my family.

---

**mit dem Auto** [mit dehm ow-to] expression            **by car**

*Er fährt mit dem Auto.*
He'll go by car.

---

**das Mitglied** [MIT-gleed] noun, neut.                **member**

*Er ist ein Mitglied der Mannschaft.*
He is a member of the team.

---

**mit der U-Bahn** [mit dair oo-bahn] expression    **by subway**

*Die Krankenschwester fährt mit der U-Bahn.*
The nurse takes the subway.

---

**der Mittag** [MIT-tahg] noun, masc.                   **noon**

---

**das Mittagessen**          **lunch, the warm midday meal**
   [MIT-tahg-es-sen] noun
**zu Mittag essen** [tsu MIT-tahg-es-sen] expression

*Wir essen zu Mittag um ein Uhr.*
We eat lunch at one o'clock.

---

**in der Mitte** [in-dair MIT-te] expression       **in the middle**

*Wo soll ich sitzen? In der Mitte.*
Where should I sit? In the middle.

---

**die Mitternacht** [MIT-ter-na·h·t] noun, fem.     **midnight**
**um Mitternacht**     **at midnight**
    [um MIT-ter-na·h·t] expression
*Um Mitternacht? Ich schlafe dann.*
At midnight? I am asleep then.

---

**der Mittwoch** [MIT-vo·h·] noun, masc.     **Wednesday**
*Am Mittwoch gehe ich zur Bibliothek.*
On Wednesday I'll go to the library.

---

**möchte** [MOE·h·-te] verb     **would like**
    ich/er/sie/es möchte     wir/sie/Sie möchten
    du möchtest     ihr möchtet
*Sie möchte Astronautin sein und auf den Mond fliegen.*
She would like to be an astronaut and go to the moon.

---

**mögen** [MOE-gen] verb     **to like, to want**
    see also **gern haben**    expression     **to like**
    ich/er/sie/es mag    wir/sie/Sie mögen
    du magst    ihr mögt
*Ich mag Märchen mit Riesen.*
I like fairy tales with giants.

---

**die Möhre** [MOE-re] noun, fem.     **carrot**
**die Karotte** [ka-ROT-te] noun, fem.
*Kaninchen fressen Möhren.*
Rabbits eat carrots.

---

**der Monat** [MOH-nat] noun, masc.     **month**

*Die Sommer Monate in Europa sind Juni, Juli, und August.*
The summer months in Europe are June, July, and August.

**der Mond** [MONT] noun, masc.      **moon**

*Die Erde hat nur einen Mond.*
The earth has only one moon.

---

**der Montag** [MON-tag] noun, masc.      **Monday**

*Was machst du am Montag?*
What are you doing on Monday?

---

**morgen** [MOR-gen] adverb      **tomorrow**

*Morgen fliege ich nach Australien.*
Tomorrow I am flying to Australia.

---

**der Morgen** [MOR-gen] noun, masc.      **morning**

*Wann stehst du jeden Morgen auf?*
What time do you get up every morning?

---

**die Mücke** [MUIK-e] noun, fem.      **mosquito**

*Da ist eine Mücke in meinem Schlafzimmer!*
There is a mosquito in my bedroom!

---

**müde** [MUI-de] adjective      **tired**

*Nach einem Tennisspiel bin ich müde.*
After a game of tennis I am tired.

---

**der Mund** [MUNT] noun, masc.      **mouth**

*Der Junge öffnet seinen Mund und singt.*
The boy opens his mouth and sings.

---

**die Murmeln** [MOOR-meln] noun, pl.      **marbles**
**Murmel spielen** expression      **to play marbles**

*Jungen spielen gern mit Murmeln.*
Boys like to play marbles.

**die Muschel** [MOOSH-el] noun, fem.         **shell**

*Ich suche Muscheln am Strand.*
I am looking for shells on the shore.

**das Museum** [moo-ZEH-um] noun, neut.     **museum**
*Das Museum ist montags geschlossen.*
The museum is closed on Mondays.

**die Musik** [moo-ZIK] noun, fem.         **music**
*Die Musik ist laut, aber angenehm.*
The music is loud, but pleasant.

**der Musiker** [MOO-zee-ker] noun, masc.    **musician**
**die Musikerin** [MOO-zee-ker-in] noun, fem.
*Der Junge möchte Musiker werden.*
The boy wants to become a musician.

**müssen** [MUIS-sen] verb         **have to, must**

  ich/er/sie/es muss    wir/sie/Sie müssen
  du musst            ihr müsst

*Du musst deine Hände waschen, Jupp.*
You must wash your hands, Joey.

**mutig** [MOO-tig] adjective     **courageous, brave**
*Feuerwehrleute sind mutig.*
Firefighters are courageous.

**die Mutter** [MUT-ter] noun, fem.       **mother**
*Heute hat meine Mutter Geburtstag.*
Today is my mother's birthday.

# N

**nach** [NA'h'] preposition                              **after, to**

*Der Oktober kommt nach dem September.*
October comes after September.

*Sie reisen nach Brasilien.*
They are traveling to Brazil.

---

**nach** [NAH'h'] expression                             **according to**

*Meinem Bruder nach schneit es morgen.*
According to my brother it is going to snow
tomorrow.

---

**der Nachbar** [NAH'h'-bar] noun, masc.                  **neighbor**
**die Nachbarin** [NAH'h'-bar-in] noun, fem.

*Mein Nachbar hilft mir.*
My neighbor helps me.

---

**der Nachmittag** [NAH'h'-mit-tag] noun, masc.          **afternoon**

*Es ist zwei Uhr am Nachmittag.*
It is 2:00 in the afternoon.

---

**nächst** [NE'h'ST] adjective                           **next**

*Der Lehrer sagt, "Nächste Woche gibt es eine
Prüfung."*
The teacher says, "Next week we are having
a test."

**die Nacht** [NA'h'T] noun, fem.          **night**

*In der Nacht kann man viele
Sterne sehen.*
At night one can see many stars.

---

**der Nachtisch** [NA'h'-tish] noun, masc.          **dessert**
*Ich nehme Bayrische Creme zum Nachtisch.*
I'll have Bavarian Creme for dessert.

---

**die Nadel** [NAH-del] noun, fem.          **needle**
**die Nähnadel** [NEH-nah-del] noun, fem.     **sewing needle**
**nähen** [NEH-en] verb          **to sew**
*Die Schüler lernen mit einer Nähnadel zu nähen.*
The students are learning to sew with a sewing needle.

---

**der Nagel** [NAH-gel] noun, masc.          **nail**
*Wir spielen mit Nägeln und einem Hammer.*
We play with nails and a hammer.

---

**der Nagel, der Fingernagel**          **fingernail**
     [NAH-gel, FIN-gair-NAH-gel] noun, masc.
**die Nagelbürste** [NAH-gel-BUIR-steh] noun, fem.     **nailbrush**
*Ich schäme mich. Meine Fingernägel sind schmutzig.*
I am ashamed. My fingernails are dirty.

---

**in der Nähe** [in-dair NEH-e] expression     **close by, near**
*Der Bahnhof ist in der Nähe.*
The train station is close by.

---

107

**der Name** [NAH-me] noun, masc.                    **name**

*Was ist sein Name?*
What is his name?

---

**nass** [NASS] adjective                    **wet**

*Mein Haar ist nass, wenn ich schwimme.*
My hair is wet when I swim.

---

**Na, so etwas!** [nah, ZOH-et-vas] expression                    **Well!**

---

**die Nation** [nah-TSYOHN] noun, fem.                    **nation**

*Es gibt viele Flaggen am Hauptsitz der Vereinten Nationen.*
There are many flags at the United Nations headquarters.

---

**national** [nah-tsyon-AHL] adjective                    **national**

*Der vierte Juli ist der Nationalfeiertag der Vereinigten Staaten.*
The Fourth of July is the national holiday of the United States.

---

**die Naturwissenschaft**                    **natural science**
        [na-TOOR-vis-sen-shaft] noun, fem.
**die Biologie, die Chemie, die Physik**

*Dieses Jahr haben wir Biologie und Physik aber keine Chemie.*
This year we have biology and physics, but no chemistry.

---

**der Naturwissenschaftler**                    **scientist**
        [na-TOOR-vis-sen-shaft-ler] noun, masc.
**die Naturwissenschaftlerin** [na-TOOR-vis-sen-shaft-ler-in]
        noun, fem.

*Gregor Mendel ist ein berühmter Naturwissenschaftler.*
Gregor Mendel is a famous scientist.

**der Nebel** [NEH-bel] noun, masc.    **fog**

*Im Nebel ist es schwer zu sehen.*
In the fog it is hard to see.

---

**neben** [NEH-ben] prepositon    **next to**

*Er steht neben dem Kind.*
He stands next to the child.

---

**der Neffe** [NEF-fe] noun, masc.    **nephew**

*Peter ist mein Neffe.*
Peter is my nephew.

---

**nehmen** [NEH-men] verb    **to take**

| | |
|---|---|
| ich nehme | wir/sie/Sie nehmen |
| du nimmst | ihr nehmt |
| er/sie/es nimmt | |

*Es regnet und sie nimmt einen Regenschirm mit.*
It is raining and she takes along an umbrella.

---

**nein** [NIN] adverb    **no**

*Bitte steh auf! Nein, ich will nicht aufstehen.*
Please get up. No, I do not want to get up.

---

**das Nest** [NEST] noun, neut.    **nest**

*Wie viele Eier siehst du im Nest?*
How many eggs do you see in the nest?

---

**nett** [NET] adjective    **nice, kind**

*Die Lehrerin ist nett. Sie schreit nicht.*
The teacher (fem.) is nice. She does not yell.

---

**neu** [NOI] adjective    **new**

*Mein Fahrrad ist neu.*
My bicycle is new.

---

**neun** [N<u>OI</u>N] adjective                                    **nine**

*Ich bin neun Jahre alt.*
I am nine years old.

---

**neunzehn** [N<u>OI</u>N-ts<u>eh</u>n] adjective                    **nineteen**

*Heute ist der neunzehnte September.*
Today is September nineteenth.

---

**neunzig** [N<u>OI</u>N-tsig] adjective                            **ninety**

*Jemand ist einundneunzig Jahre alt?*
Somebody is ninety-one years old?

---

**neugierig** [N<u>OI</u>-geer-ig] adjective                        **curious**

*Er ist neugierig und möchte das Paket öffnen.*
He is curious and would like to open the package.

---

**das Neujahr** [n<u>oi</u>-Y<u>AHR</u>] noun, neut.             **New Year's Day**

---

**nicht** [NĬhˑT] adverb                                          **not**

*Hans arbeitet jetzt nicht.*
Johnny is not working now.

---

**nichts** [NĬhˑTS] pronoun                                       **nothing**

*Er nimmt nichts zur Party.*
He takes nothing to the party.

---

**nicht mehr** [NĬhˑT M<u>EH</u>R] expression        **no more, no longer**

*Ich gehe in die Schule. Mein Bruder geht nicht mehr
in die Schule.*
I go to school. My brother no longer goes to school.

---

**Nicht? Nicht wahr!**               **Isn't that so! Isn't that true?**
       [NĬhˑT][niˑhˑt v<u>AHR</u>] expression

**die Nichte** [NIˈhˑ-te] noun, fem.      **niece**

*Sie ist the Nichte der Rechtsanwältin.*
She is the lawyer's (fem.) niece.

---

**nie** [NEE] adverb      **never**

*Ich spiele nie im Wald.*
I never play in the woods.

---

**niedrig** [NEE-drig] adjective      **low**

*Der Kinderstuhl ist niedrig.*
The children's chair is low.

---

**niesen** [NEE-zen] verb      **to sneeze**

*Ich niese, denn es ist kalt.*
I'm sneezing because it is cold.

---

**noch** [NOˈhˑ] adverb      **still**

*Ja, es ist acht Uhr und ich bin noch zu Hause.*
Yes, it is eight o'clock and I am still at home.

---

**noch ein** (masc. & neut.) [NOˈhˑin] expression   **another one**
**noch eine** (fem.) [NOˈhˑin-e]

*Hier ist noch ein Stück Brot.*
Here is another piece of bread.

---

**noch einmal** [NOˈhˑ in-mahl] expression      **once again**

*Sie erzählt uns die Geschichte noch einmal.*
She tells us the story once again.

---

**der Norden** [NOR-den] noun, masc.      **north**

*Ist der Berg im Norden oder im Süden?*
Is the mountain in the north or the south?

---

**die Note** [NOH-te] noun, fem.                    **(musical) note,**
   see **das Zeugnis**                              **grade (in school)**

*Hier sind die Noten zu Mozarts "Zauberflöte."*
Here are the musical notes for Mozart's *Magic Flute.*

*Meine Zeugnisse in Mathe sind sehr gut.*
My grades in math are very good.

---

**der November** [no-VEM-ber] noun, masc.            **November**

*Erntedankfest ist ein amerikanischer Feiertag im
November.*
Thanksgiving is an American holiday in November.

---

**notwendig** [NOHT-ven-dig] adjective               **necessary**

*Es ist notwendig, in die Schule zu gehen.*
It is necessary to go to school.

---

**die Null, die Zero** [NOOL, ZEH-ro] noun, fem.       **zero**

*Die Zahl zehn hat eine Eins und eine Null.*
The number ten has a one and a zero.

---

**die Nummer** [NUM-mer] noun, fem.                   **number**

*Was ist deine Telefonnummer?*
What is your telephone number?

---

**nur** [NUR] adverb                                   **only**

*Ich esse nur Gemüse.*
I eat only vegetables.

---

**nützlich** [NUITS-li·h·] adjective                   **useful**

*Manche Insekten sind nützlich.*
Some insects are useful.

---

## O

**ob** [OP] conjunction                                    **whether, if**

*Er fragt, ob das Geschäft offen ist.*
He asks if the shop is open.

---

**oben** [OH-ben] adverb                                    **upstairs**

*Meine Wohnung ist oben.*
My apartment is upstairs.

---

**das Obst** [OBST] noun                                    **fruit**

*Hier ist das Obst. Was hast du lieber, eine Birne
oder eine Banane?*
Here is the fruit. Do you prefer a pear or a banana?

---

**oder** [O-der] conjunction                                    **or**

*Möchtest du Brot oder ein Brötchen?*
Do you want bread or a roll?

---

**offen** [OF-fen] adjective                                    **open**

*Die Tür ist offen.*
The door is open.

---

**öffnen** [OEF-nen] verb                                    **to open**

*Sie öffnet den Brief.*
She is opening the letter.

---

**oft** [OFT] adverb                                    **often**

*Ich fahre oft mit dem Bus.*
I often go by bus.

---

**ohne** [OH-neh] preposition                                    **without**

*Sie reist oft ohne ihre Familie.*
She often travels without her family.

---

**das Ohr** [OHR] noun, neut.        **ear**

*Elefanten haben große Ohren.*
Elephants have large ears.

---

**der Oktober** [OK-t<u>oh</u>-ber] noun, masc.    **October**

*Der Oktober ist der zehnte Monat des Jahres.*
October is the tenth month of the year.

---

**das Öl** [OEL] noun, neut.        **oil**

*Die Köchin gibt das Öl in den Salat.*
The cook (fem.) adds oil to the salad.

---

**der Onkel** [ON-kel] noun, masc.        **uncle**

*Mein Onkel ist der Bruder meiner Mutter.*
My uncle is my mother's brother.

---

**die Orange** [oh-R<u>AHN</u>-zhe] noun, fem.   **orange (fruit)**

*Welche Farbe hat die Orange?*
What color is the orange?

---

**orange** [oh-R<u>AHN</u>SH] adjective    **orange (color)**

*Dieser Kürbis ist orange.*
This pumpkin is orange.

**der Orangensaft** noun, masc.     **orange juice**

---

**ordnen** [ORD-nen] verb        **to arrange,
to organize**

*Der Lehrer ordnet seine Bücher.*
The teacher arranges his books.

---

**der Osten** [OST-en] noun, masc.       **east**

*Die Sonne geht im Osten auf.*
The sun rises in the east.

**der Ozean** [OH-tseh-ahn] noun, masc.                    **ocean**

*Die Ozeane bedecken fast die ganze Erde.*
The oceans cover almost all of the world.

## P

**das Paar** [PAHR] noun, neut.                            **pair, couple**

*Ich möchte ein Paar Handschuhe kaufen.*
I would like to buy a pair of gloves.

**das Paket** [pa-KET] noun, neut.                         **package**

*Toll! Ein Paket für mich!*
Great! A package for me!

**die Pampelmuse (die Grapefruit)**                        **grapefruit**
    [PAHM-pel-moo-zeh] noun, fem.

*Die Pampelmuse ist nicht süß.*
The grapefruit is not sweet.

**Papa** [PA-pa] noun, masc.                               **daddy, dad**

*Papa sagt, "Guten Morgen!"*
Daddy says, "Good morning!"

**der Papagei** [pa-pa-GI] noun, masc.                     **parrot**

*Das ist mein Papagei.*
This is my parrot.

**das Papier** [pa-PEER] noun, neut.                       **paper**

*Ich habe noch Papier in meinem Heft.*
I still have paper in my notebook.

**das Papiertaschentuch**                    **paper handkerchief**
  [pa-PEER-TASH-en-tu'h'] noun, neut.

*Er nimmt ein Papiertaschentuch, wenn er niest.*
He uses a paper handkerchief when he sneezes.

---

**die Parade** [pah-RAH-de] noun, fem.                    **parade**

*Wir machen bei der Parade mit.*
We join in the parade.

---

**der Park** [PARK] noun, masc.                              **park**

*Es gibt einen Park in der Nähe.*
There is a park near by.

---

**die Party (die Fete, das Fest)**                          **party**
    [PAHR-tee] noun, fem.

*Ist das Fest am Samstag?*
Is the party on Saturday?

---

**Pass auf!** [pass OWF] expression          **Pay attention!**

---

**passieren** [pas-SEE-ren] verb                      **to happen**

*Was passiert jetzt?*
What is happening now?

---

**die Pastete** [pas-TEH-te] noun, fem.              **pie, pastry**

*In Amerika macht man Apfelpasteten.*
In America they make apple pies.

---

**der Pfad** [PFAHD] noun, masc.                            **path**
    see **der Weg**

---

**der Planet** [PLAHN-et] noun, masc.      **planet**

*Es gibt viele Planeten.*
There are many planets.

**pfeiffen** [PFI-fen] verb      **to whistle**

*Sie pfeift, denn sie ist froh.*
She whistles because she is happy.

**das Pferd** [PFEHRD] noun, neut.      **horse**

*Der Junge reitet ein Pferd.*
The boy is riding a horse.

**der Pfirsich** [PFEER-zi'h'] noun, masc.      **peach**

*Der Pfirsicht ist noch nicht reif.*
The peach is not ripe yet.

**die Pflanze** [PFLAHN-ze] noun, fem.      **plant**

*Es gibt Pflanzen in unserem Klassenzimmer.*
There are plants in our classroom.

**pflücken** [PFLUIK-en] verb      **to pick**

*Sie pflücken Kirschen heute.*
They are picking cherries today.

**die Pfote** [PFOH-te] noun, fem.      **paw**

*Der Löwe hat vier Pfoten.*
The lion has four paws.

**das Picknick** [PIK-nik] noun, neut.      **picnic**

*Wir haben ein Picknick auf dem Land.*
We'll have a picnic in the country.

**der Pilot** [pee-LOHT] noun, masc.      **pilot**
**die Pilotin** [pee-LOHT-in] noun, fem.

*Die Pilotin fliegt das Flugzeug.*
The pilot (fem.) flies the airplane.

---

**die Pistole** [pees-TOH-le] noun, fem. ·    **pistol**

*Eine Pistole ist gefährlich.*
A pistol is dangerous.

---

**das Plätzchen** [PLETS-'h'en] noun, neut.    **cookie**

*Sie bäckt viele Plätzchen.*
She bakes a lot of cookies.

---

**plötzlich** [PLOETS-li'h'] adverb      **suddenly**

*Plötzlich sind die Lichter aus.*
Suddenly the lights go out.

---

**der Polizist** [po-lee-TSIST] noun, masc.    **policeman**
**die Polizistin** [po-lee-TSIST-tin] noun, fem.   **policewoman**

*Der Polizist hilft den Leuten.*
The policeman helps people.

---

**das Postamt** [POST-amt] noun, neut.   **the post office**
**die Post** [POST] noun, fem.

*Wo ist die Post?*
Where is the post office?

---

**die Postkarte** [POST-kar-te] noun, fem.    **postcard**

*Das sind aber schöne Postkarten.*
These are pretty postcards.

**mit der Post schicken**                    **to send in the mail**
  [mit dair POST shik-en] expression

---

**der Präsident** [pre-zee-DENT] noun, masc.                    **president**
**die Präsidentin** [pre-zee-DENT-in] noun, fem.

*Wer ist der Präsident der Vereinigten Staaten?*
Who is the president (masc.) of the United States?

---

**Prima!** [PREE-ma] expression                    **Great!**
  see **ausgezeichnet**

---

**der Prinz** [PRINTS] noun, masc.                    **prince**
**die Prinzessin** [prin-TSES-sin] noun, fem.                    **princess**

*Die Prinzessin wohnt im Schloss.*
The princess lives in the palace.

---

**die Prüfung** [PRU̱-fung] noun, fem.                    **examination, test**

*Gibt es eine Prüfung heute?*
Is there an examination today?

---

**das Pult** [PULT] noun, neut.                    **(pupil's) desk**

*Die Pulte der Schüler stehen in einem Kreis.*
The pupils' desks are in a circle.

---

**die Puppe** [PUP-eh] noun, fem.                    **doll**

*Die Puppe ist auf dem Stuhl.*
The doll is on the chair.

---

**das Puppenhaus** [PUP-en-ho̱ws] noun, neut.                    **dollhouse**

**der Purpur (lila)** [PUR-pur] noun, masc.     **purple**

*Blau und rot macht purpur.*
Blue and red make purple.

---

**putzen** [PUTS-en] verb     **to clean**

*Wer putzt das Haus?*
Who cleans the house?

---

**der Pyjama** [pui-JAHM-a] noun, masc.     **pajamas**

*Erichs Pyjama ist auf dem Bett.*
Eric's pajamas are on the bed.

## R

**das Rad** [RAHT] noun, neut.     **bicycle, bike, wheel**
**Rad fahren** [RAHT FAH-ren] expression     **to ride a bike**

*Wenn das Wetter gut ist, fährt Bernhard Rad.*
When the weather is good, Bernard rides his bike.

---

**der Radiergummi**     **eraser**
      [ra-DEER-goom-ee] noun, masc.

*Hast du einen Radiergummi am Bleistift?*
Do you have an eraser on your pencil?

---

**das Radio** [RAH-dee-o] noun, neut.     **radio**

*Das Radio ist kaputt.*
The radio is broken.

**der Rasen** [R<u>AH</u>-zen] noun, neut.      **lawn, grass**

*Der Rasen ist grün.*
The lawn is green.

---

**raten** [R<u>AH</u>-ten] verb      **to guess, to advise**

*Sie rät sein Alter.*
She will guess his age.

---

**die Ratte** [R<u>A</u>-te] noun, fem.      **rat**

*Ich habe Angst vor Ratten.*
I am afraid of rats.

---

**rauchen** [R<u>OW</u>-`h˙en] verb      **to smoke**

*Unsere Familie raucht nicht.*
Our family does not smoke.

---

**Rauchen verboten!**    **Smoking forbidden! No smoking!**
     [R<u>OW</u>-`h˙en fair-B<u>OH</u>-ten] expression

---

**das Raumschiff** [R<u>OWM</u>-shif] noun, neut.     **spaceship**
**die Raumstation**      **space station**
     [R<u>OWM</u>-shta-tsee-ohn] noun, fem.

*Astronauten arbeiten im Weltraum in einer Raumstation.*
Astronauts work in space in a spacestation.

---

**die Rechnung** [R<u>E</u>`h˙-nung] noun, fem.      **bill, check**

*Die Rechnung, bitte.*
Please bring the bill now.

---

**Du hast Recht.**                          **You are right.**
    [du hast RE'h'T] expression
**rechts** [RE'h'TS] adverb                  **on/to the right**

---

**die Regel** [REH-gel] noun, fem.                    **rule**

*Warum gibt es so viele Regeln?*
Why are there so many rules?

---

**der Regenbogen** [REH-gen-bo-gen] noun, masc.    **rainbow**

*Ich habe die Farben des Regenbogens gern.*
I like the colors of the rainbow.

---

**der Regenmantel**                               **raincoat**
    [REH-gen-man-tel] noun, masc.

*Ich trage meinen Regenmantel, denn es regnet.*
I'll wear my raincoat because it is raining.

---

**der Regenschirm**                               **umbrella**
    [REH-gen-shirm] noun, masc.

*Das ist aber ein schöner Regenschirm.*
That's a pretty umbrella.

---

**Es regnet.** [es REHG-net] expression        **It is raining.**

*Es regnet heute.*
It is raining today.

---

**reich** [RI'h'] adjective                    **rich, wealthy**

*Der Schauspieler ist reich.*
The actor is rich.

---

**reif** [RIF] adjective **ripe**
*Wenn die Erdbeere rot ist, ist sie reif.*
When the strawberry is red, it is ripe.

**die Reihe** [RI-e] noun, fem. **row**
*Es gibt viele Reihen im Klassenzimmer.*
There are many rows in the classroom.

**der Reis** [RIS] noun, masc. **rice**
*Der Reis ist schon auf dem Tisch.*
The rice is already on the table.

**reisen** [RI-zen] verb **to travel**
*Wir reisen heute mit dem Auto.*
We will travel by car today.

**eine Reise machen** **to take a trip**
　　[i-ne RI-ze ma·h·-en] expression
*Ich mache die Reise alleine.*
I am taking the trip alone.

**der Reisende** [RI-zen-de] noun, masc. **traveler**
**die Reisende** [RI-zen-de] noun, fem.
**die Reisenden** [RI-zen-den] noun, pl. **travelers**
*Die Reisende trägt ihren Computer.*
The traveler (fem.) carries her computer.

**reiten** [RI-ten] verb **to ride (a horse)**
*Sie reitet gern.*
She likes to ride (a horse).

**reparieren** [re-pa-REER-en] verb **to repair**
*Meine Schwester repariert meinen Computer für mich.*
My sister is fixing my computer for me.

**das Restaurant** [rest-t<u>ow</u>-r<u>ah</u>nt] noun, neut.    **restaurant**

*Mein Onkel arbeitet in einem Restaurant.*
My uncle works in a restaurant.

---

**retten** [ret-ten] verb    **to rescue**

*Meine Tante rettet die Katze aus dem Baum*
My aunt rescues the cat from the tree.

---

**richtig** [riʿhʿ-tig] adjective    **correct**

*Welche Antwort ist richtig?*
Which answer is correct?

---

**in Richtung** [riʿhʿ-tung] expression    **toward**

*Gehen wir doch in Richtung Krankenhaus.*
Let's go toward the hospital.

---

**riechen** [ree-ʿhʿen] verb    **to smell**

*Beate riecht die Blumen.*
Beate smells the flowers.

---

**der Riese** [ree-zeh] noun, masc.    **giant**

*Ich mag Märchen mit Riesen.*
I like stories with giants.

---

**der Rindsbraten** [rints-br<u>ah</u>-ten] noun, masc.    **roast beef**

*Sie isst Rindsbraten im Restaurant.*
She is eating roast beef in the restaurant.

---

**der Ring** [RING] noun, masc. **ring**

*Dieser Ring ist schön!*
This ring is pretty!

**der Rock** [ROK] noun, masc. **skirt**

*Elfriedas Rock ist neu.*
Elfrieda's skirt is new.

**die Rolle** [ROL-le] noun, fem. **role**

*Ich möchte die Rolle des Prinzen spielen.*
I want to play the role of the prince.

**rollen** [ROL-len] verb **to roll**

*Ich rolle das Rad über die Straße.*
I roll the bicycle across the street.

**der Rollschuh** [ROLL-shoo] noun, masc. **roller skate**
**Rollschuh laufen** [ROLL-shoo LOW-fen] verb **to roller skate**

*Lass uns Rollschuh laufen!*
Let's go roller skating.

**rosa** [ROH-za] adjective **pink**

*Anna und Arthur haben die Farbe Rosa gern.*
Anne and Arthur like the color pink.

**rot** [ROHT] adjective **red**

*Autos müssen halten, wenn die Ampel rot ist.*
Cars must stop when the light is red.

**das Rotkraut** [ROHT-krowt] noun, neut.          **red cabbage**
**der Rotkohl** [ROHT-kohl] noun, masc.

*Ist das Rotkraut frisch?*
Is the red cabbage fresh?

---

**der Rücken** [RUIK-en] noun, masc.                      **back**

*Ist das Andreas? Ich sehe nur den Rücken.*
Is it Andreas? I only see his back.

---

**rufen** [ROO-fen] verb                               **to call (out)**

*Maria sieht und ruft ihren Freund.*
Mary sees and calls her friend.

---

**ruhig** [ROO-ig] adjective                              **quiet**

*In der Nacht ist alles ruhig.*
In the night all is quiet.

---

**rund** [RUNT] adjective                                 **round**

*Unsere Welt ist rund.*
Our world is round.

---

**rutschen** [ROOT-shen] verb                          **to slide**

*Das Kind rutscht auf dem Teppich.*
The child slides on the rug.

---

## S

**die Sache** [ZAˑhˑ-e] noun, fem.      **thing**

*Man verkauft allerhand Sachen hier.*
They sell all sorts of things here.

---

**der Sack** [ZAK] noun, masc.      **sack, bag**

*Die Kartoffeln sind im Sack.*
The potatoes are in the sack.

---

**der Saft** [ZAFT] noun, masc.      **juice**

*Es gibt Himbeersaft in der Bowle.*
There is raspberry juice in the punch.

---

**der Samstag** [ZAMS-taˑhˑ] noun, masc.      **Saturday**

*Machen wir doch ein Picknick am Samstag.*
Let's have a picnic on Saturday.

---

**das Sandwich** [SAND-<u>w</u>ich] noun, neut.      **sandwich**

*Das Sandwich hat zwei Stück Brot.*
The sandwich has two pieces of bread.

---

**sanft** [ZANFT] adjective      **gentle**

*Die Kuh ist ein sanftes Tier.*
The cow is a gentle animal.

---

**der Satz** [ZATS] noun, masc.      **sentence**

*Ich schreibe einen Satz in mein Heft.*
I am writing a sentence in my notebook.

---

**sauber** [ZAU-ber] adjective      **clean**

*Meine Hände sind sauber.*
My hands are clean.

---

**die Schachtel** [SHA'h'-tel] noun, fem.      **box**

*Dort ist eine Schachtel Pralinen.*
There is a box of candy.

---

**Schade!** [SHAH-de] expression      **Too bad!**

*Er ist krank. Schade!*
He is sick. Too bad!

---

**das Schaf** [SHAHF] noun, neut.      **sheep**

*Das Schaf ist auf dem Feld.*
The sheep is in the field.

---

**der Schalter** [SHAL-ter] noun, masc.      **switch**

*Er knipst den Schalter sofort an.*
He turns the light switch on right away.

---

**sich schämen** [ZI'h' SHEH-men] verb      **to be ashamed**

*Wir sind schlimm und wir schämen uns.*
We are naughty and we are ashamed.

---

**der Schatten** [SHAT-ten] noun, masc.      **shadow**

*Mein Schatten tanzt mit mir.*
My shadow dances with me.

**die Schaufel** [SHOW-fell] noun, fem.                          shovel

*Die Schaufel ist im Eimer.*
The shovel is in the pail.

---

**das Schaufenster**                                    store window
  [SHOW-fens-ter] noun, neut.

---

**die Schaukel** [SHOW-kel] noun, fem.                         swing

*Das kleine Mädchen ist auf der Schaukel.*
The little girl is on the swing

---

**der Schauspieler** [SHOW-shpeel-er] noun, masc.            actor
**die Schauspielerin** [SHOW-shpeel-er-in] noun, fem.     actress

*Der Schauspieler ist gut aussehend.*
The actor is handsome.

---

**der Schein** [SHINE] noun, masc.     bill (money), certificate

*Ich bin reich. Ich habe einen Zwanzigmarkschein.*
I'm rich. I have a twenty-mark bill.

---

**die Schere** [SHEH-re] noun, fem.                          scissors

*Ich schneide das Papier mit der Schere.*
I cut the paper with scissors.

---

**schicken** [SHICK-en] verb                                 to send

*Ich schicke meinen Eltern einen Brief.*
I am sending my parents a letter.

---

**schieben** [SHEE-ben] verb                                 to push

*Die Kinder schieben einander ständig.*
The children constantly push each other.

---

**das Schiff** [SHIF] noun, neut.                               ship

*Die Familie reist auf dem Schiff.*
The family travels by ship.

**die Schildkröte** [SHILD-kroe-te] noun, fem.  **turtle**

*Die Schildkröte hat die Sonne gern.*
The turtle likes the sun.

---

**schimpfen** [SHIMP-fen] verb  **to scold**
*Meine Mutter schimpft, wenn ich verspätet bin.*
My mother scolds when I am late.

---

**der Schinken** [SHIN-ken] noun, masc.  **ham**
*Sie essen Schinken.*
They are eating ham.

---

**schlafen** [SHLAHF-en] verb  **to sleep**

| | |
|---|---|
| ich schlafe | wir/sie/Sie schlafen |
| du schläfst | ihr schlaft |
| er/sie/es schläft | |

*Schläfst du? I möchte mit dir sprechen.*
Are you sleeping? I would like to talk to you.

---

**schläfrig sein** [SHLEHF-rig zin] expression  **to be sleepy**
*Katzen sind immer schläfrig.*
Cats are always sleepy.

---

**das Schlafzimmer** [SHLAHF-tsim-mer] noun, neut.  **bedroom**
*Diese Wohnung hat drei Schlafzimmer.*
This apartment has three bedrooms.

---

**der Schlag** [SHLAG] noun, masc.  **blow, hit**
*Er gibt einen Schlag auf die Schulter.*
He gives a blow in the shoulder.

---

130

**schlagen** [SHLAHG-en] verb                    **to hit**

*Sie schlägt den Nagel hart mit dem Hammer.*
She hits the nail with the hammer hard.

---

**der Schlamm** [SHLAM] noun, masc.              **mud, dirt**

*Meine Schuhe sind voller Schlamm.*
My shoes are covered with mud.

---

**die Schlange** [SHLANG-e] noun, fem.           **snake**

*Ich habe Angst vor Schlangen.*
I am afraid of snakes.

---

**schlau** [SHLOW] adjective                     **cunning, sly**

*Der Fuchs ist schlau.*
The fox is cunning.

---

**schlecht** [SHLE·h·T] adjective                **bad**

*Das Wetter ist schlecht.*
The weather is bad.

---

**schließen** [SHLEES-sen] verb                  **to close**

*Bitte schließen Sie das Fenster.*
Please close the window.

---

**schlimm** [SHLIMM] adjective                   **naughty**

*Robby schlägt die Katze. Er ist schlimm.*
Robby hits the cat. He is naughty.

---

**der Schlitten** [SHLIT-ten] noun, masc.                                **sled**

*Der Schlitten macht Spaß.*
The sled is fun.

---

**der Schlittschuh** [SHLIT-shoo] noun, masc.          **ice skate**
**Schlittschuh laufen** [SHLIT-shoo LOW-fen] verb    **to ice skate**

*Die Kinder laufen Schlittschuh.*
The children are ice skating.

---

**das Schloss** [SHLOSS] noun, neut.                          **palace**

*Dieses Schloss ist groß.*
This palace is large.

---

**der Schlüssel** [SHLUIS-sel] noun, masc.                          **key**

*Wo ist denn mein Schlüssel?*
Where is my key?

---

**der Schmuck** [SHMOOK] noun, masc.                         **jewelry**

*Der Dieb findet den Schmuck.*
The burglar finds the jewelry.

---

**schmücken** [SHMUIK-en] verb                           **to decorate**

*Sie schmücken das Hochzeitsauto.*
They are decorating the wedding car.

---

**schmutzig** [SHMOOT-tsig] adjective                          **dirty**

*Diese Straße ist nicht schmutzig.*
This street is not dirty.

---

**der Schnabel** [SHN<u>AH</u>-bel] noun, masc.        **beak**

*Der Schnabel des Papageis ist groß.*
The parrot's beak is big.

---

**der Schnee** [SHN<u>EH</u>] noun, masc.             **snow**

*Ich spiele gern im Schnee.*
I like to play in the snow.

---

**der Schneemann** [SHN<u>EH</u>-man] noun, masc.     **snowman**

*Die Kinder spielen mit der Schneemann.*
The children play with the snowman.

---

**schneiden** [SHN<u>I</u>-den] verb                 **to cut**

*Bernhard schneidet die Melone.*
Bernard is cutting the melon.

---

**der Schneider** [SHN<u>I</u>-der] noun, masc.      **tailor**
**die Schneiderin** [SHN<u>I</u>-der-in] noun, fem.  **seamstress**

*Die Schneiderin besitzt den Laden.*
The seamstress owns the shop.

---

**Es schneit!** [ess SHN<u>I</u>T] expression        **It is snowing!**

*Ein Sturm kommt. Es schneit schon.*
A storm is coming. It is snowing already.

---

**schnell** [SHNELL] adjective                       **fast**

*Der Hund rennt schnell, wenn er die Katze sieht.*
The dog runs fast when he sees the cat.

---

**die Schnur** [SHNOOR] noun, fem.                    **string**

*Eine Schnur liegt auf dem Fußboden.*
A string is on the floor.

---

**die Schokolade** [SHO-ko-LAH-de] noun, fem.                    **chocolate**

*Was, du magst keine Schokolade?*
What, you don't like chocolate?

---

**schon** [SHON] adverb                    **already**

*Ist es schon Zeit fürs Mittagessen?*
Is it already dinner time?

---

**schön** [SHOEN] adjective                    **pretty, beautiful**

*Das ist eine schöne Puppe.*
That is a pretty doll.

---

**der Schrank** [SHRANK] noun, masc.                    **cupboard, closet**

*Die Teller sind im Schrank.*
The plates are in the cupboard.

---

**schreiben** [SHRI-ben] verb                    **to write**

ich schreibe          wir/sie/Sie schreiben
du schreibst          ihr schreibt
er/sie/es schreibt

*Sie schreiben Briefe im Internet.*
They write letters on the Internet.

---

**die Schreibkraft** [SHRIB-kraft] noun, fem.                    **typist**

*Die Schreibkraft benutzt einen Computer mit Textverarbeitungssystem.*
The typist uses a computer with a word processor.

---

**die Schreibmaschine**                    **typewriter**
     [SHRIB-ma-SHEE-ne] noun, fem.
**die elektrische Schreibmaschine**                    **electric typewriter**
     noun, fem.

---

**der Schreibtisch** [SHRIB-tish] noun, masc.     **desk**

*Der Schreibtisch der Lehrerin ist in der Ecke.*
The teacher's (fem.) desk is in the corner.

---

**schreien** [SHRI-en] verb     **to scream**

*Mutti schreit, "Komm doch schnell!"*
Mom shouts, "Come quickly!"

---

**der Schritt** [SHRITT] noun, masc.     **step**

*Die Kinder gehen drei Schritte vorwärts.*
The children take three steps forward.

---

**die Schublade** [SHOOP-lah-de] noun, fem.     **drawer**

*Dorothee legt ihren Schmuck in eine Schublade.*
Dorothy puts her jewelry in a drawer.

---

**der Schuh** [SHOO] noun, masc.     **shoe**

*Ich habe diese Schuhe gar nicht gern.*
I don't like these shoes.

---

**die Schule** [shoo-le] noun, fem.     **school**

*Wir haben samstags keine Schule.*
We don't have school on Saturdays.

---

**der Schüler** [SHUI-ler] noun, masc.     **pupil, student**
**die Schülerin** [SHUI-ler-in] noun, fem.     **pupil, student**

*Der Schüler antwortet richtig.*
The pupil answers correctly.

---

**die Schulferien**     **school holidays, vacation**
    [SHOOL-fair-ee-en] noun, pl.

*Was machst du in den Schulferien?*
What are you doing during the summer vacation?

---

**die Schulter** [SHOOL-ter] noun, fem.                    **shoulder**

*Der Ball trifft Claudias Schulter.*
The ball hits Claudia's shoulder.

---

**die Schürze** [SHUIR-tse] noun, fem.                     **apron**

*Papa trägt eine Schürze, wenn er kocht.*
Dad wears an apron when he cooks.

---

**die Schüssel** [SHUI-sel] noun, fem.                     **bowl**

*Wo ist die Schüssel für den Salat?*
Where is the bowl for the salad?

---

**schwach** [SHVA'h'] adjective                            **weak**

*Der Junge ist schwach, denn er ist krank.*
The boy is weak because he is sick.

---

**der Schwanz** [SHVANTS] noun, masc.                      **tail**

*Mein Hund wedelt den Schwanz, wenn ich nach Hause komme.*
My dog wags his tail when I come home.

---

**schwarz** [SHVARTS] adjective                            **black**

*Meine Schuhe sind schwarz.*
My shoes are black.

---

**das Schwein** [SHVIN] noun, neut.                        **pig**

*Der Bauer hat drei Schweine.*
The farmer has three pigs.

---

**schwer** [SHVEHR] adjective                              **heavy, difficult**

*Der Koffer ist schwer.*
The suitcase is heavy.

*Deutsch ist nicht schwer.*
German is not difficult.

---

**die Schwester** [SHVES-ter] noun, fem.                    **sister**

*Meine Tante ist die Schwester meiner Mutter.*
My aunt is my mother's sister.

---

**schwimmen** [SHVIM-en] verb                          **to swim**

*Ich schwimme im Sommer.*
I swim in the summer.

---

**das Schwimmbad**                              **swimming pool**
   [SHVIM-bad] noun, neut.

*Wir schwimmen im Schwimmbad.*
We are swimming in the pool.

---

**sechs** [ZEKS] adjective                                **six**

*Es gibt sechs Eier im Kühlschrank.*
There are six eggs in the refrigerator.

---

**sechzehn** [ZE˙h˙-tzehn] adjective                    **sixteen**

*Sie ist sechzehn Jahre alt. "Alles Gute."*
She is sixteen years old. "Best wishes."

---

**sechzig** [ZE˙h˙-tsig] adjective                       **sixty**

*Eine Stunde hat sechzig Minuten.*
An hour has sixty minutes.

---

**der See** [zeh] noun, masc.                            **lake**

*Da ist ein Boot in der Mitte des Alpensees.*
There is a boat in the middle of the Alpine lake.

---

**sehen** [ZEH-en] verb                                  **to see**

| | |
|---|---|
| ich sehe | wir/sie/Sie sehen |
| du siehst | ihr seht |
| er/sie/es sieht | |

*Ich sehe mich in dem Spiegel.*
I see myself in the mirror.

---

**sehr** [ZEHR] adverb  **very**

*Das Schloss ist sehr groß.*
The palace is very large.

---

**die Seife** [ZI-fe] noun, fem.  **soap**

*Ich wasche mir die Hände mit Seife.*
I wash my hands with soap.

---

**das Seil** [ZIL] noun, fem.  **rope**

*Dieses Seil ist dick.*
This rope is thick.

---

**Seil springen** [ZIL SHPRING-en] expression  **jump rope**

---

**sein** [ZIN] verb  **to be**

| | |
|---|---|
| ich bin | wir/sie/Sie sind |
| du bist | ihr seid |
| er/sie/es ist | |

---

**die Seite** [ZIT-e] noun, fem.  **page, side**
**auf die rechte Seite** expression  **on the right side**

---

**der Sekretär** [zek-re-TAIR] noun, masc.  **secretary**
**die Sekretärin** [zek-re-TAIR-in] noun, fem.

*Der Sekretär verteilt die Post.*
The secretary distributes the mail.

---

**selbst** [ZELBST] pronoun                                    **myself**

*Ich mache es schon selbst.*
I'll do it myself.

---

**der Sellerie** [ZEL-er-ee] noun, fem.                        **celery**

*Da ist Sellerie für den Salat.*
Here is the celery for the salad.

---

**die Semmel (das Brötchen)** [ZEM-el] noun, fem.             **roll**

*Susanne isst frische Semmeln zum Frühstück.*
Susan eats fresh rolls for breakfast.

---

**der September** [ZEP-tem-ber] noun, masc.          **September**

*Der September hat dreißig Tage.*
September has thirty days.

---

**servieren** [ser-VEER-en] verb                          **to serve**

*Sie servieren den Kindern den Kuchen zuerst.*
They are serving the cake to the children first.

---

**die Serviette** [ser-vee-ET-te] noun, fem.               **napkin**

*Ihre Serviette ist auf dem Tisch.*
Her napkin is on the table.

---

**Servus!** [SER-voos] expression                    **hello, goodbye**

---

**der Sessel** [ZES-sel] noun, masc.                      **armchair**

*Der Sessel ist bequem.*
The armchair is comfortable.

---

**sich setzen** [zi͡'h· ZET-tsen] verb                    **to sit down**

*Meine Großmutter setzt sich auf das Sofa.*
My grandmother sits down on the sofa.

---

**sicher** [ZI͡'h·-er] adverb                    **sure, certain**

*Heute ist Dienstag. Bist du sicher?*
Today is Tuesday. Are you sure?

---

**sie** [ZEE] pronoun                    **she & her, they & them (subject & acc.)**

*Sie ist meine Kusine. Kennst du sie?*
She is my cousin. Do you know her?

---

**Sie** [ZEE] pronoun                    **you**
**Sie sind** [ZEE zint] expression                    **you are**

---

**sieben** [ZEE-ben] adjective                    **seven**

*Es ist schon sieben Uhr dreißig abends.*
It is already seven thirty in the evening.

---

**siebzehn** [ZEEP-tsehn] adjective                    **seventeen**

*Neun und acht macht siebzehn.*
Nine and eight are seventeen.

---

**siebzig** [ZEEP-tsig] adjective                    **seventy**

*Leos Großvater ist siebzig Jahre alt.*
Leo's grandfather is seventy years old.

---

**das Silber** [ZIL-ber] noun, neut.                    **silver**

*Der Ring ist aus Silber.*
The ring is made of silver.

---

**der Silvesterabend**                    **New Year's Eve**
    [sil-VE-ster AH-bent] noun, masc.

---

**sitzen** [ZITS-en] verb          **to sit**

*Wir sitzen um den Tisch.*
We are sitting around the table.

**singen** [ZING-en] verb          **to sing**

*Welches Lied singst du lieber?*
Which song would you rather sing?

**so** [ZOH] adverb          **so**

*Das Baby isst so langsam.*
The baby is eating so slowly.

**die Socke** [ZOK-e] noun, fem.          **sock**

*Ich möchte ein Paar Socken kaufen.*
I would like to buy a pair of socks.

**das Sofa** [ZOH-fah] noun, neut.          **sofa**

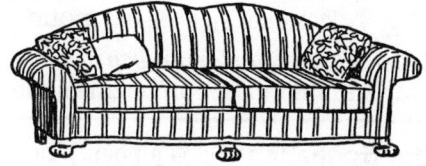

*Das Sofa ist bequem.*
The sofa is comfortable.

**sofort** [ZO-fort] adverb          **right away, immediately**

*Wenn der Papa mich ruft, gehe ich sofort.*
When Daddy calls me, I go immediately.

**der Softdrink** [SOFT-drink] noun, masc.          **soda, pop**

*Ich nehme einen Softdrink, bitte.*
I'll have a soda, please.

**der Sohn** [ZOHN] noun, masc.                    **son**

*Ich kenne seinen Sohn.*
I know his son.

---

**der Soldat** [sol-DAT] noun, masc.          **soldier**

*Der Soldat geht vor dem Jeep.*
The soldier walks in front of the jeep.

---

**der Sommer** [ZOM-mer] noun, masc.          **summer**

*Was hast du lieber, Sommer oder Winter?*
Do you prefer summer or winter?

**das Sommerlager**                         **summer camp**
    [ZOM-mer LAH-ger] noun, neut.
**die Sommerferien**                    **summer vacation**
    [ZOM-mer FEHR-ee-en] noun, pl.          **(from school)**

*Unsere Sommerferien beginnen bald.*
Our summer vacation begins soon.

---

**der Sonnabend** [ZON-AH-bent] noun, masc.          **Saturday**
**der Samstag** [ZAMS-tAHG]

*Machen wir doch ein Picknick am Samstag.*
Let's have a picnic on Saturday.

---

**die Sonne** [ZON-ne] noun, fem.                    **sun**

*Wann geht die Sonne auf?*
What time does the sun rise?

---

142

**das Sonnenbad** [ZON-nen-bad] noun, neut.          **sunbath**
**Es ist sonnig.** [es ist ZON-ni·h˙] expression      **It is sunny.**
**Die Sonne scheint.**                          **The sun is shining.**
[dee ZON-neh SHINT] expression

---

**sorgfältig, vorsichtig** [ZOHRG-fehl-tig] adverb      **carefully**
*Tabia trägt die Flaschen vorsichtig.*
Tabia carries the bottles carefully.

---

**so sehr** [zoh zehr] adverb                         **so very**
**so viel** [zoh feel] expression                     **so much**
**so viele** [zoh feel-e] expression                  **so many**

---

**spanisch** [SHPAH-nish] adjective                   **Spanish**
*Die Spanische Reitschule ist in Wien.*
The Spanish Riding School is in Vienna.

---

**das Sparschweinchen**                              **piggy bank**
[SHPAHR-shvin-·h˙en] noun, fem.
*Peter hat ein Sparschweinchen.*
Peter has a piggy bank.

---

**sparen** [SHPAHR-en] verb                      **to save (money)**
*Der Junge spart Geld im Sparschweinchen.*
The boy saves money in the piggy bank.

---

**spät** [SHPEHT] adjective                            **late**
*Frank kommt selten spät.*
Frank seldom comes late.

---

**später** [SHPEHT-er] adverb                         **later**
*Es ist acht Uhr. Der Briefträger kommt später.*
It is eight o'clock. The mailman comes later.

---

**spazieren gehen**        **to take a walk,**
    [shpa-ts-EER-en GEH-en] verb     **to go for a walk**

*Sie gehen im Park spazieren.*
They are walking in the park.

---

**die Speisekarte** [SHPI-ze-KAHR-te] noun, fem.     **menu**

*Ich lese die Speisekarte.*
I am reading the menu.

---

**der Spiegel** [SHPEE-gel] noun, masc.      **mirror**

*Da ist ein Spiegel im Schlafzimmer.*
There is a mirror in the bedroom.

---

**das Spiel** [SHPEEL] noun, neut.      **game**

*Welches Spiel hast du lieber?*
Which game do you prefer?

---

**spielen** [SHPEE-len] verb     **to play a sport, game,**
                        **musical instrument**

*Lass uns Basketball spielen!*
Let's play basketball.

---

**die Spielkarte** [SHPEEL-kar-te] noun, fem.    **playing card**

*Spielt er Karten?*
Does he play cards?

---

**der Spielplatz** [SHPEEL-plats] noun, masc.    **playground**

*Die Rutschbahn ist auf dem Spielplatz.*
The slide is on the playground.

---

**das Spielzeug** [SPEEL-ts<u>oig</u>] noun, neut.                    **toys**

*Was für Spielzeug hast du?*
What kind of toys do you have?

---

**der Spinat** [shpi-N<u>AH</u>T] noun, masc.                  **spinach**

*Spinat hat viele Vitamine und Mineralien.*
Spinach has many vitamins and minerals.

---

**die Spinne** [SHPIN-ne] noun, fem.                          **spider**

*Wer hat Angst vor Spinnen?*
Who is afraid of spiders?

---

**der Sport** [SHPORT] noun, masc.                             **sport**

*Baseball ist ein amerikanischer Sport.*
Baseball is an American sport.

---

**sprechen** [SHPRE `h`en] verb                              **to speak**

   ich spreche        wir/sie/Sie sprechen
   du sprichst        ihr sprecht
   er/sie/es spricht

*Ich spreche jetzt mit dir, Erik.*
I'll speak with you now, Eric.

---

**springen** [SHPRIN-gen] verb                               **to jump**

*Der Junge springt von der Treppe.*
The boy jumps from the stairs.

---

**der Staat** [SHT<u>AH</u>T] noun, masc.                   **state, country**

*Das ist eine Karte von den Vereinigten Staaten von Amerika.*
Here is a map of the United States of America.

---

**die Stadt** [SHTAT] noun, fem.               **city**

*Die Stadt ist groß.*
The city is large.

**der Staubsauger**              **vacuum cleaner**
      [SHTOWB-ZOW-ger] noun, masc.
*Der Staubsauger ist sehr praktisch.*
The vacuum cleaner is very practical.

**stechen** [SHTE'h'en] verb        **to sting, to bite**
*Mücken stechen mich oft.*
Mosquitoes bite me often.

**die Stecknadel** [SHTEK-nah-del] noun, fem.    **straight pin**

**stehen** [SHTEH-en] verb        **to stand (there)**
*Er steht vor dem Hotel.*
He is standing in front of the hotel.

**stehlen** [SHTEH-len] verb          **to steal**
*Die Maus stiehlt den Käse.*
The mouse steals the cheese.

**der Stein** [SHTIN] noun, masc.         **stone**

*Es gibt viele Steine in der Wüste.*
There are many stones in the desert.

**stellen** [SHTEL-len] verb      **to put, to place (down)**

*Legt bitte das Besteck auf den Tisch.*
Please put the silverware on the table.

---

**die Stereoanlage**          **stereo system**
    [STEH-re-oh-AHN-lag-e] noun, fem.

*Wir haben eine Stereoanlage.*
We have a stereo system.

---

**der Stern** [SHTEHRN] noun, masc.        **star**

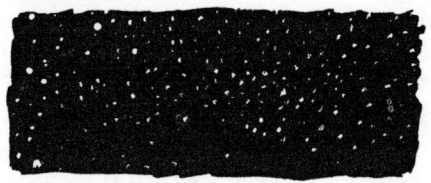

*Sieh mal die Sterne!*
Look at the stars!

---

**der Stiefel** [SHTEE-fel] noun, masc.      **boot**

*Wenn es schneit, ziehe ich meine Stiefel an.*
When it snows, I put on my boots.

---

**die Stimme** [STIM-me] noun, fem.      **voice**

*Die Stimme meiner Tante ist angenehm.*
My aunt's voice is pleasant.

---

**mit leiser Stimme**     **in a low voice, in a quiet voice**
    [mit LIZ-er SHTIM-me] expression

---

**der Stock** [SHTOK] noun, masc.        **stick**

*Der Polizist trägt einen Stock.*
The policeman carries a stick.

---

**der Stock (die Etage)**        **floor (of building)**
    [SHTOK] noun, masc.

---

**stoßen** [SHT<u>OH</u>-sen] verb　　　　　　　　**to kick**

*Ich stoße gegen den Stein (mit dem Fuss).*
I kick the stone (with the foot).

---

**der Strand** [SHTR<u>AH</u>NT] noun, masc.　　　**beach, shore**

*Wir spazieren gern am Strand.*
We like to walk on the shore.

---

**die Straße** [SHTR<u>AH</u>-se] noun, fem.　　　　**street**

*Es ist gefährlich, auf der Straße zu spielen.*
It is dangerous to play on the street.

---

**der Straßenkehrer**　　　　　　　　**street cleaner**
　　　　[SHTR<u>AH</u>-sen-C<u>EHR</u>-er] noun, masc.
**die Straßenkehrerin** [SHTR<u>AH</u>-sen-C<u>EHR</u>-er-in] noun, fem.

*Es gibt Straßenkehrer und Straßenkehrerinnen.*
There are men and women street cleaners.

---

**das Streichholz** [SHTR<u>I</u>˙h˙-holts] noun, neut.　　**match**

*Streichhölzer sind gefährlich für Kinder.*
Matches are dangerous for children.

---

**stricken** [SHTRIK-en] verb　　　　　　　　**to knit**

*Ellen strickt einen Pullover.*
Ellen is knitting a sweater.

---

**der Strumpf** [SHTROOMPF] noun, masc.　　　**stocking**

*Wo kann ich denn Strümpfe kaufen, bitte?*
Where can I buy stockings, please?

---

**die Strumpfhose**          **pantyhose**
[SHTROOMPF-h<u>oh</u>-ze] noun, fem.

---

**das Stück** [SHT<u>UI</u>K] noun, neut.          **piece**
*Ich möchte ein Stück Kuchen, bitte.*
I would like a piece of cake, please.

---

**ein Stück Papier**          **a piece of paper**
[<u>in</u> SHT<u>UI</u>K pah-P<u>EE</u>R] expression

---

**der Student**          **student (at the university)**
[shtoo-DENT] noun, masc.
**die Studentin** [shtoo-DENT-in] noun, fem.
*Meine Schwester ist Studentin an einer*
*Universität in Berlin.*
My sister is a student at a university in Berlin.

---

**studieren**          **to study (at the university)**
[shtoo-D<u>EE</u>R-en] verb
*Er studiert Jura.*
He is studying law.

---

**der Stuhl** [SHTOOL] noun, masc.          **chair**
*Fünf Stühle sind im Esszimmer.*
Five chairs are in the dining room.

---

**die Stunde** [SHTOON-deh] noun, fem.          **hour**
*Ein Tag hat vierundzwanzig Stunden.*
A day has twenty-four hours.

---

**eine halbe Stunde**          **half an hour**
[<u>I</u>-neh HAL-beh SHTOON-deh] expression
*Ich warte schon eine halbe Stunde auf dich!*
I have been waiting for you for half an hour already!

---

**der Sturm** [SHTOORM] noun, masc.      **storm**

*Wenn es Stürme gibt, schließen die Schulen.*
When there are storms, the schools close.

---

**suchen** [ZOO-ʼhˑen] verb      **to look for**
*Papa sucht immer seine Schlüssel.*
Dad is always looking for his keys.

---

**der Süden** [ZUI-den] noun, masc.      **the south**
*München ist im Süden Deutschlands.*
Munich is in the south of Germany.

---

**Super!** [zoo-per] interjection      **Great! Super!**

---

**der Supermarkt**      **food market, supermarket**
    [ZOOP-er-markt] noun, masc.
*Ich gehe mit meiner Freundin zum Supermarkt.*
I'm going to the supermarket with my girlfriend.

---

**die Suppe** [ZUP-pe] noun, fem.      **soup**

*Meine Schwester serviert meinem Bruder die Suppe.*
My sister serves soup to my brother.

---

**süß** [ZUISS] adjective      **sweet, darling**
*Manche Kirschen sind süß.*
Some cherries are sweet.

---

## T

**die Tafel** [TAH-fel] noun, fem.        **blackboard**

*Der Schüler schreibt an die Tafel.*
The student writes on the blackboard.

---

**die Taille** [TAL-ye] noun, fem.        **waist**

*Man misst meine Taille für den neuen Gürtel.*
They measure my waist for the new belt.

---

**das Tal** [TAHL] noun, neut.        **valley**

*Der See ist in einem Tal.*
The lake is in a valley.

---

**die Tante** [TAHN-te] noun, fem.        **aunt**

*Meine Tante ist Ärztin.*
My aunt is a physician.

---

**tanzen** [TANTS-en] verb        **to dance**

*Meine Schwester tanzt gern.*
My sister likes to dance.

---

**die Tasche** [TA-she] noun, fem.        **pocket, purse**

*Die Handtasche liegt auf dem Sessel.*
The pocketbook is on the armchair.

*Ich habe nichts in meiner Manteltasche.*
I have nothing in my coat pocket.

---

**das Taschentuch**        **handkerchief**
    [TA-shen-tu'h'] noun, neut.
**das Papiertaschentuch** noun, neut.        **tissue**

*Er nimmt ein Papiertaschentuch, wenn er niest.*
He uses a paper handkerchief when he sneezes.

---

**die Tasse** [TAS-se] noun, fem.      **cup**

*Ich wasche die Tasse und die Untertasse.*
I wash the cup and the saucer.

**tausend** [TOW-zent] adjective      **thousand**

*Ich möchte tausend Dollar haben.*
I would like to have a thousand dollars.

**das Taxi** [TAX-ee] noun, neut.      **taxi**

*Meine Schwester fährt ein Taxi.*
My sister drives a taxi.

**der Tee** [TEH] noun, masc.      **tea**

*Meine Tante trinkt immer Tee.*
My aunt always drinks tea.

**das Telefon** [TEL-e-fon] noun, neut.      **telephone**

*Unser Telefon klingelt oft.*
Our telephone rings often.

**der Teller** [TEL-ler] noun, masc.      **plate**

*Der Teller ist auf dem Tisch.*
The plate is on the table.

**der Teppich** [TEP-pi'h'] noun, masc.      **rug**

*Der Teppich ist auf dem Fußboden.*
The rug is on the floor.

**teuer** [TOI-er] adjective           **expensive**

*Dieses Fahrrad ist zu teuer.*
This bicycle is too expensive.

---

**das Textverarbeitungssystem**      **word processor**
    [TEXT-fer-ahr-bi-tungs-SUIS-tehm] noun, neut.

*Ich benutze das Textverarbeitungssystem oft.*
I use the word processor often.

---

**das Theater** [teh-AH-ter] noun, neut.     **theater**

*Dieses Stück ist im neuen Theater.*
This play is in the new theater.

---

**tief** [TEEF] adjective               **deep**

*Ist der See tief?*
Is the lake deep?

---

**das Tier** [TEER] noun, neut.          **animal**

*Die Tiere sind im Wald.*
The animals are in the forest.

---

**der Tiger** [TEE-ger] noun, masc.        **tiger**

*Ein Tiger kann sehr weit springen.*
A tiger can jump very far.

---

**der Tisch** [TISH] noun, masc.          **table**

*Der Malkasten ist auf dem Tisch.*
The paintbox is on the table.

---

**den Tisch decken**       **to set the table**
    [den TISH dek-en] expression

*Georg deckt den Tisch für die Familie gern.*
George likes to set the table for the family.

**die Tischdecke** [TISH-dek-e] noun, fem.    **tablecloth**

---

**der Toast** [TOAST] noun, masc.      **toast**

*Der Toast ist noch heiß.*
The toast is still hot.

---

**Toll!** [TOL] interjection      **Great!**

---

**die Tomate** [to-MAH-te] noun, fem.      **tomato**

*Die Tomate ist rot, wenn sie reif ist.*
The tomato is red when it is ripe.

---

**die Torte** [TOR-te] noun, fem.      **cake**

*Mutti bäckt mir eine Torte. Sie ist so schön.*
Mom makes me a cake. It is so pretty.

---

**töten** [TOE-ten] verb      **to kill**

*Mutti tötet die Fliege.*
Mom kills the fly.

---

**tragen** [TRAH-gen] verb      **to carry, to wear**

| ich trage | wir/sie/Sie tragen |
|---|---|
| du trägst | ihr tragt |
| er/sie/es trägt | |

*Der Hund trägt eine Zeitung.*
The dog is carrying a newspaper.

*Sie trägt meinen Hut.*
She is wearing my hat.

---

**die Träne** [TRE-ne] noun, fem.      **tear**

*Es tut so sehr weh, dass er Tränen in den Augen hat.*
It hurts so much that there are tears in his eyes.

---

**die Traube** [TROW-be] noun, fem.      **grape**

*Der Fuchs betrachtet die Trauben.*
The fox looks at the grapes.

---

**träumen** [TROI-men] verb                    **to dream**

*Er träumt, dass er in den Alpen ist.*
He dreams that he is in the Alps.

---

**traurig** [TROW-ri'h'] adjective                    **sad**

*Ich kann nicht mit dir gehen. Ich bin traurig.*
I cannot go with you. I am sad.

---

**treffen** [TREF-en] verb                    **to meet**

| | |
|---|---|
| ich treffe | wir/sie/Sie treffen |
| du triffst | ihr trefft |
| er/sie/es trifft | |

*Wer trifft Rotkäppchen im Wald?*
Who meets Little Red Riding Hood in the forest?

---

**die Treppe** [TREP-pe] noun, fem.          **stairs, staircase**

*Jetzt gehe ich die Treppe hinunter.*
I am now going down the stairs.

---

**trinken** [TRIN-ken] verb                    **to drink**

*Das Kind trinkt Orangensaft.*
The child is drinking orange juice.

---

**das Trinkgeld** [TRINK-gelt] noun, neut.          **tip**

*Die Frau gibt dem Kellner ein Trinkgeld.*
The woman gives the waiter a tip.

---

**trocken** [TROK-en] adjective                    **dry**

*Ist der Fussboden trocken, Anton?*
Is the floor dry, Anthony?

---

**die Trommel** [TROM-mel] noun, fem.                     **drum**

*Wenn ich Trommel spiele, ist es sehr laut.*
When I play the drum, it is very loud.

**die Tür** [TUIR] noun, fem.                                **door**
*Schließen Sie bitte die Tür!*
Please close the door!

**die Türklinke** [TUIR-klin-ke] noun, fem.              **doorknob**
*Diese Türklinke ist anders.*
This doorknob is different.

**der Turm** [TURM] noun, masc.                            **tower**
*Der Turm stammt aus dem Mittelalter.*
The tower is from the Middle Ages.

**die Tüte** [TUI-te] noun, fem.                  **bag, sack (paper)**
*Die Kartoffeln sind im Sack.*
The potatoes are in the sack.

## U

**überall** [ui-ber-AHL] adverb                          **all over**
*Ich suche meine Armbanduhr überall.*
I look for my watch all over.

**überholen** [ui-ber-HOHL-en] verb                       **to pass**
*Das Auto überholt den Lastwagen auf der Autobahn.*
The car passes the truck on the expressway.

**überqueren** [ui-ber-KVEHR-en] verb **to cross**

*Können wir den Fluss überqueren?*
Can we cross the river?

---

**überraschend** [ui-ber-RAH-shend] adjective **surprising**

*Die Nachricht ist nicht überraschend.*
The news is not surprising.

---

**die Überraschung** [ui-ber-RAHSH-ung] noun, fem. **surprise**

*Sie hat die Überraschung gern.*
She likes the surprise.

---

**Uhr** [OOR] expression **o'clock**

*Es ist drei Uhr.*
It is three o'clock.

---

**die Uhr** [OOR] noun, fem. **clock**

*Die Uhr ist kaputt.*
The clock is broken.

---

**um** [UM] preposition **around, at (time)**

*Ich möchte eine Reise um die Welt machen.*
I would like to take a trip around the world.

*Wann beginnt die Schule? Um acht Uhr dreißig.*
When does school begin? At eight thirty.

---

**der Umschlag** [UM-shlag] noun, masc. **envelope**

*Der Umschlag hat schon eine Briefmarke.*
The envelope already has a stamp.

---

**umsteigen** [UM-shti-gen] verb **to change (train, bus)**

*In München steigen wir um.*
In Munich we change trains.

---

---

**um...zu** [um...tsu] expression                    **in order to**

*Er geht ins Museum, um Kunstwerke zu sehen.*
He goes to the museum in order to see artwork.

---

**und** [UNT] conjunction                              **and**

*Margarete und ihre Freundin spielen.*
Margaret and her girlfriend are playing.

---

**ungewöhnlich** [UN-ge-voen-li`h`] adjective        **unusual**

*Die Geschichte hat ein ungewöhnliches Ende.*
The story has an unusual ending.

---

**unglücklich** [UN-gluik-li`h`] adjective          **unhappy**

*Sie ist unglücklich, denn sie darf nicht Ball spielen.*
She is unhappy because she may not play ball.

---

**die Universität**                                  **university**
     [u-nee-vehr-zee-TEHT] noun, fem.

*Die Universität ist nicht weit vom Stadtzentrum.*
The university is not far from the center of the city.

---

**unmöglich** [un-MOEG-li`h`] adjective             **impossible**

*Es ist unmöglich diesen Felsen zu rollen.*
It is impossible to roll this rock.

---

**uns** [UNS] pronoun                                **us, to us**

*Sie sieht uns sofort.*
She sees us at once.

*Er gibt uns Bonbons.*
He gives (to) us candy.

---

**unser** [UN-ser] adjective                           **our**

*Unser Hund liebt Kekse, Hundekekse.*
Our dog loves cookies, dog cookies.

---

**unter** [UN-ter] preposition　　　　　**under**

*Wir stellen unsere Schuhe unter das Bett.*
We put our shoes under the bed.

---

**die Untergrundbahn, die U-Bahn**　　　　**subway**
　　　[UN-ter-grunt-b<u>ah</u>n] noun, fem.
**mit der Untergrundbahn**　　　**to go on the subway**
　　**(mit der U-Bahn) fahren** expression

*Die Krankenschwester fährt mit der U-Bahn.*
The nurse takes the subway.

---

**sich gut unterhalten**　　　**to have a good time**
　　　[SI'h' GOOT un-ter-H<u>AHL</u>-ten] expression

*Ich unterhalte mich gut.*
I am having a good time.

---

**der Unterricht** [UN-ter-ri'h't] noun, masc.　　**lesson, class**

*Der Matheunterricht ist sehr interessant.*
The math class is very interesting.

---

**unterrichten** [un-ter-RI'h'-ten] verb　　　**to teach**

*Sie unterrichtet Deutsch gern.*
She likes teaching German.

---

**die Untertasse** [UN-ter-ta-se] noun, fem.　　**saucer**

*Die Frau stellt die Tasse auf die Untertasse.*
The woman puts the cup on the saucer.

---

**der Urlaub** [OOR-l<u>ow</u>b] noun, masc.　　**vacation**

*Wohin geht ihr in eurem Familienurlaub?*
Where are you going on your family vacation?

## V

**die Vanille** [va-NIL-le] noun, fem.                    **vanilla**

*Es gibt kein Vanilleeis heute.*
There is no vanilla ice cream today.

---

**der Vater** [FAH-ter] noun, masc.                    **father**

*Mein Vater ist ein Feuerwehrmann.*
My father is a fireman.

---

**der Ventilator**                              **fan (mechanical)**
    [ven-tee-LAH-tor] noun, masc.

*Der Ventilator ist praktisch, wenn es heiß ist.*
The fan is handy when it is hot.

---

**verboten** [fer-BOH-ten] adjective              **forbidden**

*Es ist verboten, im Lift zu rauchen.*
It is forbidden to smoke in the elevator.

---

**Das ist verboten!**                        **This is forbidden!**
    [DAS IST fer-BOT-en] expression

---

**verbrennen** [fer-BREN-nen] verb          **to burn (something)**

*Der Mann verbrennt Papiere im Kamin.*
The man is burning papers in the fireplace.

---

**verbringen** [fer-BRING-en] verb              **to spend time**

*Ich verbringe den ganzen Tag in der Bibliothek.*
I will spend all day in the library.

**verdienen** [fer-DEEN-en] verb                                  **to earn**
*Ich verdiene noch kein Geld.*
I do not earn money yet.

**vergessen** [fer-GESS-en] verb                                  **to forget**
*Manchmal vergisst er seine Karte.*
Sometimes he forgets his ticket.

**das Vergnügen** [ver-GNUI-gen] noun, neut.                      **pleasure**
*Kommst du mit uns? Mit Vergnügen!*
Are you going with us? With pleasure!

**verhaften** [fer-HAHF-ten] verb                                 **to arrest**
*Die Polizistin verhaftet den Dieb.*
The policewoman arrests the thief.

**vereinigt** [fer-I-nigt] adjective                              **united**
**vereint** [fer-INT] adjective                                   **united, joined**

**die Vereinigten Staaten von Amerika**         **United States of America**

**die Vereinten Nationen**                      **United Nations**

**verkaufen** [fer-KOW-fen] verb                                  **to sell**
*Sie verkauft Spielzeug in diesem Geschäft.*
She sells toys in this store.

**der Verkäufer** [fer-KOI-fer] noun, masc.                       **salesman**
**die Verkäuferin** [fer-KOI-fer-in] noun, fem.                   **saleslady**
*Der Verkäufer zeigt ihm einen Pullover.*
The salesman is showing him a sweater.

**der Verkehr** [fer-KEHR] noun, masc.                            **traffic**
*Der Verkehr hält bei Rot.*
The traffic stops for the red light.

**verlassen** [fer-LAS-sen] verb     **to leave (a place)**

*Sie verlässt das Büro um fünf Uhr.*
She leaves the office at five o'clock.

---

**verlieren** [fer-LEER-en] verb     **to lose**

*Pass auf, sonst verlierst du deinen Schal.*
Careful, you are going to lose your scarf.

---

**verrückt** [fer-RUIKT] adjective     **crazy**

*Dieser Plan ist verrückt.*
This plan is crazy.

---

**verschütten** [fer-SHUIT-ten] verb     **to spill**

*Das Baby verschüttet die Milch.*
The baby spills the milk.

---

**versprechen** [fer-SHPREH'h'en] verb     **to promise**

*Er verspricht, seine Hausaufgaben zu machen.*
He promises to do his homework.

---

**verstecken** [fer-SHTEK-en] verb     **to hide**

*Sie versteckt das Geschenk in der Schublade.*
She hides the present in the drawer.

---

**Verstecken spielen** expression     **to play hide and seek**

*Die Kinder spielen Verstecken.*
The children play hide and seek.

---

**verstehen** [fer-SHTEH-en] verb     **to understand**

*Er versteht die Frage, aber hat keine Antwort.*
He understands the question but has no answer.

---

**versuchen** [fer-SOO-'h'en] verb     **to try**

*Ich versuche das neue Kuchenrezept.*
I am trying the new cake recipe.

---

162

**Verzeihung!** [fer-TSI-ung] expression      **Excuse me!**
**Entschuldigung!**      **Beg your pardon!**

---

**der Vetter** [FET-ter] noun, masc.      **cousin**

*Mein Vetter Paul ist elf Jahre alt und meine*
*Kusine Maria ist siebzehn.*
My cousin Paul is eleven years old and my
cousin Mary is seventeen.

---

**viel, viele** [FEEL, FEEL-e] adverb      **much, many**

*Lernst du viel jeden Tag?*
Do you study much every day?

*Ja, ich habe viele Aufgaben.*
Yes, I have many assignments.

---

**vielleicht** [feel-LIʼhʼT] adverb      **perhaps, maybe**

*Gehen wir heute Abend ins Kino? Vielleicht.*
Are we going to the movies tonight? Maybe.

---

**vier** [FEER] adjective      **four**

*Es gibt vier Plätzchen auf dem Teller.*
There are four cookies on the plate.

---

**viereckig** [FEER-ek-iʼhʼ] adjective      **square**

*Der Tisch ist viereckig.*
The table is square.

---

**das Viertel** [FEER-tel] noun, neut.      **quarter**

*Es ist (ein) Viertel nach sechs.*
It is a quarter after six.

---

**vierzig** [FEER-tsiʼhʼ] adjective      **forty**

*Lesen wir das Märchen von den vierzig Dieben.*
Let's read the tale of the forty thieves.

---

**vierzehn** [FEER-ts<u>eh</u>n] adjective        **fourteen**
*Es gibt vierzehn Schüler in meiner Klasse.*
There are fourteen pupils in my class.

---

**das Violett** [vee-<u>oh</u>-LET] noun       **violet, purple**
*Blau und Rot macht Violett.*
Blue and red make purple.

---

**die Violine** [vee-<u>oh</u> LEEN-eh] noun, fem.     **violin**
*Die Violine liegt auf dem Klavier.*
The violin is on the piano.

---

**der Vogel** [F<u>OH</u>-gel] noun, masc.       **bird**
*Der Vogel ist im Baum.*
The bird is on the tree.

---

**voll** [FOL] adjective       **full**
*Der Koffer ist voll mit Kleidern.*
The suitcase is full of clothes.

---

**von** [FON] preposition       **of, from**
*Hier, der Apfel ist von deinem Großvater.*
Here, the apple is from your grandfather.

---

**vor** [FOR] preposition       **before, in front of**
*Das Mädchen sitzt vor dem Jungen.*
The girl is sitting in front of the boy.

---

**vor allem** [for AL-em] expression       **above all**
*Ich sehe gern fern, Samstag morgens vor allem.*
I like to watch television, Saturday mornings above all.

---

**der Vorhang** [F<u>OH</u>R-hang] noun, masc.     **curtain, drape**
*Die Vorhänge in meinem Zimmer sind zu lang.*
The curtains in my room are too long.

---

**vorlesen** [FOHR-leh-zen] verb     **to read aloud**

*Er liest die Geschichte vor.*
He reads the story aloud.

---

**vorstellen** [FOHR-shtel-en] verb     **to introduce**

| ich stelle vor | wir/sie/Sie stellen vor |
|---|---|
| du stellst vor | ihr stellt vor |
| er/sie/es stellt vor | |

*Sie stellt uns ihren Enkel vor.*
She is introducing her grandson to us.

---

## W

**wachsen** [VAKS-en] verb     **to grow**

*Viele Pflanzen wachsen in diesem Garten.*
Many plants are growing in this garden.

---

**die Waffe** [VAF-e] noun, fem.     **gun, weapon**

*Eine Waffe ist gefährlich.*
A gun is dangerous.

---

**wagen** [VAH-gen] verb     **to dare**

*Ich wage es, mit dem Schauspieler zu sprechen.*
I dare to speak with the actor.

---

**der Wagen** [VAH-gen] noun, masc.     **car**
**das Auto** [OW-to] noun, neut.

*Das Auto ist in der Garage.*
The car is in the garage.

---

**der Waggon** [va-GOHN] noun, masc.     **car (of train)**

*Dieser Zug hat sechs Waggons.*
This train has six cars.

**wählen** [VEH-len] verb              **to choose, dial, vote**

*Wir wählen Schokolade oder Vanille.*
We are choosing chocolate or vanilla.

---

**wahr** [VAHR] adjective                    **true**

*Ist es wahr, dass Katzen und Hunde streiten?*
Is it true that cats and dogs fight?

---

**Nicht wahr?** [NEE'H'T VAHR] expression    **Isn't that true?**

*Die Hauptstadt Österreichs ist Wien, nicht wahr?*
The capital of Austria is Vienna, isn't that true?

---

**während** [VEH-rend] preposition          **during**

*Es gibt meistens keine Schule während des Sommers.*
There is usually no school during the summer.

---

**der Wald** [VALT] noun, masc.             **forest**

*Der Wald ist voll mit Bäumen.*
The forest is full of trees.

---

**der Walkman**         **Walkman®, cassette recorder**
       [WALK-man] noun, masc.

*Wo ist dein Walkman?*
Where is your Walkman?

---

**wann** [VAN] adverb                    **when**

*Wann kommen sie?*
When are they coming?

---

**warm** [vAHRM] adjective             **warm**

*Das Essen ist noch warm.*
The meal is still warm.

---

**warten auf** [vAHR-ten owf] expression      **to wait for**

*Sie wartet auf ihren Vater.*
She is waiting for her father.

---

**warum?** [va-RUM] interrogative         **why?**

*Warum ist er denn verspätet?*
Why is he late?

---

**waschen** [va-shen] verb             **to wash**

*Sie wäscht das Auto.*
She is washing the car.

---

**die Waschmaschine**         **washing machine**
    [vASH-ma-shee-ne] noun, fem.

---

**was für ein** (masc. & neut.)    **what type, what kind of**
    [vAS für IN] expression
**was für eine** (fem.) [vas für AIN-e] expression

*Was für ein Computer ist denn das?*
What type of computer is that?

---

**Was ist los?**             **What's the matter?**
    [vAS ist LOHS] expression

*Du siehst traurig aus. Was ist denn los?*
You look sad. What's the matter?

---

**das Wasser** [VAS-ser] noun, neut. **water**

*Da ist Wasser im Waschbecken.*
There is water in the sink.

---

**die Wassermelone** **watermelon**
    [VAS-ser-mel-OH-ne] noun, fem.

*Das Mädchen trägt eine Wassermelone.*
The girl is carrying a watermelon.

---

**der Wecker** [VEK-ker] noun, masc. **alarm clock**

*Ihr Wecker klingelt um sieben Uhr.*
Her alarm clock rings at seven o'clock.

---

**wedeln** [VEH-deln] verb **to wag**

*Der Hund wedelt mit seinem Schwanz, wenn er froh ist.*
The dog wags his tail when he is happy.

---

**der Weg** [VEHG] noun, masc. **way, path**

*Dieser Weg führt zur Brücke.*
This path leads to the bridge.

---

**weich** [VĪh'] adjective **soft**

*Der Sessel ist weich.*
The armchair is soft.

---

**weinen** [VĪ-nen] verb **to cry**

*Ich weine, wenn mich jemand neckt.*
I cry when someone teases me.

---

**weise** [VI-ze] adjective      **wise**

*Mein Großvater ist weise.*
My grandfather is wise.

---

**weit** [VIT] adverb      **far**

*Ist Washington weit von New York?*
Is Washington far from New York?

---

**der Weizen** [VI-tsen] noun, masc.      **wheat**

*Ich sehe Weizen auf den Feldern.*
I see wheat in the fields.

---

**die Welt** [VELT] noun, fem.      **world**

*Wie viele Nationen gibt es in der Welt?*
How many nations are there in the world?

---

**der Weltraum** [VELT-rowm] noun, masc.      **space**

*Astronauten arbeiten im Weltraum in einer Raumstation.*
Astronauts work in space in a space station.

---

**welcher** [VEL-'h˙er] adjective, masc.      **which**
**welche** [VEL-'h˙e] fem. & pl.
**welches** [VEL-'h˙es] neut.

*Welches Buch lesen wir?*
Which book are we reading?

---

**die Welle** [VEL-le] noun, fem.      **wave**

*Wir sehen die Wellen am Ozean.*
We see the waves at the ocean.

---

**der Wellensittich**      **parakeet**
> [VEL-len-zi-ti·h'] noun, masc.

*Haben sie einen Wellensittich?*
Do they have a parakeet?

---

**wem** [VEHM] pronoun      **to whom**

*Wem gibst du das Geschenk?*
To whom are you giving the present?

---

**wen** [VEHN] pronoun      **whom**

*Wen kennst du hier?*
Whom do you know here?

---

**weniger** [VEHN-ee-ger] adverb      **less, fewer**

*Zwölf weniger zwei macht zehn.*
Twelve less two makes ten.

---

**wenn** [VEN] conjunction      **when, whenever**

*I lese ein Buch, wenn es regnet.*
I read a book when it rains.

---

**wer** [VER] pronoun      **who**

*Wer ist der Gast?*
Who is that guest?

---

**werden** [VER-den] verb      **to become**

| | |
|---|---|
| ich werde | wir/sie/Sie werden |
| du wirst | ihr werdet |
| er/sie/es wird | |

*Sie wird Polizistin.*
She is becoming a policewoman.

---

170

**werfen** [VER-fen] verb      **to throw**

| | |
|---|---|
| ich werfe | wir/sie/Sie werfen |
| du wirfst | ihr werft |
| er/sie/es wirft | |

*Sie wirft den Ball.*
She is throwing the ball.

---

**der Westen** [VES-ten] noun, masc.      **the west**

*Wenn ich von Dresden nach Köln fahre, fahre ich nach Westen.*
When I go from Dresden to Cologne, I go toward the west.

---

**das Wetter** [VET-ter] noun, neut.      **weather**

*Wie ist denn das Wetter?*
How is the weather?

---

**wichtig** [VI'h'-tig] adjective      **important**

*Es ist wichtig, Gemüse zu essen.*
It is important to eat vegetables.

---

**Wie bitte?** [VEE BIT-te] interjection      **What's that?**

*Wie bitte? Noch einmal, ja!*
What's that please? Repeat it!

---

**wiederholen** [vee-der-HOL-en] verb      **to repeat**

*Die Lehrerin sagt, "Wiederhole deine Frage, Georg!"*
The teacher (fem.) says, "Repeat your question, George!"

---

**wiedersehen** [VEE-der-zeh-en] verb      **to see again**

*Ich sehe den Film nächste Woche wieder.*
I am going to see the film again next week.

---

**Auf Wiedersehen!**      **Until we see each other again!**
                            **Good-bye!**
**Wiedersehen!** expression      **Good-bye for now!**

---

**Wie geht's?**              **How are you? (informal)**
[VEE GEHTS] expression
**Wie geht es Ihnen?**         **How are you? (formal)**
[VEE GEHT es EE-nen] expression

---

**der Wein** [VIN] noun, masc.            **wine**
*Der Kellner bringt den Wein.*
The waiter brings the wine.

---

**weiß** [VIS] adjective                 **white**
*Seine Schuhe sind weiß.*
His shoes are white.

---

**wie viel** [vee FEEL] expression      **how much**
*Wie viel kostet das?*
How much does that cost?

---

**wie viele** [vee FEEL-e] expression     **how many**
*Wie viele Spiele hast du?*
How many games do you have?

---

**die Wiege** [VEE-ge] noun, fem.        **cradle**
*Das Baby schläft in der Wiege.*
The baby is sleeping in the cradle.

---

**wild** [VILD] adjective                 **wild**
*Der Förster fängt den wilden Bären.*
The ranger catches the wild bear.

---

**der Wind** [VINT] noun, masc.          **wind**

*Im Sturm ist der Wind lauter als der Donner.*
In the storm the wind is louder than the thunder.

---

**der Winter** [VIN-ter] noun, masc.                **winter**

*Der Winter kommt nach dem Herbst.*
Winter comes after fall.

---

**die Wippe** [VIP-pe] noun, fem.                   **seesaw**

*Die Jungen sind auf der Wippe.*
The boys are on the seesaw.

---

**wir** [VEER] pronoun                                **we**

*Wir fahren oft aufs Land.*
We often drive to the country.

---

**der Wischer**                          **eraser (for blackboard)**
         [VISH-er] noun, masc.

*Haben wir einen Wischer für die Tafel?*
Do we have an eraser for the blackboard?

---

**wissen** [VIS-sen] verb                            **to know**

   ich/er/sie/es weiß    wir/sie/Sie wissen
   du weißt          ihr wisst

*Sie weiß, wie die Hauptstadt von der Schweiz heißt, Bern.*
She knows the name of the capital of Switzerland, Bern.

---

**wo** [VOH] adverb                                  **where**

*Wo ist der Eingang?*
Where is the entrance?

---

**die Woche** [VO-'h'eh] noun, fem.                  **week**

*Ein Monat hat vier Wochen.*
A month has four weeks.

---

**sich wohl fühlen**        **to feel well**
     [zi·h· VOHL FUI-len] expression

*Ich fühle mich nicht wohl heute.*
I do not feel well today.

---

**wohnen** [VOH-nen] verb      **to dwell, to live**

*Wir wohnen in einer Wohnung.*
We live in an apartment.

---

**die Wohnung** [VOH-nung] noun, fem.    **dwelling, apartment**

*Meine Wohnung ist im Erdgeschoss.*
My apartment is on the ground floor.

---

**das Wohnzimmer**        **living room**
     [VOHN-tsim-mer] noun, neut.

*Wer ist denn im Wohnzimmer?*
Who is in the living room?

---

**der Wolf** [VOLF] noun, masc.      **wolf**

*Rotkäppchen hat keine Angst vor dem Wolf.*
Red Riding Hood is not afraid of the wolf.

---

**die Wolke** [VOL-ke] noun, fem.      **cloud**

*Die Sonne ist hinter den Wolken.*
The sun is behind the clouds.

---

**die Wolle** [VOL-le] noun, fem.      **wool**

*Meine Socken sind aus Wolle.*
My socks are made of wool.

**wollen** [VOL-len] verb                  **to want to**

ich/er/sie/es will      wir/sie/Sie wollen
du willst               ihr wollt

*Die Krankenschwester will dem Kind helfen.*
The nurse wants to help the child.

---

**das Wort** [VORT] noun, neut.               **word**

*Wie schreibt man das Wort "Wörterbuch"?*
How do you spell the word "dictionary"?

---

**Wunderbar! Ausgezeichnet!**       **Great! Excellent!**
[VOON-der-bar] interjection

---

**wunderbar** [VOON-der-bar] adjective      **wonderful**

*Es ist eine wunderbare Party.*
It is a wonderful party.

---

**der Wunsch** [VUNSH] noun, masc.          **wish**

*Hast du einen Wunsch für deinen Geburtstag?*
Do you have a wish for your birthday?

---

**der Wurm** [VOORM] noun, masc.           **worm**

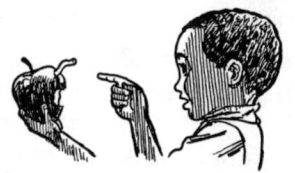

*Da ist ein Wurm in meinem Apfel.*
There is a worm in my apple.

---

**die Wurst** [VURST] noun, fem.           **sausage**

*Wer kocht die Wurst?*
Who will cook the sausage?

**die Wüste** [VUI-steh] noun, fem.      **desert**

*In der Wüste gibt es viel Sand.*
In the desert there is a lot of sand.

---

## Z

**zählen** [TSEH-len] verb      **to count**

*Die Kinder zählen die Ballons.*
The children are counting the balloons.

---

**der Zahn** [TSAHN] noun, masc.      **tooth**

*Ich putze meine Zähne täglich.*
I clean my teeth daily.

---

**der Zahnarzt** [TSAHN-artst] noun, masc.    **dentist**
**die Zahnärztin** [TSAHN-erts-tin] noun, fem.    **dentist**

*Frieda möchte Zahnärztin werden.*
Frieda would like to become a dentist.

---

**die Zahnbürste** [TSAHN-buir-ste] noun, fem.   **toothbrush**
**die Zahnpaste** [TSAHN-pas-te] noun, fem.    **toothpaste**
**Zahnschmerzen haben**    **to have a toothache**
     [TSAHN-shmer-tsen HAH-ben] expression

*Man geht zum Zahnarzt, wenn man Zahnschmerzen hat.*
You go to the dentist when you have a toothache.

---

**das Zebra** [TSEH-bra] noun, neut.      **zebra**

*Ein Zebra hat schwarze und weiße Streifen.*
A zebra has black and white stripes.

---

**der Zeh** [TSEH] noun, masc.      **toe**

*Das Baby fasst seine Zehen an.*
The baby touches its toes.

---

**zehn** [TSEHN] adjetive                                    **ten**

*Ich habe zehn Finger und zehn Zehen.*
I have ten fingers and ten toes.

**zeichnen** [TSIʻh-nen] verb                               **to draw**

*Charlotte zeichnet ein Bild von einem Haus.*
Charlotte is drawing a picture of a house.

**zeigen** [TSI-gen] verb                                   **to show**

*Anna zeigt mir ihren Computer.*
Anna is showing me her computer.

**die Zeitung** [TSI-tung] noun, fem.                       **newspaper**

*Sonntagmorgens lesen wir die Zeitung.*
On Sunday mornings we read the newspaper.

**das Zelt** [TSELT] noun, neut.                            **tent**

*Wenn wir campen, schlafe ich in einem Zelt.*
When we go camping, I sleep in a tent.

**zelten** [TSEL-ten] verb                                  **to camp**

*Meine Familie zeltet sehr gern.*
My family loves to camp.

**die Zero, die Null** [ZEH-ro, NUL] noun, fem.             **zero**

*Die Zahl zehn hat eine Eins und eine Null.*
The number ten has a one and a zero.

**das Zeugnis** [TSOOIG-nis] noun, neut.                    **grade**

*Meine Zeugnisse in Mathe sind sehr gut.*
My grades in math are very good.

**die Zigarette** [tsi-ga-RET-te] noun, fem.               **cigarette**

*Raucht dein Onkel Zigaretten?*
Does your uncle smoke cigarettes?

**die Ziege** [TSEE-ge] noun, fem.                                     **goat**

*Die Ziege frisst Gras auf dem Berg.*
The goat is eating grass on the mountain.

---

**ziehen** [TSEE-en] verb                                     **to pull**

*Bert zieht den Esel.*
Bert is pulling the donkey.

---

**das Zimmer** [TSIM-mer] noun, neut.                                     **room**

*Unsere Wohnung hat drei Zimmer.*
Our apartment has three rooms.

---

**der Zirkus** [TSEER-koos] noun, masc.                                     **circus**

*Es gibt viele Tiere im Zirkus.*
There are many animals in the circus.

---

**die Zitrone** [tsit-ROH-ne] noun, fem.                                     **lemon**

*Zitronen sind gelb.*
Lemons are yellow.

---

**der Zoo** [tsoo] noun, masc.                                     **zoo**

*Wann öffnet der Zoo?*
What time does the zoo open?

---

**zu** [TSOO] preposition                                     **to**

    **zum** (masc. & neut.)                                     **to the**
    **zur** (fem.)                                     **to the**
    **zu den** (pl.)                                     **to the**

*Sie fährt zum Flughafen.*
She is going to the airport.

---

**der Zucker** [TSUK-er] noun, masc.                                     **sugar**

*Er nimmt Zucker mit dem Tee.*
He takes sugar with the tea.

**der Zug** [TSOOG] noun, masc.                      **train**

*Züge sind bequem und nicht zu teuer.*
Trains are comfortable and not too expensive.

---

**zu Hause sein** [tsoo HOW-ze] expression          **be at home**

*Wo ist denn deine Schwester? Sie ist zu Hause.*
Where is your sister? She is at home.

---

**die Zukunft** [TSOO-kunft] noun, fem.             **future**

*In der Zukunft werde ich Ägypten besuchen.*
In the future I am going to visit Egypt.

---

**die Zunge** [TSOON-geh] noun, fem.                **tongue**

*Heiße Suppe verbrennt meine Zunge.*
Hot soup burns my tongue.

---

**zurückbringen**                    **to bring back, to return**
     [tsoo-RUIK-bring-en] verb

*Sie bringt das Buch in die Bibliothek zurück.*
She returns the book to the library.

---

**zurückgeben** [tsoo-RUIK-geh-ben] verb            **to give back**

*Er gibt meine Rollschuhe zurück.*
He gives my roller skates back.

**zurückgehen** [tsoo-RUIK-geh-en] verb             **to go back**

*Ich gehe zur Bibliothek zurück.*
I am going back to the library.

**zurückkommen** [tsoo-RUIK-kom-men] verb      **to come back**

---

**zusammen** [tsoo-ZAM-en] adverb                   **together**

*Lass uns doch zusammen zur Schule gehen.*
Let's go to school together.

---

**Zutritt verboten!**                    **No entrance!**
[TSOO-trit fer-BOHT-en]  expression

---

**zwanzig** [TSVAN-tsi'h˙] adjective                    **twenty**
*Wir haben nur zwanzig Gläser.*
We have only twenty glasses.

---

**zwei** [TSVI] adjective                    **two**
*Er hat zwei Hunde.*
He has two dogs.

---

**zweimal** [TSVI-mahl] adverb                    **twice**
*Sag das Wort zweimal, bitte.*
Please say the word twice.

---

**zwischen** [TSVISH-en] preposition                    **between**
*Das Auto steht zwischen der Kirche und dem Rathaus.*
The car stands (is) between the church and the city hall.

---

**zwölf** [TSVOELF] adjective                    **twelve**
*Ein Jahr hat zwölf Monate.*
A year has twelve months.

---

# Englisch-Deutsch

# (English-German)

# Aussprache des Englischen, für einen Deutschsprechenden

*(English Pronunciation Key for German Speakers)*

## Note

**1.** Im Gegensatz zum Deutschen, wo man fast alles geschriebene ausspricht, ist Englisch anders. Ein "e" am Ende eines Wortes ist meistens lautlos.

**2.** Die angegebene Aussprache des Englischen ist eher eine Annäherung, als eine exakte Aussprache.

| KONSONANTEN | | | |
|---|---|---|---|
| Englische Buchstabe | Phonetisch Geschrieben | Englisches Beispiel | Deutsches Beispiel |
| b | b | boat | **B**aby |
| c | k *oder* ss | close, piece | **C**afé, da**ss** |
| ch | tsch | chase | **K**itsch |
| d | d | director | **D**irektor |
| f | f *oder* v | fast, vapor | für, **V**ater |
| g | g | gap | **g**ut |
| h | h | hammer | **H**ammer |
| j | dg | joy | **J**eans |
| k | k | key | **K**ind |
| kn | n | knee | **n**ein |
| i | i | lost | **L**eute |
| m | m | mine | **M**utter |
| n | n | mine | **N**ame |
| p | p | pipe | **P**apa |
| qu | qu | queen | **Q**uadrat |
| r | r | Es gibt nicht kein gleichwertiges beispiel | |
| s | s | song | **C**ity |
| sh | sch | wish | **Sch**atten |
| t | t | tea | **T**ee |
| tion | shen | sta**tion** | Wa**schen** |
| v | w | have | **w**enn |
| w | w̲ | week | **W**alkman |
| x | ks | si**x** | ni**x** |
| y | j | **y**ou | **j**ung |
| z | s | la**z**y | **S**onne |

| VOKALE UND DOPPELVOKALE | | | |
|---|---|---|---|
| Englische Buchstabe | Phonetisch Geschrieben | Englisches Beispiel | Deutsches Beispiel |
| a | a | what | **A**ntwort |
| | eh | baby | gehen |
| | oh | ball | Kohl |
| | ah | father | haben |
| | ä | jazz | Jazz |
| e | e | bed | nett |
| | ie | Egypt | die |
| i | i | will | bitte |
| | ei | wide | sein |
| o | o | cost | Sommer |
| | oh | whole | Sohn |
| | a | lot | alle |
| | uh | move | Shuh |
| | u | do | du |
| u | u | stupid | Mutter |
| | uh | truth | Blume |
| | ju | usual | jung |
| | a | bus | Mann |
| | i | busy | Bild |
| | ü | turn | für |
| ai, ei | eh | rain, weigh | zehn |
| ea, ee | ie | peach, agree | wie |

## A

**a, an** [ä, än] Artikel und Adjektiv                              **ein, eine**
*A monkey is in the tree.*
Ein Affe ist in im Baum.

**to be able to, can** [EH-bel tu, KÄN] Verb                       **können**
*I can't do the puzzle. It is too difficult.*
Ich kann das Puzzle nicht machen. Es ist zu schwer.

**above all** [ä-BOV OHL] Ausdruck                                **vor allem**
*I like to watch television, Saturday mornings
above all.*
Ich sehe gern fern, Samstag morgens vor allem.

**absent** [ÄP-sint] Adjektiv                                      **abwesend**
*George is absent today.*
Georg ist heute abwesend.

**according to** [ä-KOHR-ding tu] Ausdruck                         **nach**
*According to my brother, it is going to snow
tomorrow.*
Meinem Bruder nach schneit es morgen.

**actor** [ÄK-ter] Substantiv                          **der Schauspieler**
**actress** [ÄK-tres] Substantiv                      **die Schauspielerin**

*The actor is handsome.*
Der Schauspieler ist gut aussehend.

**(to be) acquainted with, to know**          **kennen**
[e-KWEHN-ted with, tu nou]  Verb

*He knows my friend.*
Er kennt meinen Freund.

---

**addition** [ä-DI-shen] Substantiv          **die Addierung**

*We learn addition in school.*
Wir lernen Addierung in der Schule.

---

**address** [äh-DRES] Substantiv          **die Adresse**

*What is your address?*
Was ist deine Adresse?

---

**adventure** [äd-WEN-tscher] Substantiv          **das Abenteuer**

*I like to read the adventures of Puss in Boots.*
Ich lese gern die Abenteuer vom Gestiefelten Kater.

---

**(to be) afraid of** [a-FREHD] Ausdruck          **Angst haben vor**

*Are you afraid of the lion?*
Hast du Angst vor dem Löwen?

---

**after** [ÄF-ter] Präposition          **nach**

*October comes after September.*
Der Oktober kommt nach dem September.

---

**afternoon** [äf-ter-NUHN] Substantiv          **der Nachmittag**

*It is 2:00 in the afternoon.*
Es ist zwei Uhr am Nachmittag.

**again** [a-GEN] Adverb                        **noch einmal**

*Read the letter again, please.*
Lies den Brief noch einmal, bitte!

---

**against** [a-GENST] Präposition                    **gegen**

*Uwe puts the mirror against the wall.*
Uwe stellt den Spiegel gegen die Wand.

---

**age** [EHDZH] Substantiv                        **das Alter**

*What's the age of this vase?*
Was ist das Alter von dieser Vase?

---

**Don't you agree?**                            **Nicht wahr?**
  [dohnt ju ä-GRIE] Ausdruck

*My aunt is beautiful, don't you agree?*
Meine Tante ist hübsch, nicht wahr?

---

**agreed** [ä-GRIED] Interjektion            **einverstanden, gut**

*Shall we leave at twelve o'clock? Agreed.*
Gehen wir um zwölf Uhr? Einverstanden!

---

**to aid, to help** [EHD] Verb                      **helfen**

*We'll help you, Mrs. Harris.*
Wir helfen Ihnen, Frau Harris.

---

**(by) airmail** [bei EHR-mehl] Ausdruck         **per Luftpost**

*My letter is going by airmail.*
Mein Brief geht per Luftpost.

---

**airplane** [EHR- plehn] Substantiv            **das Flugzeug**
**(airplane) pilot** [PAI-lot] Substantiv            **der Pilot**
                                                **die Pilotin**

*The pilot flies the airplane.*
Der Pilot fliegt das Flugzeug.

---

**airport** [EHR-port] Substantiv        **der Flughafen**

*My uncle works at the airport.*
Mein Onkel arbeitet am Flughafen.

---

**alarm clock** [a-LAHRM KLAK] Substantiv     **der Wecker**

*Her alarm clock rings at seven o'clock.*
Ihr Wecker klingelt um sieben Uhr.

---

**alike, similar** [a-LEIK] Adjektiv        **ähnlich**

*The dogs look alike.*
Die Hunde sehen ähnlich aus.

---

**all** [ohl] Pronomen              **alle**
**all over** [ohl OW-WER] Adverb      **überall**

*I look for my watch all over.*
Ich suche meine Armbanduhr überall.

---

**all right** [ohl REIT] Interjektion     **gut, na gut**

*Are you coming along? All right, I'll come along.*
Kommst du mit? Gut, ich komme mit.

---

**almost** [ohl-MOWST] Adverb          **fast**

*It is almost ten o'clock.*
Es ist fast zehn Uhr.

---

**alone** [a-LOWN] Adjektiv           **allein**

*I am alone in the kitchen.*
Ich bin allein in der Küche.

---

**alphabet** [ÄL-fa-bet] Substantiv **das Alphabet**

*Can you say the alphabet in German?*
Kannst du das Alphabet auf Deutsch sagen?

**already** [ohl-RE-di] Adverb **schon**

*Is it dinner time already?*
Ist es schon Zeit fürs Mittagessen?

**also** [OHL-so] Adverb **auch**

*We also have a Volkswagen.*
Wir haben auch einen Volkswagen.

**always** [OHL-wehs] Adverb **immer**

*The leaves always change color in the fall.*
Die Blätter verändern immer im Herbst die Farbe.

**ambulance** [AM-bju-lans] Substantiv **der Krankenwagen**

*The ambulance is at the hospital.*
Der Krankenwagen ist am Krankenhaus.

**American** [a-MER-i-ken] Adjektiv **amerikanisch**

*The camera is American.*
Der Fotoapparat ist amerikanisch.

**amusing (funny)** [a-MJUS-ing] Adjektiv **lustig**

*The bear is amusing.*
Der Bär ist lustig.

**and** [ÄND] Konjunktion **und**

*Margaret and her girlfriend are playing.*
Margarete und ihre Freundin spielen.

**angry** [ÄNG-grie] Adjektiv                          **ärgerlich, böse**

*Mom is angry because I make a lot of noise.*
Mutti ist böse, denn ich mache viel Lärm.

---

**animal** [Ä-ni-mel] Substantiv                              **das Tier**

*The animals are in the forest.*
Die Tiere sind im Wald.

---

**anniversary**                                    **der Hochzeitstag**
      [a-ni-WER-se-rie] Substantiv

*Today is my parents' wedding anniversary.*
Heute ist der Hochzeitstag meiner Eltern.

---

**annoyed** [a-NOID] Adjektiv                            **verärgert**

*Dad is annoyed when I sing while eating.*
Papa ist verärgert, wenn ich beim Essen singe.

---

**another one** [a-NATH-er] Ausdruck               **noch ein(e)**

*Here is another piece of bread.*
Hier ist noch ein Stück Brot.

---

**answer** [ÄN-ser] Substantiv                        **die Antwort**

*He writes the answer on the blackboard.*
Er schreibt die Antwort an die Tafel.

---

**to answer** [ÄN-ser] Verb                              **antworten**

*The child answers quickly.*
Das Kind antwortet schnell.

---

**ant** [ÄNT] Substantiv                                **die Ameise**

*The ant is very small.*
Die Ameise ist sehr klein.

**antenna** [an-TE-na] Substantiv      **die Antenne**

*Television antennas are on the roof of the building.*
Fernsehantennen sind auf dem Dach des Gebäudes.

---

**apartment** [a-PART-ment] Substantiv      **die Wohnung**

*My apartment is on the ground floor.*
Meine Wohnung ist im Erdgeschoss.

---

**to appear, to look** [a-PIER] Verb      **aussehen**

*The cow looks friendly.*
Die Kuh sieht freundlich aus.

---

**appearance** [a-PIER-ens] Substantiv      **das Aussehen**

*The tiger has a ferocious appearance.*
Der Tiger hat ein wildes Aussehen.

---

**appetite** [ÄH-pe-teit] Substantiv      **der Appetit**

*We have no appetite now.*
Wir haben keinen Appetit jetzt.

---

**Enjoy your meal!** Ausdruck      **Guten Appetit!**

---

**apple** [ÄH-pel] Substantiv      **der Apfel**

*I eat an apple every day.*
Ich essen jeden Tag einen Apfel.

---

**apricot** [EH-pri-kat] Substantiv          **die Aprikose, die Marille**

*Is the apricot ripe?*
Ist die Aprikose reif?

---

**April** [EH-pril] Substantiv                          **der April**

*There are thirty days in April.*
Der April hat dreißig Tage.

---

**apron** [EH-prin] Substantiv                        **die Schürze**

*Dad wears an apron when he cooks.*
Papa trägt eine Schürze, wenn er kocht.

---

**aquarium** [ah-KWÄ-rie-em] Substantiv          **das Aquarium**

*There is a turtle in the aquarium.*
Es gibt eine Schildkröte im Aquarium.

---

**aren't you** [ahrnt ju] Ausdruck          **nicht/nicht wahr**

*You are leaving tomorrow, aren't you?*
Du gehst doch morgen, nicht wahr?

---

**arm** [ARM] Substantiv                                **der Arm**

*The baby has strong arms.*
Das Baby hat kräftige Arme.

---

**armchair** [ARM-tschehr] Substantiv          **der Sessel**

*The armchair is comfortable.*
Der Sessel ist bequem.

---

**army** [AHR-mie] Substantiv                        **die Armee**

*The army brings food after the flood.*
Die Armee bringt Lebensmittel nach dem Hochwasser.

---

**around** [a-ROWND] Präposition                          **um**

*I would like to take a trip around the world.*
Ich möchte eine Reise um die Welt machen.

---

**to arrange** [a-REHNDG] Verb                **ordnen, arrangieren**

*The teacher arranges his books.*
Der Lehrer ordnet seine Bücher.

---

**to arrest** [a-REST] Verb                        **verhaften**

*The policewoman arrests the thief.*
Die Polizistin verhaftet den Dieb.

---

**to arrive** [a-REIV] Verb                        **ankommen**

*The train arrives at two fifteen in the afternoon.*
Der Zug kommt um vierzehn Uhr fünfzehn an.

---

**artist** [AHR-tist] Substantiv              **der Künstler**
                                              **die Künstlerin**
*My mother is an artist.*
Meine Mutter ist Künstlerin.

---

**as, since, because** [ÄS] Konjunktion            **denn**

*He invites us for cake, because it is his birthday.*
Er lädt uns zum Kuchen ein, denn er hat Geburtstag.

---

**as** [ÄS] Adverb                                     **als**

*He is going to the party dressed as the wolf.*
Er geht zur Party als Wolf verkleidet.

---

**to be ashamed** [a-SHEHMD] Verb          **sich schämen**

*We are naughty and we are ashamed.*
Wir sind schlimm und wir schämen uns.

---

**to ask** [ÄSK] Verb                                **fragen**

*She asks, "What is today's date?"*
Sie fragt, "Was ist denn das Datum heute?"

---

**to ask for** [ÄSK vor] Ausdruck              **bitten um**

*The girl asks for her allowance.*
Das Mädchen bittet um ihr Taschengeld.

**astronaut** [ÄS-tra-noht] Substantiv          **der Astronaut**
                                                **die Astronautin**

*The astronaut takes a trip in a spaceship.*
Der Astronaut macht eine Reise in einem Raumschiff.

---

**at** [ÄT] Präposition                                           **um**

*When does school begin? At eight thirty.*
Wann beginnt die Schule? Um acht Uhr dreißig.

---

**(to be) at home** [ÄT ho<u>w</u>m] Ausdruck     **zu Hause (sein)**

*They are at home.*
Sie sind zu Hause.

---

**to attend, to go to** [a-TEND] Verb                   **besuchen**

*We attend the soccer game.*
Wir besuchen das Fussballspiel.

---

**to pay attention** [PEH a-TEN-shen] Ausdruck     **aufpassen**

*Pay attention, Fritz!*
Pass auf, Fritz!

*Class, this is important. Please pay attention!*
Kinder, das ist wichtig. Passt bitte auf!

---

**August** [OH-gest] Substantiv                       **der August**

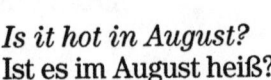

*Is it hot in August?*
Ist es im August heiß?

---

**aunt** [ÄNT] Substantiv | **die Tante**

*My aunt is a physician.*
Meine Tante ist Ärztin.

---

**Austria** [OHS-trie-ja] Substantiv | **Österreich**

*His mother comes from Austria.*
Seine Mutter kommt aus Österreich.

---

**auto(mobile), car** | **das Auto, der Wagen**
  [OH-to] Substantiv

*Our car is old.*
Unser Auto ist alt.

---

**autumn (fall)** [OH-tem] Substantiv | **der Herbst**

*Do you prefer spring or fall?*
Was hast du lieber, Frühling oder Herbst?

---

**avenue** [ÄV-en-ju] Substantiv | **die Allee, der Damm**

*I like to walk on the avenue.*
Ich gehe auf der Allee gern spazieren.

---

**right away** [reit a-WEH] Adverb | **sofort**

*I am going to take a bath right away.*
Ich bade sofort.

---

## B

**baby** [BEH-bie] Substantiv | **das Baby**

*Maria plays with the baby.*
Maria spielt mit dem Baby.

---

**baby carriage**          **der Kinderwagen**
[BEH-bie KÄR-idg] Substantiv

*The baby is in the carriage.*
Das Baby ist im Kinderwagen.

---

**back** [BÄK] Substantiv       **der Rücken**

*Is it Andreas? I only see his back.*
Ist das Andreas? Ich sehe nur den Rücken.

---

**to give back** [giv BÄK] Verb      **zurückgeben**

*She's giving the book back today.*
Sie gibt das Buch heute zurück.

---

**bad** [BÄD] Adjektiv      **schlimm, schlecht**

*The weather is bad.*
Das Wetter ist schlecht.

**Too bad!** [tu BÄD] Ausdruck      **Schade!**

*He is sick. Too bad!*
Er ist krank. Schade!

---

**bag** [BÄG] Substantiv      **die Tüte**

*Here are the oranges. Do you have a bag?*
Da sind die Orangen. Hast du eine Tüte?

---

**baggage** [BÄG-idg] Substantiv      **das Gepäck**

*The baggage is ready for the trip.*
Das Gepäck ist fertig für die Reise.

---

**baker** [BEH-ker] Substantiv      **der Bäcker**
                                   **die Bäckerin**

*The baker makes bread.*
Der Bäcker macht Brot.

---

**bakery** [BEH-ke-rie] Substantiv           **die Bäckerei**

*The baker is in the bakery.*
Der Bäcker ist in der Bäckerei.

**ball** [BOHL] Substantiv           **der Ball**
*The soccer ball is black and white.*
Der Fussball ist schwarz und weiß.

**to play ball** Ausdruck           **Ball spielen**
*Let's play ball.*
Spielen wir doch Ball.

**balloon** [ba-LUHN] Substantiv           **der Ballon**
*The balloon is not heavy.*
Der Ballon ist nicht schwer.

**ballpoint pen**       **der Kugelschreiber, der Kuli**
    [BOHL peunt PEN] Substantiv
*May I borrow your ballpoint pen?*
Darf ich deinen Kuli borgen?

**banana** [ba-NANA] Substantiv           **die Banane**
*The monkey is eating a banana.*
Der Affe frisst eine Banane.

**bank** [BÄNK] Substantiv           **die Bank**
*I have to change money. Where is the bank?*
Ich muss Geld wechseln. Wo ist die Bank?

**baseball** [BEHS-bohl] Substantiv      **Baseball**

*Let's play baseball.*
Spielen wir doch Baseball!

---

**basement** [BEHS-ment] Substantiv      **der Keller**

*The basement is dry.*
Der Keller ist trocken.

---

**basket** [BÄS-ket] Substantiv      **der Korb**

*There are three apples in the basket.*
Es gibt drei Äpfel im Korb.

---

**basketball** [BÄS-ket-bohl] Substantiv      **Basketball**

*Do you know how to play basketball?*
Kannst du Basketball spielen?

---

**bath, bathroom**      **das Bad, das Badezimmer**
     [BÄTH, BÄTH-rum] Substantiv

*Where is the bathroom?*
Wo ist das Badezimmer?

---

**to bathe** [BEHTH] Verb      **baden**

*Mom is bathing the baby.*
Mutti badet das Baby.

**to sunbathe** [SAN-behth] Verb      **sich sonnen**

*He is careful when he sunbathes.*
Er passt auf, wenn er sich sonnt.

---

**bathing suit** [BEHTH-ing suht] Substantiv      **der Badeanzug**
**swim trunks**      **die Badehose**

*I wear a bathing suit at the beach.*
Ich trage einen Badeanzug am Strand.

**to be** [BIE] Verb                **sein**

| | |
|---|---|
| I am | we are |
| you are | you are |
| he/she/it is | they are |

*I am finished.*
Ich bin fertig.

*It is late.*
Es ist spät.

---

**to be acquainted with, to know**     **kennen**
    [a-KWEHN-ted] Verb

*He knows my friend.*
Er kennt meinen Freund.

---

**beach** [BIETSCH] Substantiv        **der Strand**

*We go to the beach in the summer.*
Wir gehen im Sommer an den Strand.

---

**beak** [BIEK] Substantiv          **der Schnabel**

*The parrot's beak is big.*
Der Schnabel des Papageis ist groß.

---

**bear** [BEHR] Substantiv             **der Bär**

*The bear is playing in the water.*
Der Bär spielt im Wasser.

---

**beard** [BIERD] Substantiv           **der Bart**

*The president does not have a beard.*
Der Präsident hat keinen Bart.

---

**beast, pest** [BIEST] Substantiv      **das Biest**

*Mosquitoes are pests everywhere.*
Mücken sind überall Biester.

---

**beautiful** [BJU-tie-ful] Adjektiv                    **hübsch, schön**

*Snow White's stepmother, the queen, is beautiful but cruel.*
Schneewittchens Stiefmutter, die Königin, ist hübsch, aber
grausam.

**because** [bie-KOHS] Konjunktion                         **denn**

*I am not going to the pool, because I don't have a bathing
suit.*
Ich gehe nicht zum Schwimmbad, denn ich habe keinen
Badeanzug.

**to become** [bie-KAM] Verb                              **werden**

*She is becoming a policewoman.*
Sie wird Polizistin.

**bed** [BED] Substantiv                                 **das Bett**

*The cat is on my bed.*
Die Katze ist auf meinem Bett.

**to go to bed** Ausdruck                           **zu Bett gehen**

*She is tired and is going to bed now.*
Sie ist müde und geht jetzt zu Bett.

**bedroom** [BED-ruhm] Substantiv            **das Schlafzimmer**

*This apartment has three bedrooms.*
Diese Wohnung hat drei Schlafzimmer.

**bee** [BIE] Substantiv                              **die Biene**

*The bee is dangerous.*
Die Biene ist gefährlich.

**beefsteak** [BIEF-stehk] Substantiv                    **das Beefsteak**
*I would like beefsteak, please.*
Ich möchte Beefsteak, bitte.

**roast beef** [ROWST-bief] Substantiv                    **der Rindsbraten**
*The roast beef is delicious.*
Der Rindsbraten ist lecker.

**before** [bie-FOHR] Präposition                    **vor**
*My brother comes home before my sister.*
Mein Bruder kommt vor meiner Schwester nach Hause.

**to begin** [be-GIN] Verb                    **beginnen**
*The German film is beginning now.*
Der deutsche Film beginnt jetzt.

**Beg your pardon!**          **Engschuldigung! Verzeihung!**
     see **Excuse me!**

**to behave** [be-HEHV] Verb                    **sich benehmen**
*The children are behaving very well.*
Die Kinder benehmen sich sehr gut.

**behind** [bie-HEIND] Präposition                    **hinter**
*The cat is behind the sofa.*
Die Katze ist hinter dem Sofa.

**before (in front of)** [bie-FOHR] Präposition                    **vor**
*The girl is sitting in front of the boy.*
Das Mädchen sitzt vor dem Jungen.

**to believe, to think** [bie-LIEV] Verb          **glauben, meinen**
*She thinks that she can go to the concert.*
Sie glaubt, dass sie ins Konzert gehen kann.

**to believe (a person)** [bie-LIEV] Verb　　**glauben**

*We believe Mr. Blau.*
Wir glauben Herrn Blau.

---

**bell** [BEL] Substantiv　　　　　　　　**die Glocke**

*This bell rings at twelve o'clock noon.*
Diese Glocke läutet um zwölf Uhr mittags.

---

**doorbell** [DOHR-bel] Substantiv　　　**die Klingel**

*The doorbell is not loud enough.*
Die Klingel ist nicht laut genug.

---

**belt** [BELT] Substantiv　　　　　　　**der Gürtel**

*Great! You've got a new belt.*
Toll! Du hast einen neuen Gürtel.

---

**bench** [BENTSCH] Substantiv　　　　　**die Bank**

*Let's find a bench in the park.*
Lass uns doch eine Bank im Park finden.

---

**Best wishes!** [best WISCH-es] Ausdruck　**Alles Gute!**
**Congratulations!**

---

**better** [BET-er] Adjektiv　　　　　　　**besser**

*I think that the cherries are better than the grapes.*
Ich finde, dass die Kirschen besser als die Trauben sind.

---

**between** [be-TWIEN] Präposition　　　**zwischen**

*The car stands (is) between the church and the city hall.*
Das Auto steht zwischen der Kirche und dem Rathaus.

---

**bicycle** [BEI-sik-el] Substantiv　　　**das Fahrrad**
**bike** [BEIK] Substantiv　　　　　　　　**das Rad**
**to ride a bike** [REID a BEIK] Ausdruck　**Rad fahren**

*When the weather is good Bernard rides his bike.*
Wenn das Wetter gut ist, fährt Bernhard Rad.

**big** [BIG] Adjektiv                                                                    **groß**

*The elephant is very big.*
Der Elefant ist sehr groß.

**bigger** [BIG-ger] Adjektiv                                                        **größer**

*My pencil is bigger than your pencil.*
Mein Bleistift ist größer als dein Bleistift.

**bike,** see **bicycle**

**bill** [BIL] Substantiv                                                            **der Schein**

*I'm rich. I have a twenty-mark bill.*
Ich bin reich. Ich habe einen Zwanzigmarkschein.

**bill** [BIL] Substantiv                                                         **die Rechnung**

*Please bring the bill now.*
Die Rechnung, bitte.

**bird** [BÜRD] Substantiv                                                         **der Vogel**

*The bird is in the tree.*
Der Vogel ist im Baum.

**birthday** [BÜRTH-deh] Substantiv        **der Geburtstag**

*Come to my house. My birthday is on Saturday.*
Komm zu mir. Mein Geburtstag ist am Samstag.

---

**Happy birthday!**              **Alles Gute zum Geburtstag!**
[HÄP-ie BÜRTH-deh] Ausdruck
**Herzlichen Glückwunsch zum Geburtstag!**

---

**to bite** [BEIT] Verb                                  **beißen**

*This dog does not bite.*
Dieser Hund beißt nicht.

---

**to bite** [BEIT] Verb                                  **stechen**

*Mosquitoes bite me often.*
Mücken stechen mich oft.

---

**black** [BLÄK] Adjektiv                               **schwarz**

*My shoes are black.*
Meine Schuhe sind schwarz.

---

**blackboard**                    **die Tafel, die Schultafel**
[BLÄK-bohrd] Substantiv

*The pupil writes on the blackboard.*
Der Schüler schreibt an die Tafel.

---

**blanket, cover**                 **die Decke, die Bettdecke**
[BLÄN-kit] Substantiv

*The blanket is very warm.*
Die Decke ist sehr warm.

---

**Bless you!** [BLESS ju] Ausdruck              **Gesundheit!**

---

**blind** [BLEIND] Adjektiv                              **blind**

*Beethoven was not blind, but deaf.*
Beethoven war nicht blind, sondern taub

**to play blindman's bluff** Ausdruck     **blinde Kuh spielen**

*Let's play blindman's bluff.*
Lass uns doch blinde Kuh spielen!

---

**blond** [BLAHND] Adjektiv       **blond**

*She is blond. She has blond hair.*
Sie ist blond. Sie hat blonde Haare.

---

**blood** [BLAD] Substantiv       **das Blut**

*My foot hurts. Look at the blood.*
Mein Fuß tut weh. Sieh nur das Blut!

---

**a blow, a hit** [BLOW] Substantiv       **der Schlag**

*He gives a blow on the shoulder.*
Er gibt einen Schlag auf die Schulter.

---

**blue** [BLUH] Adjektiv       **blau**

*The Alpine lake is blue.*
Der Alpensee ist blau.

---

**boat** [BOHT] Substantiv       **das Boot**

*I see a boat in the water.*
Ich sehe ein Boot im Wasser.

---

**book** [BUK] Substantiv       **das Buch**

*We are looking for German books.*
Wir suchen deutsche Bücher.

---

**boot** [BUHT] Substantiv　　　　　　**der Stiefel**

*When it snows, I put on my boots.*
Wenn es schneit, ziehe ich meine Stiefel an.

---

**to be bored** [BOHRD] Verb　　　　**sich langweilen**

*I am never bored.*
Ich langweile mich nie.

---

**to be born** [BORN] Ausdruck　　　　**bin geboren**

*My mother was born in Switzerland. (She is living.)*
Meine Mutter ist in der Schweiz geboren.

---

**to be born** [BORN] Ausdruck　　　　**wurde geboren**

*Beethoven was born in Bonn. (He is dead now.)*
Beethoven wurde in Bonn geboren.

---

**to borrow** [BAHR-ow] Verb　　　　　**borgen**

*I'll borrow a pencil from the teacher.*
Ich borge einen Bleistift vom Lehrer.

---

**bottle** [BAT-l] Substantiv　　　　　**die Flasche**

*Be careful! The bottle is made of glass.*
Pass auf! Die Flasche ist aus Glas.

---

**boulevard, avenue**　　　　**der Damm, die Allee**
　　　　[BU-le-wahrd] Substantiv

*I like to walk on the boulevard.*
Ich gehe gern auf dem Damm spazieren.

---

**bouquet** [bu-KEH] Substantiv            **der Blumenstrauß**
*"Here is a bouquet of flowers, Margie," he says.*
"Hier ist ein Blumenstrauß, Gretchen," sagt er.

**bowl** [BOWL] Substantiv                  **die Schüssel**
*Where is the bowl for the salad?*
Wo ist die Schüssel für den Salat?

**box** [BAKS] Substantiv                    **die Schachtel**

*There is a box of candy.*
Dort ist eine Schachtel Pralinen.

**boy** [BOI] Substantiv              **der Junge, der Bub**
*The boy is playing with his siblings.*
Der Junge spielt mit seinen Geschwistern.

**branch** [BRÄNTSCH] Substantiv                **der Ast**
*The tree has many large branches.*
Der Baum hat viele große Äste.

**brave** [BREHV] Adjektiv                        **mutig**
*The prince is brave when he saves the princess.*
Der Prinz ist mutig, wenn er die Prinzessin rettet.

**bread** [BRÄD] Substantiv                    **das Brot**
*The loaf of bread is fresh.*
Das Brot ist frisch.

**to break** [BREHK] Verb                      **brechen**
*Be careful! Don't break the glass, Anne.*
Pass auf! Brich das Glas nicht, Anne!

**breakfast** [BREK-fest] Substantiv                    **das Frühstück**

*Is breakfast the biggest meal?*
Ist das Frühstück die größte Mahlzeit?

---

**bridge** [BRIDG] Substantiv                            **die Brücke**

*The Adenauer Bridge crosses the Rhine in Bonn.*
Die Adenauer Brücke führt in Bonn über den Rhein.

---

**briefcase** [BRIEF-kehs] Substantiv            **die Aktentasche**

*He forgets his briefcase often.*
Er vergisst seine Aktentasche oft.

---

**to bring** [BRING] Verb                                     **bringen**

*I am bringing sandwiches for the picnic.*
Ich bringe Brote für das Picknick.

---

**broad, wide** [BROHD] Adjektiv                           **breit**

*The table is wide.*
Der Tisch ist breit.

---

**broom** [BRUHM] Substantiv                           **der Besen**

*We sweep the floor with a broom.*
Wir kehren den Fußboden mit dem Besen.

---

**brother** [BRATH-er] Substantiv                    **der Bruder**

*How many brothers does George have?*
Wie viele Brüder hat Georg?

---

**brown** [BRAUN] Adjektiv                                  **braun**

*She has brown eyes.*
Sie hat braune Augen.

---

**brush** [BRASCH] Substantiv                        **die Bürste**

hairbrush          die Haarbürste
toothbrush         die Zahnbürste

| | |
|---|---|
| clothesbrush | die Kleiderbürste |
| nailbrush | die Nagelbürste |

*The hairbrush is bigger than the toothbrush.*
Die Haarbürste ist größer als die Zahnbürste.

---

**to brush** [BRASCH] Verb                      **bürsten**

*The girl is brushing her hair.*
Das Mädchen bürstet ihre Haare.

---

**bucket, pail** [BAK-it] Substantiv            **der Eimer**

*The farmer fills the pail with milk.*
Der Bauer füllt den Eimer mit Milch.

---

**building** [BIL-ding] Substantiv            **das Gebäude**

*The buildings are very tall in the city.*
Die Gebäude in der Stadt sind sehr groß.

---

**bunny,** see **rabbit**

---

**burglar, thief** [BÜR-gler] Substantiv           **der Dieb**

*They are looking all over for the burglar.*
Man sucht den Dieb überall.

---

**to burn** [BÜRN] Verb                   **verbrennen**

*The man is burning papers in the fireplace.*
Der Mann verbrennt Papiere im Kamin.

---

**bus** [BAS] Substantiv                       **der Bus**

*The children go by bus.*
Die Kinder fahren mit dem Bus.

---

**busy** [BIS-ie] Adjektiv           **beschäftigt**

*My grandfather is always busy.*
Mein Großvater ist immer beschäftigt.

---

**but** [BAT] Konjunktion          **aber**

*I want to go to the movies, but Dad says, "no!"*
Ich möchte ins Kino gehen, aber Papa sagt, "nein!"

---

**butcher**          **der Metzger, der Fleischer**
    [BUTSCH-er] Substantiv

*The butcher sells meat.*
Der Metzger verkauft Fleisch.

---

**butcher shop**          **die Metzgerei, die Fleischerei**
    [BUTSCH-er SCHAP] Substantiv

*You go to the butcher shop to buy meat and sausage.*
Man kauft Fleisch und Würste in der Metzgerei.

---

**butter** [BAT-er] Substantiv          **die Butter**

*Pass the butter, please!*
Die Butter, bitte!

---

**button** [BAT-en] Substantiv          **der Knopf**

*This coat has only three buttons.*
Dieser Mantel hat nur drei Knöpfe.

---

**to buy** [BEI] Verb          **kaufen**

*I would like to buy an orange.*
Ich möchte eine Orange kaufen.

---

**by** [BEI] Präposition          **bei**
    see **near**

**by airmail** Ausdruck **per Luftpost**

*The letter will go by airmail.*
Der Brief geht per Luftpost.

**by car** Ausdruck **mit dem Auto**

*He'll go by car.*
Er fährt mit dem Auto.

**by subway** **mit der Untergrundbahn,**
　　Ausdruck **mit der U-bahn**

*I'll go by subway.*
Ich fahre mit der U-bahn.

---

## C

**cabbage** [KÄB-idsch] Substantiv **das Kraut, der Kohl**

*Do you prefer cabbage or carrots?*
Was hast du lieber Kraut oder Karotten?

**red cabbage** **das Rotkraut, der Rotkohl**
　　[RED KÄB-idsch] Substantiv

*Is the red cabbage fresh?*
Ist der Rotkohl frisch?

---

**café** [ka-FEH] Substantiv **das Café, die Konditorei**

*The café is just around the coner.*
Das Café ist gleich um die Ecke.

---

**cake** [KEHK] Substantiv **der Kuchen, die Torte**

*Mom makes me a cake. It is so pretty.*
Mutti bäckt mir einen Kuchen. Er ist so schön.

---

**calendar** [KÄL-en-der] Substantiv        **der Kalender**

*The calendar is hanging on the wall.*
Der Kalender hängt an der Wand.

**to call (out)** [KOHL] Verb        **rufen**

*Mary sees and calls her friend.*
Maria sieht und ruft ihren Freund.

**to be called, named** [KOHLD] Verb        **heißen**

*He is called Frank.*
Er heißt Frank.

**to call (on the telephone)** [KOHL] Verb        **anrufen**

*He is calling his girlfriend.*
Er ruft seine Freundin an.

**calm** [KAHLM] Adjektiv        **ruhig**

*I like to go rowing when the water is calm.*
Ich rudere gern, wenn das Wasser ruhig ist.

**camera** [KÄM-er-a] Substantiv        **die Kamera**

*Look at my camera. It is new.*
Sieh mal meine Kamera an! Sie ist neu.

**camp** [KÄMP] Substantiv        **das Lager, das Sommerlager**

*The summer camp for boys is over there.*
Das Sommerlager für Jungen ist dort drüben.

**to camp** [KÄMP] Verb        **zelten**

*My family loves to camp.*
Meine Familie zeltet sehr gern.

**can, be able to** [KÄN] Verb        **können**

*Can he ski?*
Kann er Ski fahren?

**can, may** [KĂN] Verb                                                   **dürfen**

*May I go to the movies?*
Darf ich ins Kino gehen?

---

**candy** [KĂN-die] Substantiv                                           **Bonbons**

*Eric likes candy.*
Erik mag Bonbons.

---

**capital** [KĂP-it-el] Substantiv                              **die Hauptstadt**

*What is the capital of the United States?*
Wie heißt die Hauptstadt der Vereinigten Staaten?

---

**car** [KAHR] Substantiv                              **das Auto, der Wagen**

*The car is in the garage.*
Das Auto ist in der Garage.

---

**car (railroad)** [KAHR] Substantiv                            **der Waggon**

*This train has six cars.*
Dieser Zug hat sechs Waggons.

---

**card** [KAHRD] Substantiv                   **die Spielkarte, die Karte**
**to play cards** Ausdruck                              **Karten spielen**

*Does he play cards?*
Spielt er Karten?

**postcard**                        **die Ansichtskarte, die Postkarte**
   [POWST-kahrd] Substantiv

---

**to be careful, to watch out** [KEHR-ful] Verb          **aufpassen**

*Be careful, the soup is hot!*
Pass auf, die Suppe ist heiß!

---

**carefully** [KEHR-fu-lie] Adverb                              **vorsichtig**

*Tabia carries the bottles carefully.*
Tabia trägt die Flaschen vorsichtig.

---

**(baby) carriage,** see **baby**           **der Kinderwagen**

---

**carrot** [KÄR-et] Substantiv        **die Möhre, die Karotte**
*Rabbits eat carrots.*
Kaninchen fressen Karotten.

---

**to carry** [KÄR-ie] Verb                     **tragen**

*The dog is carrying a newspaper.*
Der Hund trägt eine Zeitung.

---

**castle** [KÄS-el] Substantiv                  **die Burg**
*The castle is on a hill.*
Die Burg ist auf einem Berg.

---

**cat** [KÄT] Substantiv                         **die Katze**

*The cat is playing with the girl.*
Die Katze spielt mit dem Mädchen.

---

**to catch** [KÄTSCH] Verb                      **fangen**
*Hurray! Anna catches the ball.*
Hurrah! Anna fängt den Ball.

---

**CD, compact disc** [sie-DIE] Substantiv     **die CD-Platte**
**CD player** Substantiv                 **der CD-Spieler**
*I have two CDs, but I have no CD player.*
Ich habe zwei CDs, aber ich habe keinen CD-Spieler.

---

**ceiling** [CIE-ling] Substantiv      **die Decke**
*The ceiling of the ballroom is interesting.*
Die Decke des Ballsaals ist interessant.

**celery** [CE-le-rie] Substantiv      **der Sellerie**
*Here is the celery for the salad.*
Da ist Sellerie für den Salat.

**cellar, basement** [CEL-er] Substantiv      **der Keller**
*The stairs lead to the cellar.*
Die Treppe führt zum Keller.

**certain, sure** [CÜR-ten] Adjektiv      **sicher**
*Today is Tuesday. Are you sure?*
Heute ist Dienstag. Bist du sicher?

**chair** [TSCHEHR] Substantiv      **der Stuhl**
*Five chairs are in the dining room.*
Fünf Stühle sind im Esszimmer.

**chalk** [TSCHOHK] Substatniv      **die Kreide**
*The teacher looks for the chalk.*
Die Lehrerin sucht die Kreide.

**to change** [TSCHEHNDG] Verb      **ändern**
*He changes his answer.*
Er ändert seine Antwort.

**to change (trains)** [TSCHEHNDG] verb      **umsteigen**
*In Munich we change trains.*
In München steigen wir um.

**change** [TSCHEHNDG] Substantiv      **das Wechselgeld**
*Wait, he is bringing my change.*
Moment, er bringt mein Wechselgeld.

**cheap** [TSCHIEP] Adjektiv       **billig**
*Oranges are cheap today.*
Orangen sind heute billig.

---

**cheat,** see **deceive** Verb       **betrügen**

---

**check** [TSCHEK] Substantiv       **die Rechnung**
*The waiter is bringing the check.*
Der Kellner bringt die Rechnung.

---

**cheerful** [TSCHIER-ful] Adjektiv       **gutgelaunt**
*My sister is always cheerful.*
Meine Schwester ist immer gutgelaunt.

---

**cheese** [TSCHIES] Substantiv       **der Käse**
*I would like some cheese, please.*
Ich möchte etwas Käse, bitte.

---

**cherry** [TSCHER-ie] Substantiv       **die Kirsche**
*Let us pick the cherries.*
Pflücken wir doch die Kirschen.

---

**chest,** see **closet** Substantiv       **der Schrank**

---

**chicken** [TSCHIK-en] Substantiv       **das Huhn**
*Do you prefer chicken or fish?*
Was hast lieber, Huhn oder Fisch?

---

**child** [TSCHEILD] Substantiv       **das Kind**

*The children are playing on the playground.*
Die Kinder spielen auf dem Spielplatz.

**chimney, fireplace** [TSCHIM-nie] Substantiv      **der Kamin**

*There is a fire in the fireplace.*
Es gibt ein Feuer im Kamin.

---

**chin** [TSCHIN] Substantiv      **das Kinn**

*Here is the doll's chin.*
Hier ist das Kinn der Puppe.

---

**chocolate** [TSCHOH-klat] Substantiv      **die Schokolade**

*What, you don't like chocolate?*
Was, du magst keine Schokolade?

---

**to choose** [TSCHUHS] Verb      **wählen**

*We are choosing chocolate or vanilla.*
Wir wählen Schokolade oder Vanille.

---

**church** [TSCHURTSCH] Substantiv      **die Kirche**

*The church is over there on the corner.*
Die Kirche ist dort drüben an der Ecke.

---

**cigarette** [CI-ga-ret] Substantiv      **die Zigarette**

*Does your uncle smoke cigarettes?*
Raucht dein Onkel Zigaretten?

---

**circle** [CÜR-kel] Substantiv      **der Kreis**

*They form a circle to play handball.*
Sie bilden einen Kreis, um Handball zu spielen.

---

**circus** [CÜR-kes] Substantiv      **der Zirkus**

*There are many animals in the circus.*
Es gibt viele Tiere im Zirkus.

---

**city** [CIT-ie] Substantiv　　　　　　　　　　　**die Stadt**

*Berlin is a large city.*
Die Stadt Berlin ist groß.

---

**class (students)** [KLÄS] Substantiv　　　　　　**die Klasse**

*My class has twenty-eight students.*
Meine Klasse hat achtundzwanzig Schüler.

---

**class (subject)** [KLÄS] Substantiv　　　　　**der Unterricht**

*The math class is very interesting.*
Der Matheunterricht ist sehr interessant.

---

**classroom** [KLÄS-rum] Substantiv　　　**das Klassenzimmer,**

*Where is the chemistry classroom?*
Wo ist das Chemieklassenzimmer?

---

**clean** [KLIEN] Adjektiv　　　　　　　　　　**sauber, rein**

*My hands are clean.*
Meine Hände sind sauber.

---

**to clean** [KLIEN] Verb　　　　　　　　　　　　**putzen**

*Who cleans the house?*
Wer putzt das Haus?

---

**clear** [KLIER] Adjektiv　　　　　　　　　　　　　　**klar**

*The water is clear.*
Das Wasser ist klar.

**clever** [KLEW-er] Adjektiv                           **klug**

*The cat is a clever animal.*
Die Katze ist ein kluges Tier.

---

**to climb** [KLEIM] Verb                             **klettern**

*The kitten climbs the tree.*
Das Kätzchen klettert in den Baum.

---

**clock** [KLAK] Substantiv                         **die Uhr**

*The clock is broken.*
Die Uhr ist kaputt.

    see **o'clock** and **time**

---

**to close** [KLOWS] Verb                             **schließen**

*Please close the window.*
Bitte schließen Sie das Fenster.

---

**close by** [KLOWS bei] Ausdruck               **in der Nähe**

*The train station is close by.*
Der Bahnhof ist in der Nähe.

---

**close to, near** [KLOWS tu] Präposition             **bei**

*Bremen is near the North Sea.*
Bremen ist in bei der Nordsee.

---

**closet (chest)** [KLAHS-it] Substantiv          **der Schrank**

*The closet is closed.*
Der Schrank ist zu.

---

**clothes, clothing** [KLO<u>WS</u>] Substantiv          **die Kleider**

*My clothes are in the box.*
Meine Kleider sind im Karton.

**cloud** [KLAUD] Substantiv                              **die Wolke**

*The sun is behind the clouds.*
Die Sonne ist hinter den Wolken.

**clown** [KLAUN] Substantiv                              **der Clown**

*When I'm at the circus, I say hello to the clown.*
Wenn ich im Zirkus bin, begrüße ich den Clown.

**coat** [KO<u>WT</u>] Substantiv                         **der Mantel**

*He is putting on his coat.*
Er zieht seinen Mantel an.

**coffee** [KOH-fie] Substantiv                           **der Kaffee**

*Mom drinks her coffee black.*
Mutti trinkt ihren Kaffee schwarz.

**cold** [KOHLD] Adjektiv                                 **kalt**

*He likes cold water.*
Er hat kaltes Wasser gern.

**It is cold.** Ausdruck                                  **Es ist kalt.**
**I am cold** Ausdruck                                    **Mir ist kalt.**

*I am so cold today! I need a jacket.*
Mir ist so kalt heute! Ich brauche eine Jacke.

**to have a cold** Ausdruck                               **erkältet sein**

*I cough and sneeze when I have a cold.*
Ich huste und niesse, wenn ich erkältet bin.

**color** [KAL-er] Substantiv               **die Farbe**

*My favorite color is blue.*
Meine Lieblingsfarbe ist blau.

---

**to color** [KAL-er] Verb                **anmalen**

*We color our picture with crayons.*
Wir malen unser Bild mit Farbstiften an.

---

**comb** [KOHM] Substantiv              **der Kamm**

*Where is my comb?*
Wo ist denn mein Kamm?

---

**to comb** [KOHM] Verb                **kämmen**

*I comb my hair often.*
Ich kämme meine Haare oft.

---

**to come** [KAMM] Verb                **kommen**

*My parents are coming soon.*
Meine Eltern kommen bald.

---

**to come back** [KAMM bäk] Verb      **zurückkommen**

---

**comfortable** [KAMF-te-bl] Adjektiv      **bequem**

*The sofa is comfortable.*
Das Sofa ist bequem.

---

**company** [KAM-pe-ni]              **die Firma**

*The Bayer Company is located here.*
Die Firma Bayer befindet sich hier.

---

**to complain** [kam-PLEHN] Verb **klagen**
*He is complaining again.*
Er klagt wieder.

---

**completely** [kam-PLIET-lie] Adverb **ganz**
*It is raining, and I'm completely wet.*
Es regnet und ich bin ganz nass.

---

**computer** [kam-PJUH-ter] Substantiv **der Computer**
*Do you have a computer?*
Hast du einen Computer?

---

**to continue** [kan-TIN-ju] Verb **fortsetzen**
*Let's continue the game now.*
Setzen wir das Spiel jetzt fort.

---

**to cook** [KUK] Verb **kochen**
*He cooks often.*
Er kocht oft.

---

**cookie** [KUK-ie] Substantiv **das Plätzchen**
*She bakes a lot of cookies.*
Sie bäckt viele Plätzchen.

---

**cool** [KUHL] Adjektiv **kühl**
*It is cool in the evenings.*
Es ist kühl abends.

---

**to copy** [KAP-ie] Verb **abschreiben**
*We have to copy the sentences from the blackboard.*
Wir müssen die Sätze von der Tafel abschreiben.

---

**corn** [KORN] Substantiv **der Mais**
*This corn is tasty.*
Dieser Mais ist lecker.

---

**corner** [KOR-ner] Substantiv                           **die Ecke**

*Let's cross the street at the corner.*
Überqueren wir die Strasse an der Ecke.

**correct** [ko-REKT] Adjektiv                               **richtig**

*Which answer is correct?*
Welche Antwort ist richtig?

**to cost** [KOST] Verb                                      **kosten**

*How much does this dictionary cost?*
Wie viel kostet dieses Wörterbuch?

**cotton** [KAT-en] Substantiv                       **die Baumwolle**

*The dress is made of cotton.*
Das Kleid ist aus Baumwolle.

**to cough** [KOHF] Verb                                     **husten**

*I cough when I have a cold.*
Ich huste, wenn ich erkältet bin.

**to count** [KAUNT] Verb                                    **zählen**

*The children are counting the balloons.*
Die Kinder zählen die Ballons.

**country** [KAN-trie] Substantiv                          **das Land**

*Canada is a country.*
Kanada ist ein Land.

**to go to the country** Ausdruck              **aufs Land gehen**

*Let's go to the country on the weekend.*
Lasst uns am Wochenende auf's Land gehen.

**courageous** [ka-REH-dges] Adjektiv                       **mutig**

*Firefighters are courageous.*
Feuerwehrleute sind mutig.

**of course** [av KOHRS] Ausdruck          **natürlich**

*Of course we understand German!*
Natürlich verstehen wir Deutsch!

---

**cousin** [KAS-en] Substantiv       **der Vetter, die Kusine**

*My cousin Paul is eleven years old and my cousin*
*Mary is seventeen.*
Mein Vetter Paul ist elf Jahre alt und meine Kusine
Maria ist siebzehn.

---

**cover** [KAW-er] Substantiv       **die Decke, die Bettdecke**
        see **blanket**

---

**covered** [KAW-erd] Adjektiv          **zugedeckt**

*The child is covered with a blanket.*
Das Kind ist mit einer Decke zugedeckt.

---

**cow** [KAU] Substantiv          **die Kuh**

*The cow is in the field.*
Die Kuh ist auf dem Feld.

---

**cradle** [KREHD-l] Substantiv          **die Wiege**

*The baby is sleeping in the cradle.*
Das Baby schläft in der Wiege.

---

**crayon** [KREH-an] Substantiv          **der Farbstift**

*Angela has new crayons.*
Angela hat neue Farbstifte.

---

224

**crazy** [KREH-sie] Adjektiv                                **verrückt**
*This plan is crazy.*
Dieser Plan ist verrückt.

**to cross** [KROSS] Verb                                    **überqueren**
*Can we cross the river?*
Können wir den Fluss überqueren?

**to cry** [KREI] Verb                                       **weinen**

*I cry when someone teases me.*
Ich weine, wenn mich jemand neckt.

**cunning** [KANN-ing] Adjektiv                              **schlau**
*The fox is cunning.*
Der Fuchs ist schlau.

**cup** [KAP] Substantiv                                     **die Tasse**
*I wash the cup and the saucer.*
Ich wasche die Tasse und die Untertasse.

**cupboard** [KA-berd] Substantiv                            **der Schrank**
*The plates are in the cupboard.*
Die Teller sind im Schrank.

**curious** [KJUHR-jes] Adjektiv                             **neugierig**
*He is curious and would like to open the package.*
Er ist neugierig und möchte das Paket öffnen.

**curtain** [KER-ten] Substantiv                    **der Vorhang**

*The curtains in my room are too long.*
Die Vorhänge in meinem Zimmer sind zu lang.

---

**to cut** [KAT] Verb                                      **schneiden**

*Bernard is cutting the melon.*
Bernhard schneidet die Melone.

---

**cute** [KJUT] Adjektiv                            **süss, niedlich**

*The kitten is cute.*
Das Kätzchen ist süss.

---

**cutlet** [KAT-let] Substantiv                    **das Kotelett**

*The cutlet is delicious.*
Das Kotelett ist lecker.

---

## D

**dad, daddy** [DÄD, DÄD-ie] Substantiv                    **Papa**

*Daddy says, "Good morning!"*
Papa sagt, "Guten Morgen!"

---

**damp** [DÄMP] Adjektiv                                    **feucht**

*My bathing suit is still damp.*
Mein Badeanzug ist noch feucht.

---

**to dance** [DÄNZ] Verb                                    **tanzen**

*My sister likes to dance.*
Meine Schwester tanzt gern.

---

**dangerous** [DEHN-dger-es] Adjektiv              **gefährlich**

*It is dangerous to play with matches.*
Es ist gefährlich, mit Streichhölzern zu spielen.

---

**to dare** [DEHR] Verb                           **wagen**

*I dare to speak with the actor.*
Ich wage es, mit dem Schauspieler zu sprechen.

**dark** [DARK] Adjektiv                           **dunkel**

*The sky is dark before a storm.*
Der Himmel ist dunkel vor einem Sturm.

**darling, cute** [DAHR-ling] Adjektiv            **süss**

*The baby is darling.*
Das Baby ist süss.

**date** [DEHT] Substantiv                         **das Datum**

*What is the date today?*
Was ist das Datum heute?

**dear** [DIER] Adjektiv                  **liebe, lieber, liebes**

*My letter begins, "Dear Mom and Dad."*
Mein Brief beginnt, "Liebe Mama und lieber Vati!"

**to deceive (cheat)** [die-CIEV] Verb            **betrügen**

*In the film, the robber deceives the policewoman.*
Im Film betrügt der Dieb die Polizistin.

**December** [die-SEM-ber] Substantiv        **der Dezember**

*It snows in December.*
Es schneit im Dezember.

**to decorate** [DE-ka-reht] Verb      **schmücken**

*They are decorating the wedding car.*
Sie schmücken das Hochzeitsauto.

---

**deep** [DIEP] Adjektiv      **tief**

*Is the lake deep?*
Ist der See tief?

---

**delicious** [de-LISCH-es] Adjektiv      **lecker**

*The grapes are delicious.*
Die Trauben sind lecker.

---

**delighted, happy** [de-LEI-ted] Adjektiv      **froh**

*Everyone is happy at a party.*
Auf einer Party sind alle froh.

---

**dentist** [DEN-tist]      **der Zahnarzt, die Zahnärztin**
    Substantiv

*Frieda would like to become a dentist.*
Frieda möchte Zahnärztin werden.

---

**desert** [DES-ert] Substantiv      **die Wüste**

*In the desert there is a lot of sand.*
In der Wüste gibt es viel Sand.

---

**desk** [DESK] Substantiv      **der Schreibtisch**

*The teacher's desk is in the corner.*
Der Schreibtisch der Lehrerin ist in der Ecke.

**(pupil's) desk**                                          **das Pult**

*The pupils' desks are in a circle.*
Die Pulte der Schüler stehen in einem Kreis.

---

**dessert** [die-SURT] Substantiv                **der Nachtisch**

*I'll have Bavarian Creme for dessert.*
Ich nehme Bayrische Creme zum Nachtisch.

---

**to detest (hate)** [die-TEST] Verb                **hassen**

*She hates to cut the lawn.*
Sie hasst es, den Rasen zu mähen.

---

**dictionary** [DIK-schen-er-ie] Substantiv    **das Wörterbuch**

*This dictionary is very useful.*
Dieses Wörterbuch ist sehr praktisch.

---

**different** [DIF-rent] Adjektiv                **verschieden**

*These loaves of bread are different.*
Diese Brote sind verschieden.

---

**difficult** [DIF-i-kalt] Adjektiv                **schwer**

*German is not difficult.*
Deutsch ist nicht schwer.

---

**dining room** [DEIN-ing rum] Substantiv    **das Esszimmer**

*The family seldom eats in the dining room.*
Die Familie isst selten im Esszimmer.

**to direct, conduct** [dei-REKT] Verb      **dirigieren**

*The music teacher conducts the student orchestra.*
Der Musiklehrer dirigiert das Schülerorchester.

---

**to direct, lead** [dei-REKT] Verb      **leiten**

*He leads the hiking club.*
Er leitet den Wanderklub.

---

**dirty** [DIR-tie] Adjektiv      **schmutzig**

*This street is not dirty.*
Diese Straße ist nicht schmutzig.

---

**dishes** [DISCH-es] Substantiv, pl.      **das Geschirr**

*I am washing the dishes.*
Ich spüle das Geschirr.

---

**displeased, angry** [diss-PLIESD] Adjektiv      **ärgerlich**

*The teacher is displeased when I do not pay attention.*
Der Lehrer ist ärgerlich, wenn ich nicht aufpasse.

---

**distant, far away** [DISS-tent] Ausdruck      **weit entfernt**

*The store is far away.*
Das Geschäft ist weit entfernt.

---

**to do** [DU] Verb      **machen**

*What does she do Mondays?*
Was macht sie montags?

---

**doctor (medical)** [DAK-ter] Substantiv      **der Arzt,
die Ärztin**

*Mother says, "You are sick. I'm calling the doctor."*
Die Mutter sagt, "Du bist krank. Ich rufe den Arzt an."

---

**dog** [DOHG] Substantiv          **der Hund**

*Do you have a dog?*
Hast du einen Hund?

**doll** [DAHL] Substantiv         **die Puppe**
*The doll is on the chair.*
Die Puppe ist auf dem Stuhl.

**dollhouse** [DAHL-haus] Substantiv    **das Puppenhaus**

**dollar** [DAHL-er] Substantiv       **der Dollar**
*The locker in the train station costs one dollar.*
Das Schließfach im Bahnhof kostet einen Dollar.

**Well done!** [WEL DANN] Ausdruck   **Prima! Gut gemacht!**

**dominos** [DAM-i-no<u>w</u>s] Substantiv, pl.    **der Domino**
*My aunt plays dominos well.*
Meine Tante spielt Domino gut.

**donkey** [DANK-ie] Substantiv       **der Esel**

*The donkey does not want to walk.*
Der Esel will nicht gehen.

**door** [DOHR] Substantiv         **die Tür**
*Please close the door!*
Schließen Sie bitte die Tür!

**doorbell, bell** [DOHR-bel, bel] Substantiv     **die Klingel**

*The doorbell is not loud enough.*
Die Klingel ist nicht laut genug.

---

**doorknob** [DOHR-nab] Substantiv     **die Türklinke**

*This doorknob is different.*
Diese Türklinke ist anders.

---

**Don't you think so?**     **Nicht wahr?**
   [DONT ju think so] Ausdruck

*The trains are punctual here, don't you think so?*
Die Züge sind pünktlich hier, nicht wahr?

---

**dozen** [DAHS-en] Substantiv     **das Dutzend**

*A dozen is twelve pieces.*
Ein Dutzend ist zwölf Stück.

---

**to drag, to pull** [DRÄG] Verb     **ziehen**

*They are pulling their baggage out of the compartment.*
Sie ziehen ihr Gepäck aus dem Abteil.

---

**to draw** [DROH] Verb     **zeichnen**

*Charlotte is drawing a picture of a house.*
Charlotte zeichnet ein Bild von einem Haus.

---

**drawer** [DROWER] Substantiv     **die Schublade**

*Dorothy puts her jewelry in a drawer.*
Dorothee legt ihren Schmuck in eine Schublade.

---

**to dream** [DRIEM] Verb     **träumen**

*He dreams that he is in the Alps.*
Er träumt, dass er in den Alpen ist.

---

**dress** [DRESS] Substantiv        **das Kleid**

*Joanna's dress is made of silk.*
Johannas Kleid ist aus Seide.

---

**to get dressed** [get DRESST] Verb    **sich anziehen**

*We get dressed before breakfast.*
Wir ziehen uns vor dem Frühstück an.

---

**to drink** [DRINK] Verb        **trinken**

*The child is drinking orange juice.*
Das Kind trinkt Orangensaft.

---

**to drive** [DREIV] Verb        **fahren**

*Let's drive to Munich.*
Fahren wir doch nach München.

---

**driver** [DREIV-er] Substantiv    **der Fahrer,**
**die Fahrerin**

*The driver stops when the light is red.*
Der Fahrer hält, wenn die Ampel rot ist.

---

**drugstore, pharmacy**        **die Apotheke**
   [DRAG-stohr] Substantiv

*The pharmacy is by the post office.*
Die Apotheke ist bei der Post.

---

**drum** [DRAM] Substantiv        **die Trommel**

*When I play the drum, it is very loud.*
Wenn ich Trommel spiele, ist es sehr laut.

---

**dry** [DREI] Adjektiv        **trocken**

*Is the floor dry, Anthony?*
Ist der Fussboden trocken, Anton?

**duck** [DAK] Substantiv **die Ente**

*There are many ducks in the lake.*
Es gibt viele Enten auf dem See.

**during** [DUHR-ing] Präposition **während**
*There is usually no school during the summer.*
Es gibt meistens keine Schule während des Sommers.

**dwelling** [DWÄL-ing] Substantiv **die Wohnung**
  see **apartment**

## E

**each** [IETSCH] Adjektiv **jeder, jede, jedes**
*Each tourist has a map.*
Jeder Tourist hat eine Karte.

**ear** [IER] Substantiv **das Ohr**
*Elephants have large ears.*
Elefanten haben große Ohren.

**early** [ÄR-lie] Adverb **früh**

*The rooster gets up early.*
Der Hahn steht früh auf.

**to earn** [ÄRN] Verb                    **verdienen**
*I do not earn money yet.*
Ich verdiene noch kein Geld.

---

**earth** [ÄRTH] Substantiv                **die Erde**
*When the astronaut is in space, she sees the earth.*
Wenn die Astronautin im Weltall ist, sieht sie die Erde.

---

**east** [IEST] Substantiv                **der Osten**
*The sun rises in the east.*
Die Sonne geht im Osten auf.

---

**easy** [IE-sie] Adjektiv                    **leicht**
*It is easy to learn German.*
Es ist leicht Deutsch zu lernen.

---

**to eat** [IET] Verb                          **essen**
*Linda is eating an open-faced cheese sandwich.*
Linda isst ein Käsebrot.

---

**edge, shore** [EDG, SHOHR] Substantiv    **die Küste**
*She lives at the shore.*
Sie wohnt an der Küste.

---

**egg** [EG] Substantiv                        **das Ei**
*He eats an egg for breakfast.*
Er isst ein Ei zum Frühstück.

---

**eight** [EHT] Adjektiv                        **acht**
*Here are eight buttons.*
Hier sind acht Knöpfe.

---

**eighteen** [eh-TIEN] Adjektiv            **achtzehn**
*My address is 18 Beethoven Street.*
Meine Adresse ist Beethoven Straße achtzehn.

---

**eighty** [EH-tie] Adjektiv        **achtzig**

*The capital is almost eighty kilometers from here.*
Die Hauptstadt ist fast achtzig Kilometer von hier.

---

**electric** [ä-LEK-trik] Adjektiv        **elektrisch**

*Wow! There is an electric car!*
Toll! Dort ist ein elektrisches Auto!

**electric stove**        **der Elektroherd**

**electric lawn mower**        **der Elektrorasenmäher**

**electric train**        **die elektrische Eisenbahn**

---

**elephant** [EL-e-fant] Substantiv        **der Elefant**

*The elephant has two large ears.*
Der Elefant hat zwei grosse Ohren.

---

**eleven** [ie-LEW-en] Adjektiv        **elf**

*The university student carries eleven books.*
Der Student trägt elf Bücher.

---

**empty** [EMP-tie] Adjektiv        **leer**

*This bottle is empty.*
Diese Flasche ist leer.

---

**end** [END] Substantiv        **das Ende**

*The end of the book is sad.*
Das Ende des Buches ist traurig.

---

**engineer** [en-dge-NIER] Substantiv               **der Ingenieuer,
die Ingenieuerin**

*The engineer travels a lot.*
Die Ingenieurin reist viel.

---

**enough** [ie-NAF] Adverb                             **genug**

*Do you have enough potatoes, Mr. Moritz?*
Haben Sie genug Kartoffeln, Herr Moritz?

---

**to enter** [EN-ter] Verb                             **eintreten**

*She enters the house.*
Sie tritt in das Haus ein.

---

**envelope** [AHN-we-lowp] Substantiv            **der Umschlag**

*The envelope already has a stamp.*
Der Umschlag hat schon eine Briefmarke.

---

**equal** [IE-kwel] Adjektiv                           **gleich**

*The children are equal in size.*
Die Kinder sind gleich gross.

---

**to erase** [e-REHSS] Verb                         **ausradieren**

*Oh, a mistake. I have to erase this word.*
Oh, ein Fehler. Ich muss dieses Wort ausradieren.

---

**eraser** [e-REHSS-er] Substantiv                 **der Wischer,
der Radiergummi**

*Do you have an eraser on your pencil?*
Hast du einen Radiergummi am Bleistift?

---

**error, mistake** [ER-er] Substantiv         **der Fehler**

*I make errors when I write fast.*
Ich mache Fehler, wenn ich schnell schreibe.

---

**especially** [ess-PESCH-e-lie] Adverb       **besonders**

*I love ice cream, especially lemon.*
Ich liebe Eis, besonders Zitrone.

---

**even, also** [IE-wen] Adverb                 **auch**

*She cries even when she is happy.*
Sie weint auch, wenn sie froh ist.

---

**evening** [IEW-ning] Substantiv          **der Abend**

*In the evening I sometimes watch television.*
Am Abend sehe ich manchmal fern.

---

**every** [ew-rie] Adjektiv         **jeder, jedes, jede**

*I read every day.*
Ich lese jeden Tag.

---

**everybody** [EW-rie-bad-ie] Pronomen        **alle**

*Everybody is at home.*
Alle sind zu Hause.

---

**everywhere** [EW-rie-wehr] Adverb         **überall**

*I am looking everywhere for my watch.*
Ich suche meine Armbanduhr überall.

---

**examination** [eg-sam-i-NEH-shen] Substantiv   **die Prüfung**

*Is there an examination today?*
Gibt es eine Prüfung heute?

---

**excellent** [EK-se-lent] Adjektiv         **ausgezeichnet**

*The film is excellent.*
Der Film ist ausgezeichnet.

**Excuse me!**          **Entschuldigung! Verzeihung!**
[eks-KJUSH mie] Ausdruck

*Excuse me, what time is it?*
Entschuldigung, wie viel Uhr ist es?

---

**expensive** [eks-PEN-siv] Adjectiv          **teuer**
*This bicycle is too expensive.*
Dieses Fahrrad ist zu teuer.

---

**to explain** [eks-SPLEHN] Verb          **erklären**
*She explains the map to Adam.*
Sie erklärt Adam die Karte.

---

**extraordinary, unusual**          **ungewöhnlich**
[eks-tra-OHR-di-ner-ie] Adjektiv
*We are taking an extraordinary trip to Alaska.*
Wir unternehmen eine ungewöhnliche Reise nach Alaska.

---

**eye** [EI] Substantiv          **das Auge**
*My left eye hurts.*
Mein linkes Auge tut weh.

---

## F

**face** [FEHS] Substantiv          **das Gesicht**
*She is washing her face.*
Sie wäscht ihr Gesicht.

---

**factory** [FÄK-te-rie] Substantiv          **die Fabrik**
*The factory is near our apartment.*
Die Fabrik ist bei unserer Wohnung.

---

**fair (festival)** [FEHR] Substantiv          **das Fest**
*Let's go to the fair. It will be fun.*
Gehen wir zum Fest. Das macht Spaß.

---

**fair** [FEHR] Adjektiv                                                            **fair**

*But it's my turn. It isn't fair!*
Aber ich bin dran. Das ist nicht fair!

---

**fairy** [FEHR-ie] Substantiv                                    **der Elf, die Fee**

*What's the fairy's name in the fairy tale?*
Wie heißt denn die Fee im Märchen?

---

**fairy tale** [FEHR-ie tehl] Substantiv                            **das Märchen**

*We are reading another fairy tale.*
Wir lesen noch ein Märchen.

---

**fall (autumn)** [FOHL] Substantiv                                  **der Herbst**

*Do you prefer spring or fall?*
Was hast du lieber, Frühling oder Herbst?

---

**to fall** [FOHL] Verb                                                       **fallen**

*Leaves fall from the tree when it is windy.*
Blätter fallen vom Baum, wenn es windig ist.

---

**family** [FÄM-e-lie] Substantiv                                    **die Familie**

*There are seven people in my family.*
Es gibt sieben Leute in meiner Familie.

---

**famous** [FEH-mes] Adjektiv                                           **berühmt**

*The German actress is famous.*
Die deutsche Schauspielerin ist berühmt.

---

**fan** [FÄN] Substantiv                                           **der Ventilator**

*The fan is handy when it is hot.*
Der Ventilator ist praktisch, wenn es heiß ist.

---

**far** [FAHR] Adverb                                                           **weit**

*Is Washington far from New York?*
Ist Washington weit von New York?

---

**farm** [FAHRM] Substantiv                    **der Bauernhof**

*Are there mostly vegetables or animals on this farm?*
Gibt es hauptsächlich Gemüse oder Tiere auf diesem
Bauernhof?

---

**farmer** [FAHR-mer] Substantiv          **der Bauer, die Bäuerin**

*The farmer milks the cow.*
Der Bauer melkt die Kuh.

---

**fast** [FÄST] Adverb                                     **schnell**

*The dog runs fast when he sees the cat.*
Der Hund rennt schnell, wenn er die Katze sieht.

---

**fat** [FÄT] Adjektiv                                        **dick**

*The baby is not fat.*
Das Baby ist nicht dick.

---

**father** [FAH-ther] Substantiv                   **der Vater**

*My father is a fireman.*
Mein Vater ist ein Feuerwehrmann.

---

**favorite** [FEH-wer-it] Adjektiv              **Lieblings-**

*This is my favorite song and my favorite singer.*
Das ist mein Lieblingslied und mein Lieblingssänger.

---

**February** [FEB-ru-er-ie] Substantiv        **der Februar**

*February usually has twenty-eight days.*
Der Februar hat meistens achtundzwanzig Tage.

---

**to feel well** [FIEL wel] Ausdruck          **sich wohl fühlen**

*I do not feel well today.*
Ich fühle mich nicht wohl heute.

---

**feet** [FIET] Substantiv, pl.                        **die Füße**

**ferocious, fierce** [fe-ROH-sches, FIERS] Adjectiv          **wild**

*The leopard is wounded. He is ferocious.*
Der Leopard ist verwundet. Er ist wild.

---

**fever** [FIE-wer] Substantiv                          **das Fieber**

*When I have a fever, I stay home.*
Wenn ich Fieber habe, bleibe ich zu Hause.

---

**field** [FIELD] Substantiv                             **das Feld**

*The sheep are in the field.*
Die Schafe sind auf dem Feld.

---

**fifteen** [fif-TIEN] Adjectiv                          **fünfzehn**

*There are fifteen children in the street.*
Es gibt fünfzehn Kinder auf der Straße.

---

**fifty** [FIF-tie] Adjektiv                             **fünfzig**

*The flag of the United States has fifty stars.*
Die Flagge der Vereinigten Staaten hat fünfzig Sterne.

---

**to fill** [FIL] Verb                                   **füllen**

*Susi fills the copier with paper.*
Susi füllt den Kopierer mit Papier.

---

**film** [FILM] Substantiv                               **der Film**

*Are they playing a good film at the movies?*
Läuft ein guter Film im Kino?

*I need to buy film for my camera.*
Ich muss einen Film für meine Kamera kaufen.

**finally** [FEI-nel-ie] Adverb  **endlich**
*The weather is finally good.*
Das Wetter ist endlich gut.

**to find** [FEIND] Verb  **finden**

*I like to find shells.*
Ich finde Muscheln gern.

**finger** [FIN-ger] Substantiv  **der Finger**
*I have five fingers on each hand.*
Ich habe fünf Finger an jeder Hand.

**fingernail** [FIN-ger-nehl] Substantiv  **der Fingernagel**
*I am ashamed. My fingernails are dirty.*
Ich schäme mich. Meine Fingernägel sind schmutzig.

**to finish** [FIN-isch] Verb  **beenden**
*I will finish my work before going out.*
Ich beende meine Arbeit, bevor ich ausgehe.

**fire** [FEI-er] Substantiv  **das Feuer**
*There is a fire in the forest.*
Es gibt ein Feuer im Wald.

**fireman** [FEI-er-män] Substantiv  **der Feuerwehrmann**
*The fireman is strong.*
Der Feuerwehrmann ist kräftig.

**fireplace** [FEI-er-plehs] Substantiv  **der Kamin**
*There is a fire in the fireplace.*
Es gibt ein Feuer im Kamin.

**fire truck**                                    **der Feuerwehrwagen**

---

**first** [FÜRST] Adjektiv                                          **erst**
*Breakfast is the first meal of the day.*
Das Frühstück ist die erste Mahlzeit des Tages.

---

**fish** [FISCH] Substantiv                                   **der Fisch**
*There are many fish in this lake.*
Es gibt viele Fische in diesem See.

**to go fishing** [go͟w FISCH-ing] Verb                         **angeln**
*We are fishing today.*
Wir angeln heute.

**goldfish** [GOLD-fisch] Substantiv                       **der Goldfisch**

---

**fish tank** [FISCH-tänk] Substantiv                    **das Aquarium**

*There are goldfish and plants in the fish tank.*
Es gibt Goldfische und Pflanzen im Aquarium.

---

**five** [FEIW] Adjektiv                                           **fünf**
*She has five siblings.*
Sie hat fünf Geschwister.

---

**to fix (repair)** [FIKS] Verb                              **reparieren**
*My sister fixes the lamp.*
Meine Schwester repariert die Lampe.

---

**flag** [FLÄG] Substantiv                                   **die Flagge**
*What are the colors of the Swiss flag? Red and white.*
Was sind die Farben der schweizer Flagge? Rot und weiß.

---

**flat** [FLÄT] Adjektiv                                     **flach**

*Their roof is flat.*
Ihr Dach ist flach.

---

**flight attendant** [FLEIT a-TEND-änt]          **der Flugbegleiter,**
    Substantiv                          **die Flugbegleiterin**

*My neighbor is a flight attendant with Lufthansa.*
Meine Nachbarin ist Flugbegleiterin bei Lufthansa.

---

**floor** [FLOHR] Substantiv                                **der Fußboden**

*The floor is made of wood.*
Der Fußboden ist aus Holz.

**floor (of a building)** Substantiv          **der Stock, die Etage**

**(ground) floor** Substantiv                        **der Erdgeschoß**

*I live on the ground floor.*
Ich wohne im Erdgeschoß.

---

**flower** [FLAU-er] Substantiv                             **die Blume**

*There are many flowers growing in the garden.*
Viele Blumen wachsen im Garten.

---

**fly** [FLEI] Substantiv                                   **die Fliege**

*There are flies in the kitchen!*
Da sind Fliegen in der Küche!

---

**to fly** [FLEI] Verb                                      **fliegen**

*The boy flies in the airplane for the first time.*
Der Junge fliegt zum ersten Mal im Flugzeug.

---

**fog** [FAHG] Substantiv          **der Nebel**

*In the fog it is hard to see.*
Im Nebel ist es schwer zu sehen.

---

**to follow, listen to** [FAL-o̲w̲] Verb     **folgen**

*The pupils in the class listen to the teacher.*
Die Schüler in der Klasse folgen dem Lehrer.

---

**foot** [FUT] Substantiv         **der Fuß**
**to go on foot** Ausdruck     **zu Fuß gehen**

*We are going on foot to the museum.*
Wir gehen zu Fuß zum Museum.

---

**for** [VOR] Präposition         **für**

*These gifts are for the children.*
Diese Geschenke sind für die Kinder.

---

**forbidden** [vor-BID-en] Adjektiv    **verboten**

*It is forbidden to smoke in the elevator.*
Es ist verboten, im Lift zu rauchen.

**This is forbidden!** Ausdruck    **Das ist verboten!**

---

**forest** [VOR-est] Substantiv     **der Wald**

*The forest is full of trees.*
Der Wald ist voll mit Bäumen.

---

**forever (always)** [vor-EV-er] Adverb    **immer**

*The leaves always fall in the fall.*
Die Blätter fallen immer im Herbst.

---

**to forget** [VOR-GET] Verb         **vergessen**

*Sometimes he forgets his ticket.*
Manchmal vergisst er seine Karte.

---

**fork** [VORK] Substantiv         **die Gabel**

*I eat with a knife and fork.*
Ich esse mit Messer und Gabel.

---

**forty** [VOR-tie] Adjektiv         **vierzig**

*Let's read the tale of the forty thieves.*
Lesen wir das Märchen von den vierzig Dieben.

---

**four** [VOHR] Adjektiv         **vier**

*There are four cookies on the plate.*
Es gibt vier Plätzchen auf dem Teller.

---

**fourteen** [VOR-TIEN] Adjektiv         **vierzehn**

*There are fourteen students in my class.*
Es gibt vierzehn Schüler in meiner Klasse.

---

**fox** [FAKS] Substantiv         **der Fuchs**

*The fox runs very fast.*
Der Fuchs rennt sehr schnell.

---

**France** [FRÄNZ] Substantiv         **Frankreich**

*Where is the map of France?*
Wo ist die Karte von Frankreich?

---

**French** [FRENTSCH] Adjektiv         **französisch**

*I am reading a French book.*
Ich lese ein französisches Buch.

---

**fresh** [FRESH] Adjektiv         **frisch**

*The bread is fresh.*
Das Brot ist frisch.

---

**Friday** [FREI-deh] Substantiv                    **der Freitag**

*Some people eat fish on Friday.*
Manche Leute essen Fisch am Freitag.

---

**friend** [FREND] Substantiv          **der Freund, die Freundin**

*I am your friend.*
Ich bin dein Freund.

---

**frightening** [FREIT-ning] Adjektiv              **beängstigend**

*Snakes can be frightening.*
Schlangen können beängstigend sein.

---

**frog** [FRAHG] Substantiv                        **der Frosch**

*The frog jumps into the water.*
Der Frosch springt ins Wasser.

---

**from** [FRAM] Präposition                            **von**

*Here, the apple is from your grandfather.*
Hier, der Apfel ist von deinem Großvater.

**to come from** [KAM fram] Ausdruck            **kommen aus**

*The family comes from China.*
Die Familie kommt aus China.

---

**in front of** [in FRANT av] Präposition               **vor**
        see **before**

*The girl is sitting in front of the boy.*
Das Mädchen sitzt vor dem Jungen.

**fruit** [FRUT] Substantiv      **das Obst**

*Here is the fruit. Do you prefer a pear or a banana?*
Hier ist das Obst. Was hast du lieber, eine Birne oder
eine Banane?

---

**full** [FUHL] Adjektiv      **voll**

*The suitcase is full of clothes.*
Der Koffer ist voll mit Kleidern.

---

**funny** [FAN-ie] Adjektiv      **lustig**
     see **amusing**

---

**That's fun!** [thats FAN] Ausdruck      **Das macht Spaß!**

---

**future** [FJU-tscher] Substantiv      **die Zukunft**

*In the future I am going to visit Egypt.*
In der Zukunft werde ich Ägypten besuchen.

---

## G

**game** [GEHM] Substantiv      **das Spiel**

*Which game do you prefer?*
Welches Spiel hast du lieber?

---

**garage** [ge-RAHSCH] Substantiv      **die Garage**

*The car is in the garage.*
Das Auto ist in der Garage.

---

**garden** [GAHR-den] Substantiv      **der Garten**

*Tomatoes grow in the garden.*
Tomaten wachsen im Garten.

---

**gas** [GÄS] Substantiv      **das Gas**

*You have a gas stove! We have an electric stove.*
Ihr habt einen Gasherd! Wir haben einen Elektroherd.

---

**gasoline** [gäs-e-LIEN] Substantiv      **das Benzin**

*Mom says, "We don't have enough gasoline."*
Mutti sagt, "Wir haben nicht genug Benzin."

---

**gentle** [DGEN-tl] Adjektiv      **sanft**

*The cow is a gentle animal.*
Die Kuh ist ein sanftes Tier.

---

**geography** [dgie-AHG-re-fie] Substantiv      **die Geographie**

*My favorite subject is geography.*
Mein Lieblingsfach ist Geographie.

---

**German** [DGER-man] Adjektiv      **deutsch**

*These are German children.*
Das sind deutsche Kinder.

---

**Germany** [DGER-man-ie] Substantiv      **Deutschland**

---

**to get (fetch)** [GET] Verb      **holen**

*The pupils are getting the books.*
Die Schüler holen die Bücher.

---

**to get (to receive)** [GET] Verb      **bekommen**

*I got a postcard from my sister.*
Ich bekomme eine Postkarte von meiner Schwester.

**to get up** [get AP] Verb                                    **aufstehen**

*Please get up, Eric, it is late.*
Bitte steh auf, Erik, es ist schon spät.

**giant** [DGEI-ent] Substantiv                          **der Riese**
*I like stories with giants.*
Ich mag Märchen mit Riesen.

**gift** [GIFT] Substantiv                          **das Geschenk**

*A gift for me? Thank you!*
Ein Geschenk für mich? Danke!

**girl** [GÜRL] Substantiv                          **das Mädchen**
*The girl is wearing new shoes.*
Das Mädchen trägt neue Schuhe.

**to give** [GIV] Verb                                    **geben**
*He gives me the camera.*
Er gibt mir die Kamera.

**to give back** [giv BÄK] Verb                     **zurückgeben**
*He gives my roller skates back.*
Er gibt meine Rollschuhe zurück.

**glad** [GLÄD] Adjektiv               **froh**

*When it snows the children are glad.*
Wenn es schneit, sind die Kinder froh.

---

**glass** [GLÄSS] Substantiv           **das Glas**

*I put the glass on the table carefully.*
Ich stelle das Glas sorgfältig auf den Tisch.

**(made of) glass** Ausdruck          **aus Glas**

---

**glasses** [GLÄSS-es] Substantiv      **die Brille**

*I am looking for my glasses.*
Ich suche meine Brille.

---

**glove** [GLAV] Substantiv       **der Handschuh**

*She is wearing warm gloves.*
Sie trägt warme Handschuhe.

---

**to glue** [GLUH] Verb             **kleben**

*I glue the picture on a piece of paper.*
Ich klebe das Bild auf ein Stück Papier.

---

**to go** [GOW] Verb               **gehen**

*Where are you going, Sabina? I am going home.*
Wohin gehst du, Sabina? Ich gehe nach Hause.

---

**to go to work** [GOW tu WÜRK] Ausdruck    **zur Arbeit gehen**

*She goes to work at seven thirty.*
Sie geht um sieben Uhr dreißig zur Arbeit.

---

**to go back** [GOW BÄK] Verb        **zurückgehen**

*I am going back to the library.*
Ich gehe zur Bibliothek zurück.

---

**to go to bed** [GO<u>W</u> tu BED] Ausdruck          **zu Bett gehen**

*When are you going to bed?*
Wann gehst du zu Bett?

**to go shopping** [tu GO<u>W</u> SCHOP-ing] Verb          **einkaufengehen**

*The boys are going shopping.*
Die Jungen gehen einkaufen.

**goat** [GO<u>WT</u>] Substantiv          **die Ziege**

*The goat is eating grass on the mountain.*
Die Ziege frisst Gras auf dem Berg.

**gold** [GOHLD] Substantiv          **das Gold**

*John Sutter finds gold in California.*
Johann Sutter findet Gold in Kalifornien.

**(made of) gold** Ausdruck          **aus Gold**

*I would like a watch made of gold.*
Ich möchte eine Armbanduhr aus Gold.

**goldfish** [GOHLD-fisch] Substantiv          **der Goldfisch**

**good** [GUD] Adjektiv          **gut**

*It is a good book.*
Es ist ein gutes Buch.

**Good afternoon! Good day!** Ausdruck          **Guten Tag!**
**Good-bye!** Interjektion          **Auf Wiedersehen!**
**Good evening!** Ausdruck          **Guten Abend!**
**Good luck!** Audruck          **Alles Gute!**

**Good morning!** Ausdruck     **Guten Morgen!**

**Good night!** Ausdruck     **Gute Nacht!**

---

**grandparents** [GRÄND-pär-ents] Substantiv   **die Großeltern**

   **grandmother**     **die Großmutter**
     [GRÄND-mo-ther] Substantiv

   **grandfather** [GRÄND-vah-ther] Substantiv   **der Großvater**

   **grandson** [GRÄND-san] Substantiv     **der Enkel**

   **granddaughter** [GRÄND-doh-ter] Substantiv   **die Enkelin**

   **grandchildren**     **die Enkelkinder**
     [GRÄND-tschil-dren] Substantiv

*The grandparents love their grandchildren.*
Die Großeltern lieben ihre Enkelkinder.

---

**grape** [GREHP] Substantiv     **die Traube**

*The fox looks at the grapes.*
Der Fuchs betrachtet die Trauben.

---

**grapefruit** [GREHP-frut] Substantiv     **die Pampelmuse,**
                          **die Grapefruit**

*The grapefruit is not sweet.*
Die Pampelmuse ist nicht süß.

---

**grass, the lawn** [GRÄSS] Substantiv     **der Rasen**
*The lawn is green.*
Der Rasen ist grün.

---

**grasshopper** [GRÄSS-hap-er] Substantiv     **der Grashüpfer**
*The child wants to catch the grasshopper.*
Das Kind will den Grashüpfer fangen.

**gray** [GREH] Adjektiv                                          **grau**
*The mouse is gray.*
Die Maus ist grau.

---

**Great!** [GREHT] Interjektion        **Prima! Toll! Fantastisch!**

---

**great, famous** [GREHT] Adjektiv                          **berühmt**
*Kurt Masur is a great conductor.*
Kurt Masur ist ein berühmter Dirigent.

---

**green** [GRIEN] Adjektiv                                        **grün**
*This apple is green, not red.*
Dieser Apfel ist grün, nicht rot.

---

**grocer** [GROH-ser] Substantiv        **der Lebensmittelhändler**
*The grocer sells fruits and vegetables.*
Der Lebensmittelhändler verkauft Obst und Gemüse.

---

**grocery store**                        **das Lebensmittelgeschäft**
    [GROH-ser-ie STOR] Substantiv
*One buys sugar in the grocery store.*
Man kauft Zucker im Lebensmittelgeschäft.

---

**ground, earth** [GRAUND] Substantiv    **der Boden, der Grund**
*The ground is too hard for planting.*
Der Boden ist zu hart zum Pflanzen

---

**ground floor** [GRAUND flor] Substantiv        **der Erdgeschoß**
*I live on the ground floor.*
Ich wohne im Erdgeschoß.

---

**to grow** [GROW] Verb                                        **wachsen**
*Many plants are growing in this garden.*
Viele Pflanzen wachsen in diesem Garten.

---

**to guard** [GAHRD] Verb             **bewachen, schützen**

*The dog guards the store.*
Der Hund bewacht das Geschäft.

---

**to guess** [GESS] Verb                        **raten**

*She will guess his age.*
Sie rät sein Alter.

---

**guitar** [gie-TAHR] Substantiv          **die Gitarre**

*I can play the guitar.*
Ich kann Gitarre spielen.

---

**Gummi Bears**                   **die Gummibärchen**
        [GUM-ie behrs] Substantiv, pl.

---

**gun** [GAN] Substantiv        **die Waffe, das Gewehr**

*A gun is dangerous.*
Eine Waffe ist gefährlich.

---

## H

**hair** [HEHR] Substantiv              **die Haare**

*The children have long hair.*
Die Kinder haben lange Haare.

**hairbrush** [HEHR-brasch] Substantiv    **die Haarbürste**

**half** [HÄF] Substantiv                **die Hälfte**

*Please give me half of the banana, Helene!*
Bitte gib mir die Hälfte der Banane, Helene!

---

**half an hour** [HÄF en AUER] Ausdruck    **eine halbe Stunde**

*I have been waiting for you for half an hour already!*
Ich warte schon eine halbe Stunde auf dich!

**ham** [HÄM] Substantiv                    **der Schinken**

*They are eating ham.*
Sie essen Schinken.

---

**hammer** [HÄM-er] Substantiv             **der Hammer**

*Alfred is using the hammer.*
Alfred benutzt den Hammer.

---

**hand** [HÄND] Substantiv                  **die Hand**

*My hands are dirty.*
Meine Hände sind schmutzig.

**the right hand** [tha REIT HÄND] Ausdruck   **die rechte Hand**

**the left hand** [tha LEFT HÄND] Ausdruck    **die linke Hand**

**to shake hands**                          **die Hand schütteln**
    [tu SCHEHK HÄNDS] Ausdruck

*The guests shake hands as they leave.*
Die Gäste schütteln die Hände zum Abschied.

---

**handbag (purse)** [HÄND-bäg] Substantiv   **die Handtasche**

*The handbag is on the armchair.*
Die Handtasche liegt auf dem Sessel.

---

**handkerchief**                            **das Taschentuch**
    [HÄN-ker-tschif] Substantiv

**paper handkerchief**                      **das Papiertaschentuch**

*He uses a paper handkerchief when he sneezes.*
Er nimmt ein Papiertaschentuch, wenn er niest.

---

**handsome** [HÄN-sam] Adjektiv       **gutaussehend, hübsch**

*That actor is handsome, and the actress is beautiful.*
Der Schauspieler ist gutaussehend und die Schauspielerin
ist hübsch.

---

**it happens** [HÄP-ens] Ausdruck              **es passiert**

*Is it happening now?*
Passiert es jetzt?

---

**(What is) happening?**                      **Was ist los?**
**What is the matter?**
        [what is HÄP-en-ing] Ausdruck

*I hear something. What is happening?*
Ich höre etwas. Was ist los?

---

**happy** [HÄP-ie] Adjektiv                **glücklich, froh**

*I am happy that spring is finally here.*
Ich bin glücklich, dass der Frühling endlich da ist.

---

**Happy birthday!**     **Alles Gute zum Geburtstag!**
        [HÄP-ie BÜRTH-dä] Ausdruck

---

**hard** [HAHRD] Adjektiv                            **hart**

*The chair is hard.*
Der Stuhl ist hart.

---

**hat** [HÄT] Substantiv                            **der Hut**

*The girl's hat is warm.*
Der Hut des Mädchens ist warm.

---

**to hate** [HEHT] Substantiv                      **hassen**

*The cat hates water.*
Die Katze hasst Wasser.

---

**to have** [HÄV] Verb                                **haben**

*She has a frog.*
Sie hat einen Frosch.

---

**Have a good meal!**                          **Guten Appetit!**
    [HÄV a gud MIEL] Ausdruck

**Enjoy your meal!**

---

**to have to, must** [HÄV tu] Verb                   **müssen**

*I have to write the letter.*
Ich muss den Brief schreiben.

**to have a good time, to have fun** Ausdruck    **Spaß haben**

*We are having a good time at the circus.*
Wir haben Spaß im Zirkus.

**to have a headache** Ausdruck      **Kopfschmerzen haben**

*He often has a headache.*
Er hat oft Kopfschmerzen.

---

**hay** [HEH] Substantiv                              **das Heu**

*The horse eats hay.*
Das Pferd frisst Heu.

---

**he** [HIE] Pronomen                                    **er**

*He reads well.*
Er liest gut.

---

**head** [HED] Substantiv                            **der Kopf**

*The doll's head needs hair.*
Der Kopf der Puppe braucht Haare.

---

**health** [HELTH] Substantiv            **die Gesundheit**

*Cigarettes harm your health.*
Zigaretten schaden der Gesundheit.

**to hear** [HIER] Verb                    **hören**

*I hear the music.*
Ich höre die Musik.

---

**heart** [HART] Substantiv              **das Herz**

*I see the hearts on the playing card!*
Ich sehe die Herzen auf der Spielkarte!

---

**heavy** [HEW-ie] Adjektiv              **schwer**

*The suitcase is heavy.*
Der Koffer ist schwer.

---

**helicopter** [HEL-i-kap-ter] Substantiv    **der Hubschrauber**

*What is it? A helicopter.*
Was ist es denn? Ein Hubschrauber.

---

**Hello!**                          **Hallo! Guten Tag!**
         [he-LOH] Interjektion       **Servus! Ciao!**

*When I see my freinds, I say "Hello"!*
Wenn ich meine Freunde sehe, sage ich "Hallo"!

---

**Help!** [HELP] Interjektion            **Hilfe!**

**to help** [HELP] Verb                  **helfen**

*Joanna helps the man.*
Johanna hilft dem Mann.

---

**her** [HÄR] Pronomen                    **sie**

*I know her for a year already.*
Ich kenne sie schon seit einem Jahr.

---

**to her** [HÄR] Pronomen               **ihr**

*I give my address to her.*
Ich gebe ihr meine Adresse.

---

**her** [HÄR] Adjektiv                  **ihr(e)**

*Is this her car?*
Ist das ihr Auto?

---

**here** [HIER] Adverb                    **hier**

*German is spoken here.*
Hier spricht man Deutsch.

---

**to hide** [HEID] Verb            **verstecken**

*She hides the present in the drawer.*
Sie versteckt das Geschenk in der Schublade.

**(to play) hide and go seek** Ausdruck   **Verstecken spielen**

*The children play hide and seek.*
Die Kinder spielen Verstecken.

---

**high** [HEI] Adjektiv                   **hoch**

*Manhattan has very high buildings.*
Manhattan hat sehr hohe Gebäude.

---

**highway, expressway** [HEI-weh] Substantiv   **die Autobahn**

*There are many cars on the expressway.*
Es gibt viele Autos auf der Autobahn.

---

**him** [HIM] Pronomen                  **ihn**

*I will see him in the library.*
Ich sehe ihn in der Bibliothek.

---

**to him** [HIM] Pronomen             **ihm**

*I want to give this book to him.*
Ich will ihm dieses Buch geben.

---

**his** [HIS] Adjektiv                                    **sein(e)**
*There are his parents.*
Dort sind seine Eltern.

---

**history** [HIS-te-rie] Substantiv              **die Geschichte**
*I like American history.*
Ich habe amerikanische Geschichte gern.

---

**to hit** [HIT] Verb                                    **schlagen**
*She hits the nail hard with the hammer.*
Sie schlägt den Nagel hart mit dem Hammer.

---

**hole** [HOHL] Substantiv                            **das Loch**
*I have a hole in my sock.*
Ich habe ein Loch in meiner Socke.

---

**holiday** [HA-li-deh] Substantiv              **der Feiertag**
*When is the national holiday of Switzerland?*
Wann ist der Nationalfeiertag der Schweiz?

---

**(be) at home** [bie ät HOWM] Ausdruck      **zu Hause (sein)**
*Where is your sister? She is at home.*
Wo ist denn deine Schwester? Sie ist zu Hause.

---

**(to go) home** [GOW HOWM] Ausdruck   **nach Hause (gehen)**
*I go home at four o'clock in the afternoon.*
Ich gehe um vier Uhr nachmittags nach Hause.

---

**homework** [HOWM-wurk] Substantiv      **die Hausaufgabe**
*We are doing our homework together.*
Wir machen unsere Hausaufgaben zusammen.

---

**to hope** [HOWP] Verb                                **hoffen**
*He hopes that he will get a letter.*
Er hofft, dass er einen Brief bekommt.

---

**hopscotch**                          **Himmel und Erde spielen**
  [HAP-skatsch] Ausdruck

*Let's play hopscotch!*
Lass uns Himmel und Erde spielen!

---

**hoop** [HUP] Substantiv                          **der Reifen**
*The boy is rolling a big hoop.*
Der Junge rollt einen großen Reifen.

---

**horse** [HORS] Substantiv                          **das Pferd**

*The girl is riding this horse.*
Das Mädchen reitet dieses Pferd.

---

**hospital**                  **das Krankenhaus, das Hospital**
  [HAS-pi-tl] Substantiv

*The nurse works at the hospital.*
Die Krankenschwester arbeitet im Krankenhaus.

---

**hot** [HAT] Adjektiv                          **heiß**
**It is hot.** [it is HAT] Ausdruck          **Es ist heiß.**
**(to be) hot** Ausdruck                          **heiß sein**
*She is hot in the summer.*
Ihr ist heiß im Sommer.

---

**hotel** [ho-TEL] Substantiv                          **das Hotel**
*What is the name of this hotel?*
Wie heißt dieses Hotel?

---

**hour** [AUR] Substantiv                          **die Stunde**
*A day has twenty-four hours.*
Ein Tag hat vierundzwanzig Stunden.

---

**house** [HAUS] Substantiv **das Haus**

*Here is my uncle's house.*
Hier ist das Haus meines Onkels.

**dollhouse** [DAHL-haus] Substantiv **das Puppenhaus**

*He will build the children a dollhouse.*
Er baut den Kindern ein Puppenhaus.

**How are you?** [hau AHR ju] Ausdruck **Wie geht es...?,
Wie geht's?**

*How are you, Anna?*
Wie geht es dir, Anna?

**How old are you?** **Wie alt bist du?**
     [hau OLD ahr ju] Ausdruck
*How old are you, Anna?*
Wie alt bist du, Anna?

**how much** [hau MATSCH] Ausdruck **wie viel**

*How much does that cost?*
Wie viel kostet das?

**how many** [hau MEN-ie] Ausdruck **wie viele**

*How many games do you have?*
Wie viele Spiele hast du?

**humid** [HJU-mid] Adjektiv **feucht**

*The air is humid today.*
Die Luft ist feucht heute.

**hundred** [HAN-dred] Adjektiv **hundert**

*There are one hundred people at the beach.*
Es gibt ein hundert Leute am Strand.

**(to be) hungry** [HANG-rie] Ausdruck      **hungrig sein**
*We are hungry.*
Wir sind hungrig.

**hunter** [HAN-ter] Substantiv      **der Jäger, die Jägerin**
*The hunter goes into the forest.*
Der Jäger geht in den Wald.

**Hurray!** [hu-REH] Interjektion      **Hurra! Bravo!**

**to hurry** [HA-rie] Verb      **sich beeilen**
*They hurry because they are late.*
Sie beeilen sich, denn sie sind verspätet.

**hurt** [HÜRT] Adjektiv      **verletzt**
*Oh, you are hurt, Rebecca!*
Oh, du bist verletzt, Rebekka!

**husband** [HAS-bänd] Substantiv      **der Mann**
*My aunt's husband is my uncle.*
Der Mann meiner Tante ist mein Onkel.

## I

**I** [EI] Pronomen      **ich**
*I am speaking with my friends.*
Ich spreche mit meinen Freunden.

**ice** [EIS] Substantiv      **das Glatteis**
*There is ice on the highway.*
Es gibt Glatteis auf der Autobahn.

**ice cream** [EIS kriem] Substantiv      **das Eis**
*Do you eat ice cream in the winter? No, never!*
Isst du Eis im Winter? Nein, nie!

**ice skate** [EIS-skeht] Substantiv     **der Schlittschuh**
**to ice skate** Ausdruck           **Schlittschuh laufen**

*The children are ice skating.*
Die Kinder laufen Schlittschuh.

---

**idea** [ei-DIE-a] Substantiv             **die Idee**

*She always has good ideas.*
Sie hat immer gute Ideen.

---

**if, when** [IF] Konjunktion             **wenn**

*When it rains, I take an umbrella.*
Wenn es regnet, nehme ich einen Regenschirm.

---

**immediately** [e-MIED-jet-liė] Adverb     **sofort, gleich**

*When daddy calls me, I go immediately.*
Wenn der Papa mich ruft, gehe ich sofort.

---

**important** [im-POHR-tent] Adjektiv       **wichtig**

*It is important to eat vegetables.*
Es ist wichtig, Gemüse zu essen.

---

**impossible** [im-PASS-e-bl] Adjektiv      **unmöglich**

*It is impossible to roll this rock.*
Es ist unmöglich diesen Felsen zu rollen.

---

**in, to** [IN, TU] Präposition              **in**

*They go to the school.*
Sie gehen in die Schule.

*They are now in the school.*
Sie sind jetzt in der Schule.

---

**inexpensive, cheap** [in-eks-PEN-siv] Adjektiv    **billig**

*The tomatoes are cheap, they are not expensive.*
Die Tomaten sind billig, sie sind nicht teuer.

---

**insect** [IN-sekt] Substantiv                              **das Insekt**
*A bee is an insect.*
Eine Biene ist ein Insekt.

---

**intelligent** [in-TEL-i-dgent] Adjektiv              **intelligent**
*My aunt is very intelligent.*
Meine Tante ist sehr intelligent.

---

**intentionally, on purpose**                              **absichtlich**
    [in-TEN-schen-el-lie] Adverb
*The cat teases the dog intentionally.*
Die Katze neckt den Hund absichtlich.

---

**interesting** [IN-ter-es-ting] Adjektiv              **interessant**
*Today's news is interesting.*
Die Nachrichten von heute sind interessant.

---

**to introduce** [in-tras-DUHSS] Verb                   **vorstellen**
*She is introducing her grandson to us.*
Sie stellt uns ihren Enkel vor.

---

**to invite** [in-WEIT] Verb                               **einladen**
*The man invites his grandson to the zoo.*
Der Mann lädt seinen Enkel in den Zoo ein.

---

**iron** [EI-ern] Substantiv                              **das Eisen**
*The nail is made of iron.*
Der Nagel ist aus Eisen.

---

**iron** [EI-ern] Substantiv                         **das Bügeleisen**
**to iron** [EI-ern] Verb                                     **bügeln**
*The iron is not working. He cannot iron his shirts.*
Das Bügeleisen ist kaputt. Er kann seine Hemden
nicht bügeln.

---

**is** [IS] Verb　　　　　　　　　　　**er ist / sie ist / es ist**
　　　see **be, to be**

**Isn't that true? Isn't that so?**　　**Nicht? Nicht wahr?**
　　Ausdruck

**island** [EI-länd] Substantiv　　　　　　**die Insel**

*What a beautiful island!*
So eine schöne Insel!

**it** [IT] Pronomem　　　　　　　　　　　　　　　**es**
*I like the shirt. I'll take it!*
Ich mag das Hemd. Ich nehme es!

**its** [ITS] Adjektiv　　　　　　　　　　　　　　**sein**
*The animal plays with its tail.*
Das Tier spielt mit seinem Schwanz.

**It's me!** [its MIE] Ausdruck　　　　　　**Ich bin es!**

## J

**jacket** [DGAK-it] Substantiv　　　　　　**die Jacke**
*My grandfather wears pants and a jacket.*
Mein Großvater trägt eine Hose und eine Jacke.

**jam** [DGÄM] Substantiv　　　　　**die Marmelade**
*He likes strawberry jam.*
Er mag Erdbeermarmelade.

**January** [DGÄN-ju-er-ie] Substantiv **der Januar**

*How many days are there in January?*
Wie viele Tage gibt es im Januar?

---

**jeans** [DGIENS] Substantiv **die Jeans (pl)**

*My jeans are in the wash.*
Meine Jeans sind in der Wäsche.

---

**jewelry** [DGUH-el-rie] Substantiv **der Schmuck**

*The burglar finds the jewelry.*
Der Dieb findet den Schmuck.

---

**joyful** [DGOI-fuhl] Adjektiv **fröhlich**

*She is joyful on her birthday.*
Sie ist fröhlich an ihrem Geburtstag.

---

**juice** [DGUS] Substantiv **der Saft**

*There is rasberry juice in the punch.*
Es gibt Himbeersaft in der Bowle.

**orange juice** **der Orangensaft**
      [OHR-endg dgus] Substantiv

---

**July** [dgu-LEI] Substantiv **der Juli**

*It is hot in July.*
Es ist heiß im Juli.

---

**to jump** [DGAMP] Verb **springen**

*The boy jumps from the stairs.*
Der Junge springt von der Treppe.

**to jump rope** [tu DGAMP rowp] Ausdruck **Seil springen**

---

**June** [DGUHN] Substantiv                                    **der Juni**
*My birthday is in June.*
Mein Geburtstag ist im Juni.

---

## K

**kangaroo** [käng-ge-RUH] Substantiv                **das Känguru**

*The kangaroo is an unusual animal.*
Das Känguru ist ein sonderbares Tier.

---

**to keep** [KIEP] Verb                                        **behalten**
*I want to keep the dog.*
Ich möchte den Hund behalten.

---

**key** [KIE] Substantiv                                **der Schlüssel**

*Where is my key?*
Wo ist denn mein Schlüssel?

---

**to kick** [KIK] Verb                                         **stoßen**
*I kick the stone (with the foot).*
Ich stoße gegen den Stein (mit dem Fuss).

---

**to kill** [KIL] Verb                                         **töten**
*Mom kills the fly.*
Mutti tötet die Fliege.

---

**kilometer** [kil-AH-me-ter] Substantiv        **der Kilometer**

*We live ten kilometers (six miles) from the lake.*
Wir wohnen zehn Kilometer (sechs Meilen) vom
See entfernt.

---

**kind (nice)** [KEIND] Adjektiv                        **nett**

*The teacher is nice. She does not yell.*
Die Lehrerin ist nett. Sie schreit nicht.

---

**what kind of** [wat KEIND of] Ausdruck        **was für ein(e)**

*What kind of car is that?*
Was für ein Auto ist denn das?

---

**king** [KING] Substantiv                          **der König**

*Is there a king in the United States? No, a president.*
Gibt es einen König in den Vereinigten Staaten? Nein, ein
Präsident.

---

**kiss** [KIS] Substantiv                              **der Kuss**

*I give my little brother a kiss.*
Ich gebe meinem kleinen Bruder einen Kuss.

**to kiss** [KIS] Verb                                **küssen**

*The father is kissing the child.*
Der Vater küsst das Kind.

---

**kitchen** [KITSCH-en] Substantiv               **die Küche**

*The kitchen is very small.*
Die Küche ist sehr klein.

---

**kite** [KEIT] Substantiv                          **der Drachen**

*It is windy. Let's play with our kite.*
Es ist windig. Spielen wir doch mit unserem Drachen.

---

**kitten** [KIT-en] Substantiv                      **das Kätzchen**

*The kitten sleeps a lot.*
Das Kätzchen schläft viel.

---

**knee** [NIE] Substantiv                           **das Knie**

*Do you have a sore knee? That is too bad!*
Tut dein Knie weh? Schade!

---

**knife** [NEIF] Substantiv                         **das Messer**

*I cut the bread with the knife.*
Ich schneide das Brot mit dem Messer.

---

**to knit** [NIT] Verb                              **stricken**

---

**to knock** [NAK] Verb                             **klopfen**

*The guest knocks at the door.*
Der Gast klopft an die Tür.

---

**to know (a fact)** [NOW] Verb                     **wissen**

*She knows the name of the capital of Switzerland, Bern.*
Sie weiß, wie die Hauptstadt von der Schweiz heißt, Bern.

---

**to know (a person or place)** [NOW] Verb          **kennen**

*I know his uncle.*
Ich kenne seinen Onkel.

---

**to know, to be able** [NOW] Verb                  **können**

*We know how to ski.*
Wir können Ski laufen.

---

## L

**lady** [LEH-die] Substantiv                               **die Dame**
*Who is this lady?*
Wer ist denn diese Dame?

**lake** [LEHK] Substantiv                                  **der See**

*There is a boat in the middle of the Alpine lake.*
Da ist ein Boot in der Mitte des Alpensees.

**lamb** [LÄM] Substantiv          **das Lamm, das Schaf**
    see **sheep**

**lamb chop** [LÄM-tschop] Ausdruck       **das Lammkotelett**

**lamp** [LÄMP] Substantiv                                  **die Lampe**
*The lamp is in the living room.*
Die Lampe ist im Wohnzimmer.

**large** [LAHRDG] Adjektiv                                 **groß**
*The truck in front of our house is large.*
Der Lastwagen vor unserem Haus ist groß.

**last** [LÄST] Adjektiv                                    **letzte(n)**
*This is the last stamp.*
Das ist die letzte Briefmarke.

**late** [LEHT] Adverb                                      **spät**
*Frank seldom comes late.*
Frank kommt selten spät.

**later** [LEH-ter] Adverb            **später**

*It is eight o'clock. The mailman comes later.*
Es ist acht Uhr. Der Briefträger kommt später.

---

**to laugh** [LÄF] Verb            **lachen**

*She laughs when she sees the clowns.*
Sie lacht, wenn sie die Clowns sieht.

---

**lawyer** [LOH-jer] Substantiv      **der Rechtsanwalt,
die Rechtsanwältin**

*My aunt is a lawyer.*
Meine Tante ist Rechtsanwältin.

---

**to lay (something down)**         **legen**
     see **put (down)**

---

**lazy** [LEH-sie] Adjektiv            **faul**

*Pupils are lazy when it is warm.*
Schüler sind faul, wenn es warm ist.

---

**to lead** [LIED] Verb            **leiten**

*She leads the group on a hike.*
Sie leitet die Gruppe auf einer Wanderung.

---

**leader** [LIE-der] Substantiv       **der Anführer**

*No, you are always playing the leader.*
Nein, du spielst immer den Anführer.

---

**leaf** [LIEF] Substantiv      **das Blatt**

*There are many leaves on the ground in autumn.*
Es gibt im Herbst viele Blätter auf dem Boden.

---

**to leap** [LIEP] Verb      **springen**

*When we come, the dog leaps from the sofa.*
Wenn wir kommen, springt der Hund vom Sofa.

---

**leapfrog** [LIEP-frog] Substantiv      **das Bockspringen**

*Children love leapfrog.*
Kinder lieben Bockspringen.

---

**to learn** [LÄRN] Verb      **lernen**

*He likes to learn German.*
Er lernt gern Deutsch.

---

**leather** [LETH-er] Substantiv      **das Leder**

*My brother's jacket is made of leather.*
Die Jacke meines Bruders ist aus Leder.

---

**to leave (a place, person)** [LIEV] Verb      **verlassen**

*She leaves the office at five o'clock.*
Sie verlässt das Büro um fünf Uhr.

**to leave (something)** [LIEV] Verb      **lassen**

*He often leaves his books at home.*
Er lässt seine Bücher oft zu Hause.

---

**to/on the left** [LEFT] Ausdruck      **links, auf der linken Seite**

*The bakery is on the left.*
Die Bäckerei ist links.

---

**the left hand** [tha LEFT händ] Ausdruck     **die linke Hand**

*He writes with the left hand.*
Er schreibt mit der linken Hand.

**leg** [LEG] Substantiv     **das Bein**

*Birds have two legs, cats and dogs have four paws.*
Vögel haben zwei Beine, Katzen und Hunde haben vier
Pfoten.

**lemon** [LEM-en] Substantiv     **die Zitrone**

*Lemons are yellow.*
Zitronen sind gelb.

**to lend** [LEND] Verb     **leihen**

*I'll lend you a pencil.*
Ich leihe dir einen Bleistift.

**leopard** [LEP-erd] Substantiv     **der Leopard**

*The leopard is in the forest.*
Der Leopard ist im Wald.

**less** [LESS] Adverb     **weniger**

*Twelve less two makes ten.*
Zwölf weniger zwei macht zehn.

**lesson** [LESS-en] Substantiv     **der Unterricht**

*The lesson is interesting.*
Der Unterricht ist interessant.

**Let's go!** [lets GOH] Ausdruck     **Gehen wir doch!**

**letter** [LET-er] Substantiv     **der Brief**

*I put the letter in the envelope.*
Ich stecke den Brief in den Umschlag.

**lettuce** [LE-tiss] Substantiv                     **der Kopfsalat**

*Mom makes the salad with lettuce.*
Mutti macht den Salat mit Kopfsalat.

---

**library** [LEI-brer-ie] Substantiv            **die Bibliothek**

*There are so many books in the library.*
Es gibt so viele Bücher in der Bibliothek.

---

**to lie** [LEI] Verb                                          **lügen**

*I do not lie.*
Ich lüge nicht.

---

**light** [LEIT] Substantiv                              **das Licht**

*The moon does not give much light.*
Der Mond gibt nicht viel Licht.

**light (color)** [LEIT] Adjektiv                         **hell**

*This is a light color.*
Das ist eine helle Farbe.

**light (weight)** [LEIT] Adjektiv                     **leicht**

*The box is light. It is not heavy.*
Der Karton ist leicht. Er ist nicht schwer.

**traffic light** [LEIT]                                **die Ampel**

*You cross the street when the light is green.*
Man überquert die Straße, wenn die Ampel grün ist.

---

**lightning** [LEIT-ning] Substantiv                 **das Blitzen**

*I am afraid of lightning.*
Ich habe Angst vor Blitzen.

---

**to like** [LEIK] Verb                              **gern haben**

*Mom likes her birthday gifts.*
Mutti hat ihre Geburtstagsgeschenke gern.

---

**to like, to want** [LEIK] Verb                     **mögen**

*I like fairy tales with giants.*
Ich mag Märchen mit Riesen.

    see also **would like** Verb          **möchte**

---

**lion** [LEI-en] Substantiv            **der Löwe, die Löwin**

*A lion can be ferocious.*
Ein Löwe kann grausam sein.

---

**lip** [LIP] Substantiv                              **die Lippe**

*The teacher puts his finger to his lips.*
Der Lehrer legt seinen Finger auf die Lippen.

---

**to listen (hear)** [LIS-en] Verb                   **hören**

*The boy is listening to the radio.*
Der Junge hört Radio.

    see **to follow** [FAL-ow] Verb          **folgen**

---

**little** [LĬT-l] Adjektiv                                   **klein**
*The child is little.*
Das Kind ist klein.

**a little** [ä LĬT-l] Ausdruck                              **ein Bisschen**
*Would you like some dessert? Yes, a little, please.*
Möchtest du etwas Nachtisch? Ja, ein Bisschen, bitte.

**to live (dwell)** [LĬW] Verb                               **wohnen**
*We live in an apartment.*
Wir wohnen in einer Wohnung.

**to live** [LĬW] Verb                                        **leben**
*Do wild animals live in this forest?*
Leben wilde Tiere in diesem Wald?

**living room** [LĬW-ing ruhm] Substantiv    **das Wohnzimmer**

*Who is in the living room?*
Wer ist denn im Wohnzimmer?

**lollipop** [LAL-ie-POP] Substantiv                         **der Lolli**
*The birthday child brings lollipops for the class.*
Das Geburtstagskind bringt Lollis für die Klasse.

**long** [LAŬNG] Adjektiv                                     **lang**
*Her coat is long.*
Ihr Mantel ist lang.

**no longer** [n<u>oh</u> LAUNG-ger] Ausdruck     **nicht mehr**

*He no longer plays the piano.*
Er spielt nicht mehr Klavier.

---

**to look** [LUHK] Verb                  **sehen**
      see **to see**

**to look (to appear)** [LUHK] Verb      **aussehen**

*This tiger does not look ferocious.*
Dieser Tiger sieht nicht wild aus.

**to look after, to care about**     **sich kümmern um**
       [LUHK AF-ter] Ausdruck

*The cat looks after her kittens.*
Die Katze kümmert sich um ihre Kätzchen.

**to look for** [LUHK vor] Ausdruck        **suchen**

*Dad is always looking for his keys.*
Papa sucht immer seine Schlüssel.

---

**to lose** [LUHS] Verb                **verlieren**

*Careful, you are going to lose your scarf.*
Pass auf, sonst verlierst du deinen Schal.

---

**a lot, many** [ah LAT] Adverb          **viele**

*There are many horses on this farm.*
Es gibt viele Pferde auf diesem Bauernhof.

---

**loud** [LAUD] Adjektiv                **laut**

*The balloon breaks. The bang is loud.*
Der Ballon platzt. Der Knall ist laut.

**in a loud voice**          **mit lauter Stimme**
      [in ä LAUD wOISS] Ausdruck

---

**to love** [LUV] Verb                        **lieben**

*I love my cat.*
Ich liebe meine Katze.

---

**low** [LOW] Adjektiv                 **niedrig**
*The children's chair is low.*
Der Kinderstuhl ist niedrig.

**in a low voice**                 **mit leiser Stimme**
    [in ä low WOISS] Ausdruck
*Please talk in a low voice.*
Bitte redet mit leiser Stimme.

---

**to lower** [LOH-er] Verb            **herunterlassen**
*It is dark. Let us lower the shades.*
Es ist dunkel. Lassen wir doch die Rollos herunter.

---

**luck** [LAK] Substantiv              **das Glück**
**Good luck!** Ausdruck       **Alles Gute! Viel Glück!**
*Before the examination, the teacher says, "Good luck!"*
Vor der Prüfung sagt die Lehrerin, "Viel Glück!"

---

**luggage** [LAG-idg] Substantiv       **das Gepäck**
*The baggage is ready for the trip.*
Das Gepäck ist fertig für die Reise.

---

**lunch** [LANTSCH] Substantiv         **der Lunch**
*We eat our lunch quickly.*
Wir essen unseren Lunch schnell.

**lunch** [DIN-er]                 **das Mittagessen**
*We eat at one o'clock.*
Wir essen zu Mittag um ein Uhr.

---

# M

**machine** [ma-SCHIEN] Substantiv     **die Maschine**

*The vacuum cleaner is a useful machine.*
Der Staubsauger ist eine praktische Maschine.

**washing machine**     **die Waschmaschine**
       [wasch-ing ma-SCHIEN] Substantiv

---

**be mad (angry at)** [MAD] Ausdruck     **böse sein auf**

*He is mad at his father.*
Er ist böse auf seinen Vater.

---

**made of** [MEHD aw] Ausdruck     **sein aus**

*This shirt is made of cotton.*
Dieses Hemd ist aus Baumwolle.

---

**maid** [MÄD] Substantiv     **das Dienstmädchen**

*We do not have a maid.*
Wir haben kein Dienstmädchen.

---

**to mail (a letter)** [MEHL] Verb     **mit der Post schicken**

*She mails my letters.*
Sie schickt meine Briefe mit der Post.

---

**mailbox** [MEHL-box] Substantiv     **der Briefkasten**

*I am putting the letter in the mailbox.*
Ich werfe den Brief in den Briefkasten.

---

**mail carrier** [MEHL KÄR-ie-er] Substantiv    **der Briefträger**
**die Briefträgerin**

*The mail carrier brings letters and packages.*
Der Briefträger bringt Briefe und Pakete.

---

**to make, to do** [MEHK] Verb           **machen**

*Mostly he does his homework after dinner.*
Meistens macht er seine Aufgaben nach dem Abendessen.

---

**man** [MÄN] Substantiv            **der Mann**

*The man is sitting in the park.*
Der Mann sitzt im Park.

---

**many** [MEN-ie] Adjektiv           **viele**

*Bertha has many books.*
Berta hat viele Bücher.

**so many** [so MEN-ie] Ausdruck      **so viele**

**too many** [tu MEN-ie] Ausdruck      **zu viele**

---

**map** [MÄP] Substantiv    **die Karte, die Landkarte**

*Do you have a map of the Alps?*
Hast du eine Karte von den Alpen?

---

**marbles** [MAHR-bls] Substantiv      **die Murmeln**

*Boys like to play marbles.*
Jungen spielen gern mit Murmeln.

---

**March** [MARTSCH] Substantiv        **der März**

*March is the month between February and April.*
Der März kommt zwischen Februar und April.

---

**mark, grade** [MARK] Substantiv    **das Zeugnis, die Note**

*My grades in math are very good.*
Meine Zeugnisse in Mathe sind sehr gut.

---

**market** [MAHR-kit] Substantiv      **der Markt, der Supermarkt**

*You find fresh vegetables at the market.*
Man findet frisches Gemüse auf dem Markt.

---

**marmalade** Substantiv      **die Marmelade**
    see **jam**

---

**to marry** [MÄR-ie] Verb      **heiraten**

*The prince marries the princess.*
Der Prinz heiratet die Prinzessin.

---

**Marvelous!** [MAHR-we-les] Interjektion      **Wunderbar!**

*You are going on vacation! Marvelous!*
Du machst Urlaub! Wunderbar!

---

**match** [MATSCH] Substantiv      **das Streichholz**

*Matches are dangerous for children.*
Streichhölzer sind gefährlich für Kinder.

---

**What's the matter?**      **Was ist los?**
    [WHATS tha MÄT-er] Ausdruck

*You look sad. What's the matter?*
Du siehst traurig aus. Was ist denn los?

---

**May** [MEH] Substantiv      **der Mai**

*May has thirty-one days.*
Der Mai hat einunddreißig Tage.

---

**may** [MEH] Verb      **dürfen**

*May I come along?*
Darf ich mitkommen?

**maybe** [MEH-bie] Adverb          **vielleicht**

*Are we going to the movies tonight? Maybe.*
Gehen wir heute Abend ins Kino? Vielleicht.

**me** [MIE] Pronomen          **mich**

*My mother calls me.*
Meine Mutter ruft mich.

**to me** [MIE] Pronomen          **mir**

*She gives (to) me the bread.*
Sie gibt mir das Brot.

**It's me!** [its MIE] Ausdruck          **Ich bin es!**

**meal** [MIEL] Substantiv          **die Mahlzeit**

*Which meal do you prefer?*
Welche Mahlzeit hast du lieber?

**to mean** [MIEN] Verb          **bedeuten**

*What does this word mean?*
Was bedeutet dieses Wort?

**meat** [MIET] Substantiv          **das Fleisch**

*We buy meat at the butcher shop.*
Wir kaufen Fleisch beim Metzger.

**mechanic** [me-KÄN-ik] Substantiv          **der Mechaniker,
die Mechanikerin**

*She is becoming an automobile mechanic.*
Sie wird Automechanikerin.

**medicine** [MED-e-sin] Substantiv          **die Medizin**

*The medicine helps the sick child.*
Die Medizin hilft dem kranken Kind.

**to meet** [MIET] Verb                                          **treffen**

*Who meets Little Red Riding Hood in the forest?*
Wer trifft Rotkäppchen im Wald?

---

**member** [MEM-ber] Substantiv                          **das Mitglied**

*He is a member of the team.*
Er ist ein Mitglied der Mannschaft.

---

**men** [MEN] Substantiv, pl.                              **die Männer**
    see **man**

---

**menu** [MEN-ju] Substantiv                          **die Speisekarte**

*I am reading the menu.*
Ich lese die Speisekarte.

---

**merry-go-round**                                        **das Karussell**
    [MER-ie-goh-raund] Substantiv

*We ride the horses on the merry-go-round.*
Wir reiten die Pferde auf dem Karussell.

---

**in the middle** [in tha MID-el] Ausdruck              **in der Mitte**

*Where should I sit? In the middle.*
Wo soll ich sitzen? In der Mitte.

---

**midnight** [MID-neit] Substantiv                      **die Mitternacht**
**at midnight** [ät MID-neit] Ausdruck                 **um Mitternacht**

*At midnight? I am asleep then.*
Um Mitternacht? Ich schlafe dann.

---

**mile** [MEIL] Substantiv        **die Meile**

*My cousin Erika lives one mile from here.*
Meine Kusine Erika wohnt eine Meile von hier.

**milk** [MILK] Substantiv        **die Milch**

*I drink milk and Daddy drinks coffee with milk.*
Ich trinke Milch und Vati trinkt Kaffee mit Milch.

**million** [MIL-jen] Substantiv        **die Million**

*How many CDs do you have, Anke? A million!*
Wie viele CDs hast du, Anke? Eine Million!

**Never mind!** [NE-ver MEIND] Ausdruck     **Es macht nichts!**

*You have no money? Never mind! Come anyway.*
Du hast kein Geld? Es macht nichts! Komm sowieso.

**minute** [MIN-it] Substantiv        **die Minute**

*How many minutes are there in an hour?*
Wie viele Minuten hat eine Stunde?

**mirror** [MIR-er] Substantiv        **der Spiegel**

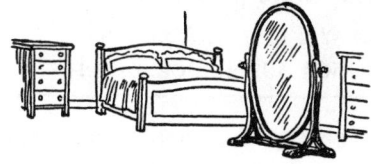

*There is a mirror in the bedroom.*
Da ist ein Spiegel im Schlafzimmer.

**Miss** [MISS] Substantiv        **das Fräulein**

*She wants to be called Miss Schmidt.*
Sie möchte, dass man sie Fräulein Schmidt nennt.

**mistake** [miss-TEHK] Substantiv                            **der Fehler**

*Martha seldom makes mistakes.*
Marta macht selten Fehler.

---

**mister, Mr., Sir** [MIS-ter] Substantiv                     **der Herr**

*The greengrocer's name is Mr. Grohe.*
Der Gemüsehändler heißt Herr Grohe.

---

**to mix** [MIKS] Verb                                         **mischen**

*Anne is mixing the ingredients for the bread.*
Anne mischt die Zutaten für das Brot.

---

**moist (damp)** [MOIST] Adjektiv                             **feucht**

*My bathing suit is still damp.*
Mein Badeanzug ist noch feucht.

---

**mom** [MAHM] Substantiv                                     **Mama, Mutti**

*Mom, here are your keys.*
Mama, hier sind deine Schlüssel.

---

**moment** [MOH-ment] Substantiv                          **der Augenblick**

*Just a moment, please!*
Einen Augenblick, bitte!

---

**Monday** [MAN-deh] Substantiv                              **der Montag**

*What are you doing on Monday?*
Was machst du am Montag?

---

**money** [MAN-ie] Substantiv                                 **das Geld**

*How much money does he have?*
Wie viel Geld hat er?

---

**monkey** [MANG-kie] Substantiv                **der Affe**

*The monkey is eating a banana.*
Der Affen frisst eine Banane.

**month** [MANTH] Substantiv                    **der Monat**
*The summer months in Europe are June, July and August.*
Die Sommer Monate in Europa sind Juni, Juli und August.

**moon** [MUHN] Substantiv                      **der Mond**
*The earth has only one moon.*
Die Erde hat nur einen Mond.

**more** [MOHR] Adverb                          **mehr**
*More salad, please.*
Mehr Salat, bitte!

**morning** [MOHR-ning] Substantiv             **der Morgen**
*What time do you get up every morning?*
Wann stehst du jeden Morgen auf?

**mosquito** [mas-KIE-ta] Substantiv           **die Mücke**
*There is a mosquito in my bedroom!*
Da ist eine Mücke in meinem Schlafzimmer!

**mother** [MATH-er] Substantiv                 **die Mutter**
*Today is my mother's birthday.*
Heute hat meine Mutter Geburtstag.

**mountain** [MAUN-ten] Substantiv　　　　　　　　**der Berg**

*The mountains in central Europe are the Alps.*
Die Berge in der Mitte Europas sind die Alpen.

**mouse** [MAUS] Substantiv　　　　　　　　　　　**die Maus**

*There are mice in this field.*
Es gibt Mäuse auf diesem Feld.

**mouth** [MAUTH] Substantiv　　　　　　　　　　**der Mund**

*The boy opens his mouth and sings.*
Der Junge öffnet seinen Mund und singt.

**Mr. (Mister)** [MIS-ter] Substantiv　　　　　　　**(der) Herr**

*Mr. Meier is on the telephone.*
Herr Meier ist am Telefon.

**Mrs.** [MISS-is] Substantiv　　　　　　　　　　　**(die) Frau**

*Mrs. Albert is our teacher.*
Frau Albert ist unsere Lehrerin.

**to move** [MUHV] Verb　　　　　　　　　　　　**bewegen**

*He moves his fingers quickly when he plays the piano.*
Er bewegt die Finger schnell, wenn er Klavier spielt.

**movie, film** [MUH-wie] Substantiv　　　　　　　**der Film**

*Is there a good film at the movies?*
Gibt es einen guten Film im Kino?

**to go to the movies** [MUH-wies] Ausdruck　　**ins Kino gehen**

*Let's go to the movies on Friday night.*
Lass uns am Freitagabend ins Kino gehen.

**Ms., Mrs.** [MIS] Substantiv　　　　　　　　　　**die Frau**

*Frieda wants to be called Ms. Braun.*
Frieda möchte, daß man sie Frau Braun nennt.

**much** [MATSCH] Adverb　　　　　　　　　　**viel**

*Do you study much every day?*
Lernst du viel jeden Tag?

**how much** Ausdruck　　　　　　　　　**wie viel**
**how many** Ausdruck　　　　　　　　**wie viele**
**too much** Ausdruck　　　　　　　　　**zu viel**
**too many** Ausdruck　　　　　　　　　**zu viele**

---

**mud** [MAD] Substantiv　　　　　　　**der Schlamm**

*My shoes are covered with mud.*
Meine Schuhe sind voller Schlamm.

---

**museum** [mju-SIE-em] Substantiv　　　**das Museum**

*The museum is closed on Mondays.*
Das Museum ist montags geschlossen.

---

**music** [MJU-sik] Substantiv　　　　　　**die Musik**

*The music is loud, but pleasant.*
Die Musik ist laut, aber angenehm.

**musical note** [MJU-si-kel NOHT] Ausdruck　　**die Note**

---

**musician** [mju-SISCH-en] Substantiv　　**der Musiker**
　　　　　　　　　　　　　　　　　　**die Musikerin**

*The boy wants to become a musician.*
Der Junge möchte Musiker werden.

---

**must, have to** [MAST] Verb　　　　　　**müssen**

*You must wash your hands, Joey.*
Du musst deine Hände waschen, Jupp.

---

**my** [mei] Adjektiv　　　　　　　　　　**mein**

*My brother is handsome.*
Mein Bruder ist gutaussehend.

**myself** [mei-SELF] Pronomen                                                      **selbst**

*I'll do it myself.*
Ich mache es schon selbst.

---

# N

---

**nail** [NEHL] Sutstantiv                                                          **der Nagel**

*We play with nails and a hammer.*
Wir spielen mit Nägeln und einem Hammer.

---

**nail, fingernail**                                                         **der Fingernagel**
    [NEHL, FIN-ger-nehl] Substantiv

*I have ten fingernails.*
Ich habe zehn Fingernägel.

---

**name** [NEHM] Substantiv                                                           **der Name**

*What is his name?*
Was ist sein Name?

---

**napkin** [NÄP-kin] Substantiv                                                   **die Serviette**

*Her napkin is on the table.*
Ihre Serviette ist auf dem Tisch.

---

**narrow** [NÄR-ow] Adjektiv                                                              **eng**

*This street is narrow.*
Diese Straße ist eng.

---

**nation** [NEH-shen] Substantiv                                                   **die Nation**

*There are many flags at the United Nations headquarters.*
Es gibt viele Flaggen am Hauptsitz der Vereinten Nationen.

---

**national** [NÄSH-en-el] Adjektiv                     **national**

*The Fourth of July is the national holiday of the
United States.*
Der vierte Juli ist der Nationalfeiertag der Vereinigten
Staaten.

---

**naughty** [NOH-tie] Adjektiv                        **schlimm**

*Robby hits the cat. He is naughty.*
Robby schlägt die Katze. Er ist schlimm.

---

**near** [NIER] Präposition                               **bei**

*Bremen is near the North Sea.*
Bremen ist in bei der Nordsee.

---

**necessary** [NESS-e-ser-ie] Adjektiv              **notwendig**

*It is necessary to go to school.*
Es ist notwendig, in die Schule zu gehen.

---

**neck** [NEK] Substantiv                              **der Hals**

*My grandmother says, "My neck hurts."*
Meine Großmutter sagt, "Mein Hals tut weh."

---

**to need** [NIED] Verb                               **brauchen**

*An astronaut needs oxygen.*
Ein Astronaut braucht Sauerstoff.

---

**needle** [NIED-l] Substantiv                        **die Nadel**

*I sew with a sewing needle.*
Ich nähe mit einer Nähnadel.

---

**neighbor** [NEH-br] Substantiv                    **der Nachbar**
                                                    **die Nachbarin**

*My neighbor helps me.*
Mein Nachbar hilft mir.

---

**nephew** [NEF-ju] Substantiv                          **der Neffe**

*Peter is my nephew.*
Peter ist mein Neffe.

---

**nest** [NEST] Substantiv                              **das Nest**

*How many eggs do you see in the nest?*
Wie viele Eier siehst du im Nest?

---

**never** [NEW-er] Adverb                               **nie**

*I never play in the woods.*
Ich spiele nie im Wald.

---

**new** [NJU] Adjektiv                                   **neu**

*My bicycle is new.*
Mein Fahrrad ist neu.

---

**New Year's Day** Ausdruck                    **(das) Neujahr**
**New Year's Eve** Ausdruck              **(der) Silvesterabend**

---

**newspaper** [NJUS-peh-per] Substantiv         **die Zeitung**

*On Sunday mornings we read the newspaper.*
Sonntagmorgens lesen wir die Zeitung.

---

**next** [NEKST] Adjektiv                                **nächst**

*The teacher says, "Next week we are having a test."*
Der Lehrer sagt, "Nächste Woche gibt es eine Prüfung."

---

**next to** [NEKST tu] Präposition                      **neben**

*He stands next to the child.*
Er steht neben dem Kind.

**nice** [NEIS] Adjektiv                                                                          **nett**

*The teacher is nice. She does not yell.*
Die Lehrerin ist nett. Sie schreit nicht.

**niece** [NIES] Substantiv                                                              **die Nichte**

*She is the lawyer's niece.*
Sie ist die Nichte der Rechtsanwältin.

**night** [NEIT] Substantiv                                                             **die Nacht**

*At night one can see many stars.*
In der Nacht kann man viele Sterne sehen.

**nine** [NEIN] Adjektiv                                                                          **neun**

*I am nine years old.*
Ich bin neun Jahre alt.

**nineteen** [nein-TIEN] Adjektiv                                                     **neunzehn**

*Today is September nineteenth.*
Heute ist der neunzehnte September.

**ninety** [NEIN-tie] Adjektiv                                                           **neunzig**

*Somebody is ninety-one years old?*
Jemand ist einundneunzig Jahre alt?

**no** [NOW] Adverb                                                                               **nein**

*Please get up. No, I do not want to get up.*
Bitte steh auf! Nein, ich will nicht aufstehen.

**No admittance!**                                                         **Zutritt verboten!**
    [NOW ad-MIT-ens] Ausdruck                                 **Kein Eingang!**

**No smoking!**　　　　　　　　　　　　**Rauchen verboten!**
　　[NO̱W s-MO̱W-king] Ausdruck

*No smoking in school.*
In der Schule ist Rauchen verboten.

---

**no longer** [NO̱W LOHNG-er] Ausdruck　　　　　　**nicht mehr**

*I go to school. My brother no longer goes to school.*
Ich gehe in die Schule. Mein Bruder geht nicht mehr
in die Schule.

---

**noise** [NOIS] Substantiv　　　　　　　　　　**der Krach**

*Thunder makes a loud noise.*
Der Donner macht einen lauten Krach.

---

**noon** [NUHN] Substantiv　　　　　　　　　　**der Mittag**

*The bell rings at noon.*
Die Glocke läutet am Mittag.

---

**north** [NORTH] Substantiv　　　　　　　　　**der Norden**

*Is the mountain in the north or the south?*
Ist der Berg im Norden oder im Süden?

---

**nose** [NO̱W̱S] Substantiv　　　　　　　　　　**die Nase**

*What a big nose you have, Grandmother.*
Was für eine große Nase du hast, Großmutter.

---

**not** [NAT] Adverb　　　　　　　　　　　　　**nicht**

*Johnny is not working now.*
Hans arbeitet jetzt nicht.

---

**not a, not an, not any**　　　　　　　　　　**kein(e)**
　　[NAT ä, NAT än, NAT äni] Adjektiv

*This is not a cat, it is a dog.*
Das ist keine Katze, es ist ein Hund.

**note** [NOWT] Substantiv         **die Note**

*Here are the musical notes for Mozart's* Magic Flute.
Hier sind die Noten zu Mozarts "Zauberflöte."

---

**note (bill)** [NOWT] Substantiv      **der Schein**

*I am rich! I have a twenty-mark bill.*
Ich bin reich! Ich habe einen Zwanzigmarkschein.

---

**notebook** [NOWT-buk] Substantiv     **das Heft**

*She writes her homework in a notebook.*
Sie schreibt ihre Aufgaben in einem Heft.

---

**nothing** [NA-thing] Pronomen       **nichts**

*He takes nothing to the party.*
Er nimmt nichts zur Party.

---

**November** [na-WEM-ber] Substantiv   **der November**

*Thanksgiving is an American holiday in November.*
Erntedankfest ist ein amerikanischer Feiertag im November.

---

**now** [NAU] Adverb             **jetzt**

*You have to go to bed now.*
Du musst jetzt zu Bett gehen!

---

**number** [NAM-ber] Substantiv     **die Nummer**

*What is your telephone number?*
Was ist deine Telefonnummer?

---

**number** [NAM-ber] Substantiv      **die Anzahl**

*You have a great number of books.*
Du hast eine große Anzahl von Büchern.

---

**nurse** [NÜRS] Substantiv          **die Krankenschwester**

*My neighbor is a nurse.*
Meine Nachbarin ist Krankenschwester.

O

**to obey** [O-BEH] Verb                                **folgen**
*When I am well behaved, I obey my parents.*
Wenn ich mich gut benehme, folge ich meinen Eltern.

**o'clock** [O-KLAK] Substantiv                          **Uhr**
*It is twelve o'clock.*
Es ist zwölf Uhr.

**occupied, busy** [AHK-ju-peid] Adjektiv          **beschäftigt**
*Walter is occupied now. He is vacuuming.*
Walters ist beschäftigt jetzt. Er staubsaugt.

**ocean** [OH-schen] Substantiv                      **der Ozean**
*The oceans cover almost all of the world.*
Die Ozeane bedecken fast die ganze Erde.

**ocean liner (steamship)**                          **der Dampfer**
     [OH-shen LEI-ner] Substantiv

*The ocean liner crosses the Atlantic Ocean.*
Der Dampfer überquert den Atlantischen Ozean.

**October** [ak-TOH-ber] Substantiv **der Oktober**
*October is the tenth month of the year.*
Der Oktober ist der zehnte Monat des Jahres.

---

**odd** [AHD] Adjektiv **komisch**
*This is an odd animal.*
Das ist ein komisches Tier.

---

**office** [OHF-fiss] Substantiv **das Büro**
*This is the office of a large company.*
Das ist das Büro einer großen Firma.

---

**often** [OHF-fen] Adverb **oft**
*I often go by bus.*
Ich fahre oft mit dem Bus.

---

**oil** [EUL] Substantiv **das Öl**
*The cook adds the oil to the salad.*
Die Köchin gibt das Öl in den Salat.

---

**O.K., all right** [o-KEH, ohl-REIT] Interjektion **gut, ja, O.K.**
*Let's play outside. O.K!*
Lass uns draußen spielen. Gut!

---

**old** [OHLD] Adjektiv **alt**
*Here is an old book and there an old watch.*
Hier ist ein altes Buch und dort eine alte Uhr.

---

**on (on top of)** [AN] Präposition **auf**
*The book is on the table.*
Das Buch liegt auf dem Tisch.

---

**once** [WANZ] Ausdruck **einmal**
**once again** [WANZ ah-GEN] Ausdruck **noch einmal**
*She tells us the story once again.*
Sie erzählt uns die Geschichte noch einmal.

---

---

**one (a, an)** [WAN] Adjektiv                               **ein(e)**

**one (a person)** [WAN] Pronomen                            **man**

*One must go to school.*
Man muss in die Schule gehen.

**one (number)** [WAN] Adjektiv                              **eins**

*The child counts: one, two, three.*
Das Kind zählt: eins, zwei, drei.

---

**onion** [AN-jen] Substantiv                          **die Zwiebel**

*I am buying the onions in the supermarket.*
Ich kaufe die Zwiebeln im Supermarkt.

---

**only** [OHN-lie] Adverb                                     **nur**

*I eat only vegetables.*
Ich esse nur Gemüse.

**only** [OHN-lie] Adjektiv                           **die einzige(n)**

*This is the only coat in the closet.*
Das ist der einzige Mantel im Schrank.

---

**open** [OH-pen] Adjektiv                                   **offen**

*The door is open.*
Die Tür ist offen.

**to open** [tu OH-pen] Verb                                **öffnen**

*She is opening the letter.*
Sie öffnet den Brief.

---

**or** [OHR] Konjunktion                                     **oder**

*Do you want bread or a roll?*
Möchtest du Brot oder ein Brötchen?

---

**orange** [OHR-indg] Substantiv                       **die Orange**

*What color is the orange?*
Welche Farbe hat die Orange?

**orange** [OHR-indg] Adjektiv                              **orange**

*This pumpkin is orange.*
Dieser Kürbis ist orange.

**orange juice**                                    **der Orangensaft**
    [OHR-indg DGUS] Substantiv

---

**to order** [OHR-der] Verb                              **bestellen**

*In the restaurant we finally order dinner.*
Im Restaurant bestellen wir endlich das Essen.

**(in) order to** [in OHR-der tu] Ausdruck              **um ... zu**

*He goes to the museum in order to see artwork.*
Er geht ins Museum, um Kunstwerke zu sehen.

---

**our** [AUR] Adjektiv                                    **unser(e)**

*Our dog loves cookies, dog cookies.*
Unser Hund liebt Kekse, Hundekekse.

---

**out of** [AUT av] Präposition                              **aus**

*The princess looks out of the window.*
Die Prinzessin sieht aus dem Fenster.

---

**outside** [AUT-seid] Adverb                            **draußen**

*The animals must stay outside.*
Die Tiere müssen draußen bleiben.

---

**over there** [oh-wer THEHR] Ausdruck              **dort drüben**

*Your brother is over there.*
Dein Bruder ist dort drüben.

---

**to overturn** [oh-wer-TERN] Verb                      **umwerfen**

*The baby overturns the cup.*
Das Baby wirft die Tasse um.

---

**owl** [AUL] Substantiv                                        **die Eule**

*One hears the owl in the night.*
Man hört die Eule in der Nacht.

---

**own** [OWN] Adjektiv                                          **eigen**

*I have my own room.*
Ich habe mein eigenes Zimmer.

---

## P

**package** [PÄK-idg] Substantiv                    **das Paket**

*Great! A package for me!*
Toll! Ein Paket für mich!

---

**page** [PEHDG] Substantiv                            **die Seite**

*The map of Europe is on page twenty-one.*
Die Karte von Europa ist auf Seite einundzwanzig.

---

**pail** [PEHL] Substantiv                              **der Eimer**

*The farmer fills the pail with milk.*
Der Bauer füllt den Eimer mit Milch.

---

**to paint** [PEHNT] Verb                               **malen**

*His sister is an artist. She paints well.*
Seine Schwester ist Künstlerin. Sie malt gut.

---

**pair** [PEHR] Substantiv                              **das Paar**

*I would like to buy a pair of gloves.*
Ich möchte ein Paar Handschuhe kaufen.

**pajamas** [pa-DGAH-mas] Substantiv, pl.     **der Pyjama**

*Eric's pajamas are on the bed.*
Erichs Pyjama ist auf dem Bett.

---

**palace** [PAHL-iss] Substantiv     **das Schloss**

*This palace is large.*
Dieses Schloss ist groß.

---

**pants** [PÄNTS] Substantiv     **die Hose**

*The boy's pants are too long.*
Die Hose des Jungen ist zu lang.

---

**paper** [PEH-per] Substantiv     **das Papier**

*I still have paper in my notebook.*
Ich habe noch Papier in meinem Heft.

---

**parachute** [PAR-e-schut] Substantiv     **der Fallschirm**

*The parachute is open.*
Der Fallschirm ist offen.

---

**parade** [pe-REHD] Substantiv     **die Parade**

*We walk in the parade.*
Wir machen bei der Parade mit.

---

**parakeet** [PAR-e-kiet] Substantiv          **der Wellensittich**

*Do they have a parakeet?*
Haben sie einen Wellensittich?

---

**Pardon me!** [PAHR-den MIE] Ausdruck        **Verzeihung!**
                                            **Entschuldigung!**

*Pardon me, where is the city hall, please?*
Verzeihung, wo ist das Rathaus, bitte?

---

**parents** [PÄHR-ents] Substantiv, pl.          **die Eltern**

*My parents go to work every morning.*
Meine Eltern gehen morgens zur Arbeit.

---

**park** [PAHRK] Substantiv                  **der Park**

*There is a park nearby.*
Es gibt einen Park in der Nähe.

---

**parrot** [PÄR-et] Substantiv             **der Papagei**

*This is my parrot.*
Das ist mein Papagei.

---

**part (role)** [PART] Substantiv           **die Rolle**

*I want to play the part of the prince.*
Ich möchte die Rolle des Prinzen spielen.

---

**party** [PAHR-tie] Substantiv    **das Fest, die Party, die Fete**

*Is the party on Saturday?*
Ist das Fest am Samstag?

---

**to pass** [PÄSS] Verb                  **überholen**

*The car passes the truck on the expressway.*
Das Auto überholt den Lastwagen auf der Autobahn.

---

**to paste** [PEHST] Verb                                  **kleben**

*He is pasting the picture in his album.*
Er klebt das Bild in sein Album.

---

**path (way)** [PÄTH] Substantiv                         **der Weg**

*This path leads to the bridge.*
Dieser Weg führt zur Brücke.

---

**paw** [POH] Substantiv                                **die Pfote**

*The lion has four paws.*
Der Löwe hat vier Pfoten.

---

**to pay** [PEH] Verb                                  **bezahlen**

*Dad pays for the meat at the butcher's.*
Vati bezahlt das Fleisch beim Metzger.

---

**Pay attention!** [peh e-TEN-schen] Ausdruck          **Pass auf!**

---

**peach** [PIETSCH] Substantiv                       **der Pfirsich**

*The peach is not ripe yet.*
Der Pfirsicht ist noch nicht reif.

---

**peanut** [PIE-nut] Substantiv                         **die Erdnuss**

*The elephant likes peanuts.*
Der Elefant hat Erdnüsse gern.

---

**pear** [PEHR] Substantiv                              **die Birne**

*Mary eats a pear for dessert.*
Maria isst eine Birne zum Nachtisch.

**peas** [PIES] Substantiv, pl.         **die Erbsen**

*The children like peas.*
Die Kinder haben Erbsen gern.

**pen (ink)** [PEN] Substantiv         **der Füller**

*I'll write the letter with an ink pen.*
Ich schreibe den Brief mit einem Füller.

**ballpoint pen**       **der Kuli, der Kugelschreiber**
    [PEN] Substantiv

**pencil** [PEN-zil] Substantiv         **der Bleistift**

*We write the assignment with a pencil.*
Wir schreiben die Aufgabe mit einem Bleistift.

**people** [PIE-pel] Substantiv, pl.         **die Leute**

*Many people are in the store.*
Viele Leute sind im Geschäft.

**perhaps (maybe)** [per-HÄPS] Adverb         **vielleicht**

*Are we going to the movies tonight? Maybe.*
Gehen wir heute Abend ins Kino? Vielleicht.

**permission** [per-MISCH-en] Substantiv       **die Erlaubnis**

*We have permission to park in the garage.*
Wir haben Erlaubnis in der Garage zu parken.

**pet** [PET] Substantiv         **das Haustier**

*Our pet, a guinea pig, is very loud.*
Unser Haustier, ein Meerschweinchen, ist sehr laut.

**pharmacy** [FAHR-me-sie] Substantiv       **die Apotheke**

*The pharmacy is near the park.*
Die Apotheke ist beim Park.

**phonograph** [FOH-ne-graf] Substantiv    **die Stereoanlage, der Plattenspieler**

see **stereo system**

---

**photo(graph)** [FOH-te-graf] Substantiv    **das Foto**

*This is a photo of you. Do you like it?*
Das ist ein Foto von dir. Hast du es gern?

---

**piano** [pie-AH-oh] Substantiv    **das Klavier**

*You have a piano? Who plays?*
Ihr habt ein Klavier? Wer spielt denn?

---

**to pick (harvest)** [PIK] Verb    **pflücken**

*They are picking cherries today.*
Sie pflücken Kirschen heute.

**to pick (choose)** [PIK] Verb    **wählen**

*We choose chocolate or vanilla.*
Wir wählen Schokolade oder Vanille.

---

**picnic** [PIK-nik] Substantiv    **das Picknick**

*We'll have a picnic in the country.*
Wir haben ein Picknick auf dem Land.

---

**picture** [PIK-tscher] Substantiv    **das Bild**

*First graders often color pictures.*
Erstklässler malen oft Bilder.

---

**pie** [PEI] Substantiv    **die Pastete**

*In America they make apple pies.*
In Amerika macht man Apfelpasteten.

---

**piece** [PIES] Substantiv    **das Stück**

*I would like a piece of cake, please.*
Ich möchte ein Stück Kuchen, bitte.

**piece of paper**                                          **das Stück Papier**
   [PIEC af PEHP-er]  Ausdruck

---

**pig** [PIG] Substantiv                                          **das Schwein**

*The farmer has three pigs.*
Der Bauer hat drei Schweine.

---

**piggy bank**                                                  **die Sparbüchse,**
   [PIG-ie-bänk] Substantiv            **das Sparschweinchen**

*Peter has a piggy bank.*
Peter hat ein Sparschweinchen.

---

**pillow** [PIL-ow] Substantiv                                   **das Kissen**

*The pillow is soft.*
Das Kissen ist weich.

---

**pin (brooch)** [PIN] Substantiv                           **die Brosche**

*Helene's brooch is from her grandmother.*
Helenes Broche ist von ihrer Großmutter.

---

**pilot** [PEI-let] Substantiv                        **der Pilot, die Pilotin**

*The pilot flies the airplane.*
Der Pilot fliegt das Flugzeug.

---

**pineapple** [PEIN-ap-el] Substantiv                        **die Ananas**

*The pineapple is ripe.*
Die Ananas ist reif.

---

**pink** [PINK] Substantiv                                    **das rosa**

*Anne and Arthur like the color pink.*
Anna und Arthur haben die Farbe Rosa gern.

---

**place (setting at table)** [PLÄS] Substantiv    **das Gedeck**

*I put a napkin at each place.*
Ich lege eine Serviette bei jedem Gedeck hin.

---

**planet** [PLÄN-it] Substantiv                              **der Planet**

*There are many planets.*
Es gibt viele Planeten.

---

**plant** [PLÄNT] Substantiv                                  **die Pflanze**

*There are plants in our classroom.*
Es gibt Pflanzen in unserem Klassenzimmer.

---

**plate** [PLEHT] Substantiv                                  **der Teller**

*The plate is on the table.*
Der Teller ist auf dem Tisch.

---

**to play** [PLEH] Verb                                       **spielen**

*Let's play basketball!*
Lass uns Basketball spielen!

**to play hide and seek**                        **Verstecken spielen**
    [PLEH heid änd SIEK] Ausdruck

*We'll play hide and seek later.*
Wir spielen Verstecken später.

---

**playground** [PLEH-graund] Substantiv          **der Spielplatz**

*The slide is in the playground.*
Die Rutschbahn ist auf dem Spielplatz.

**playing cards**                                           **die Spielkarten**
  [PLEH-ing KAHRDS]  Substantiv

*We want to play cards. Where are the cards?*
Wir wollen Karten spielen. Wo sind die Spielkarten?

---

**pleasant** [PLES-ent]  Adjektiv                              **angenehm**

*Spring is a pleasant season.*
Der Frühling ist eine angenehme Jahreszeit.

---

**please** [PLIES]  Ausdruck                            **bitte, bitte schön**

*Please give me a pencil, Mr. Braun.*
Bitte geben Sie mir einen Bleistift, Herr Braun.

---

**pleasure** [PLESCH-er]  Substantiv                       **das Vergnügen**

*Are you going with us? With pleasure!*
Kommst du mit uns? Mit Vergnügen!

---

**pocket** [PAK-it]  Substantiv                               **die Tasche**

*I have nothing in my coat pocket.*
Ich habe nichts in meiner Manteltasche.

---

**pocketbook (purse)**              **die Handtasche, die Tasche**
  [PAK-it buk]  Substantiv

*The pocketbook is on the armchair.*
Die Handtasche liegt auf dem Sessel.

---

**policeman** [pe-LIESS-män]  Substantiv                      **der Polizist**
                                                             **die Polizistin**

*The policeman helps people.*
Der Polizist hilft den Leuten.

---

**polite** [pe-LEIT]  Adjektiv                                  **höflich**

*My brother is always polite.*
Mein Bruder ist immer höflich.

---

**poor** [PUHR] Adjektiv                                           **arm**

*Poor children have few toys.*
Arme Kinder haben wenig Spielzeug.

---

**post office** [POHST OH-fiss] Substantiv                    **die Post**

*Where is the post office?*
Wo ist die Post?

---

**postal carrier**                                           **der Briefträger**
      [POHST-el KÄR-ie-er] Substantiv                         **die Briefträgerin**

---

**postcard** [POHST-kahrd] Substantiv                         **die Postkarte,
                                                               die Ansichtskarte**

*These are pretty postcards.*
Das sind aber schöne Postkarten.

---

**potato** [po-TÄ-toh] Substantiv     **die Kartoffel, der Erdapfel**

*Peter is cooking potatoes.*
Peter kocht Kartoffeln.

---

**to pour (a drink)** [POHR] Verb                            **einschenken**

*Daddy pours the children milk.*
Papa schenkt den Kindern Milch ein.

---

**to prefer** [pre-FÜR] Ausdruck                             **lieber haben**

*Do you prefer fall or winter?*
Hast du den Herbst oder den Winter lieber?

---

**present** [PRES-ent] Substantiv                            **das Geschenk**

*Here is my birthday present.*
Hier ist ja mein Geburtstagsgeschenk.

---

311

**present** [PRES-ent] Adjektiv                          **anwesend**

*Erica is not present.*
Erika ist nicht anwesend.

---

**president** [PRES-e-dent] Substantiv          **der Präsident**
                                                **die Präsidentin**

*Who is the president of the United States?*
Wer ist der Präsident der Vereinigten Staaten?

---

**pretty** [PRIT-ie] Adjektiv                              **schön**

*That is a pretty doll.*
Das ist eine schöne Puppe.

---

**prince** [PRINZ] Substantiv                          **der Prinz**

**princess** [PRIN-zess] Substantiv          **die Prinzessin**

*The princess lives in the palace.*
Die Prinzessin wohnt im Schloss.

---

**to promise** [PRAM-iss] Verb                    **versprechen**

*He promises to do his homework.*
Er verspricht, seine Hausaufgaben zu machen.

---

**to pull** [PUL] Verb                                        **ziehen**

*Bert is pulling the donkey.*
Bert zieht den Esel.

---

**pumpkin** [PAMP-kin] Substantiv              **der Kürbis**

*Where is the large pumpkin?*
Wo ist der große Kürbis?

---

**to punish** [PAN-isch] Verb                        **bestrafen**

*When I am very naughty my parents punish me.*
Wenn ich sehr schlimm bin, bestrafen mich die Eltern.

---

**pupil** [PJU-pil] Substantiv                **der Schüler**
                                              **die Schülerin**

*The pupil answers correctly.*
Der Schüler antwortet richtig.

---

**puppy** [PAP-ie] Substantiv                **das Hündchen**
*The puppy looks for its mother.*
Das Hündchen sucht seine Mutter.

---

**purple** [PÜR-pl] Substantiv                **purpur**
*Blue and red make purple.*
Blau und Rot macht Lila.

---

**on purpose** [an PÜR-pes] Adverb           **absichtlich**
*She breaks the piggy bank on purpose.*
Sie zerbricht das Sparschweinchen absichtlich.

---

**purse**                                    **die Handtasche**
        see **handbag**

---

**to push** [PUSCH] Verb                     **schieben**
*The children constantly push each other.*
Die Kinder schieben einander ständig.

---

**to put** [PUT] Verb                        **legen**
*Please put the silverware on the table.*
Legt bitte das Besteck auf den Tisch.

---

**to put on** [put AHN] Ausdruck             **anziehen**
*It is cold. I am putting on a warm coat.*
Es ist kalt. Ich ziehe einen warmen Mantel an.

## Q

**to quarrel** [KWAH-rl] Verb                          **streiten**

*My parents sometimes quarrel.*
Meine Eltern streiten manchmal.

---

**quarter** [KWOH-ter] Substantiv                    **das Viertel**
**a quarter of an hour** Substantiv              **die Viertelstunde**

*It is a quarter after six.*
Es ist (ein) Viertel nach sechs.

---

**queen** [KWIEN] Substantiv                        **die Königin**

*The queen is a good person.*
Die Königin ist ein guter Mensch.

---

**question** [KWESS-tschen] Substantiv               **die Frage**

*The pupils have many questions.*
Die Schüler haben viele Fragen.

---

**quickly** [KWIK-lie] Adverb                          **schnell**

*You eat too quickly.*
Du isst zu schnell.

---

**quiet (calm)** [KWEI-et] Adjektiv                     **ruhig**

*In the night all is quiet.*
In der Nacht ist alles ruhig.

**Be quiet!** [bie KWEI-et] Ausdruck                 **Sei ruhig!**

*Please be quiet, children!*
Seid bitte ruhig, Kinder!

---

## R

**rabbit** [RÄB-ịt] Substantiv      **das Kaninchen, der Hase**

*The little rabbit runs and hops.*
Das kleine Kaninchen rennt und hüpft.

---

**radio** [REH-die-oh] Substantiv      **das Radio**

*The radio is broken.*
Das Radio ist kaputt.

---

**It is raining.** [REH-ning] Ausdruck      **Es regnet.**

*It is raining today.*
Es regnet heute.

---

**rainbow** [REHN-bow] Substantiv      **der Regenbogen**

*I like the colors of the rainbow.*
Ich habe die Farben des Regenbogens gern.

---

**raincoat** [REHN-kowt] Substantiv      **der Regenmantel**

*I'll wear my raincoat because it is raining.*
Ich trage meinen Regenmantel, denn es regnet.

---

**to raise** [REHS] Verb      **heben**

*He raises his hand and answers the question.*
Er hebt seine Hand und beantwortet die Frage.

---

**rapid (fast)** [RÄP-id] Adjektiv      **schnell**

*My mother walks too fast.*
Meine Mutter geht zu schnell

---

**rat** [RÄT] Substantiv      **die Ratte**

*I am afraid of rats.*
Ich habe Angst vor Ratten.

---

**to read** [RIED] Verb      **lesen**

*We read in the library.*
Wir lesen in der Bibliothek.

---

**read aloud** [RIED a-LAUD] Ausdruck      **vorlesen**

*He reads the story aloud.*
Er liest die Geschichte vor.

---

**ready** [RED-ie] Adjektiv      **bereit, fertig**

*Are you ready? We are late.*
Bist du bereit? Wir sind spät dran.

---

**to receive** [rie-SIEW]      **bekommen**

*I receive a letter from my grandparents.*
Ich bekomme einen Brief von meinen Großeltern.

---

**red** [RED] Adjektiv      **rot**

*Cars must stop when the light is red.*
Autos müssen halten, wenn die Ampel rot ist.

---

**refrigerator**      **der Kühlschrank**
     [re-FRIDG-e-reh-ter] Substantiv

*The refrigerator is in the kitchen.*
Der Kühlschrank ist in der Küche.

---

**to remain, to stay** [rie-MEHN] Verb          **bleiben**

*We are staying ten days at Grandmother's house.*
Wir bleiben zehn Tage bei der Großmutter.

---

**to remember** [re-MEM-ber] Verb          **sich erinnern an**

*I don't remember his name.*
Ich erinnere mich nicht an seinen Namen.

---

**to remove** [re-MUHV] Verb          **abnehmen**

*Please remove your hat in the house, Simon.*
Bitte nimm deinen Hut im Haus ab, Simon.

---

**to repair** [re-PEHR] Verb          **reparieren**

*My sister is fixing my computer for me.*
Meine Schwester repariert meinen Computer für mich.

---

**to repeat** [re-PIET] Verb          **wiederholen**

*The teacher says, "Repeat your question, George."*
Die Lehrerin sagt, "Wiederhole deine Frage, Georg."

---

**to reply to (answer a question)**          **antworten**
   [re-PLEI] Verb

*The little girl answers the question.*
Das kleine Mädchen beantwortet die Frage.

---

**to rescue** [RES-kju] Verb          **retten**

*My aunt rescues the cat from the tree.*
Meine Tante rettet die Katze aus dem Baum.

---

**to rest** [REST] Verb          **sich ausruhen**

*Fred is tired. He is resting now.*
Fritz ist müde. Er ruht sich jetzt aus.

---

**restaurant** [RES-ter-ant] Substantiv  **das Restaurant**

*My uncle works in a restaurant.*
Mein Onkel arbeitet in einem Restaurant.

**to return (to come back)** [rie-TÜRN] Verb **zurückkommen**

*After school he returns home.*
Nach der Schule kommt er zurück nach Hause.

**to return (to bring back)** [rie-TÜRN] Verb **zurückbringen**

*She returns the book to the library.*
Sie bringt das Buch in die Bibliothek zurück.

**ribbon** [RIB-en] Substantiv **das Band**

*She is wearing a pretty ribbon in her hair.*
Sie trägt ein schönes Band im Haar.

**rice** [REIS] Substantiv **der Reis**

*The rice is already on the table.*
Der Reis ist schon auf dem Tisch.

**rich** [RITSCH] Adjektiv **reich**

*The actor is rich.*
Der Schauspieler ist reich.

**to ride** [REID] Verb **fahren**
**ride in a train** Ausdruck **im Zug fahren**
**ride on a bike** Ausdruck **Rad fahren**
**ride in a car** Ausdruck **im Auto fahren**
**to ride a horse** Ausdruck **reiten**

*She likes to ride a horse.*
Sie reitet gern.

**right** [REIT] Adjektiv               **recht**

*I show my right hand.*
Ich zeige meine rechte Hand.

**on/at the right** Ausdruck     **rechts, auf der rechten Seite**

**right away** Ausdruck            **sofort**
       see **immediately**

**You are right.** Ausdruck       **Du hast Recht.**

**ring** [RING] Substantiv         **der Ring**

*This ring is pretty!*
Dieser Ring ist schön!

**to ring** [RING] Verb            **läuten**

*The telephone rings often.*
Das Telefon läutet oft.

**ripe** [REIP] Adjektiv              **reif**

*When the strawberry is red, it is ripe.*
Wenn die Erdbeere rot ist, ist sie reif.

**river** [RIW-er] Substantiv       **der Fluss**

*Many bridges cross this river.*
Viele Brücken überqueren diesen Fluss.

**road** [ROHD]                 **die Straße**

*What is the name of this road?*
Wie heißt diese Straße?

**roast beef** [ROHST bief] Substantiv          **der Rinderbraten, das Roastbeef**

*She is eating roast beef in the restaurant.*
Sie isst Rindsbraten im Restaurant.

**to rob** [RAB] Verb                                                        **stehlen**

*Look, he is stealing my spoon!*
Sieh mal, er stiehlt meinen Löffel!

**robber** [RAB-er] Substantiv                                           **der Dieb**

*They are looking for the robber all over.*
Man sucht den Dieb überall.

**rock** [RAK] Substantiv                                                 **der Stein**

*That is a large rock over there.*
Das ist ein großer Stein dort drüben.

**rocket ship (spaceship)**                              **das Raumschiff**
      [RAK-it ship] Substantiv

*Three astronauts are in the rocket ship.*
Drei Astronauten sind im Raumschiff.

**role** [ROHL] Substantiv                                                **die Rolle**

*I want to play the role of the prince.*
Ich möchte die Rolle des Prinzen spielen.

**roll** [ROHL] Substantiv            **das Brötchen, die Semmel**

*Susan eats fresh rolls for breakfast.*
Susanne isst frische Brötchen zum Frühstück.

**to roll** [ROHL] Verb                                                       **rollen**

*I roll the bicycle across the street.*
Ich rolle das Rad über die Straße.

**to roller skate** [ROHL-er SKEHT] Ausdruck     **Rollschuh laufen**

**roof** [RUF] Substantiv     **das Dach**

*I see the city from the roof of our house.*
Ich sehe die Stadt vom Dach unseres Hauses.

**room** [RUM] Substantiv     **das Zimmer**

*Our apartment has three rooms.*
Unsere Wohnung hat drei Zimmer.

**bathroom**     **das Badezimmer,**
    [BÄTH-rum] Substantiv     **das Bad**

*The bathroom is modern.*
Das Badezimmer ist modern.

**classroom** [KLÄS rum] Substantiv     **das Klassenzimmer**

*The classroom is empty.*
Das Klassenzimmer ist leer.

**dining room** [DEI-ning rum] Substantiv     **das Esszimmer**

*The guests are in the dining room.*
Die Gäste sind im Esszimmer.

**living room** [LIV-ing rum] Substantiv     **das Wohnzimmer**

*Our living room is comfortable.*
Unser Wohnzimmer ist bequem.

**rooster** [RUHS-ter] Substantiv     **der Hahn**

*The rooster crows early.*
Der Hahn kräht früh.

**rope** [ROWP] Substantiv     **das Seil**

*This rope is thick.*
Dieses Seil ist dick.

**to jump rope** Ausdruck     **Seil springen**

**round** [RAUND] Adjektiv                       **rund**

*Our world is round.*
Unsere Welt ist rund.

---

**row** [ROW] Substantiv                     **die Reihe**

*There are many rows in the classroom.*
Es gibt viele Reihen im Klassenzimmer.

---

**rubber** [RAB-er] Substantiv                 **das Gummi**

*The boots are made of rubber, not of leather.*
Die Stiefel sind aus Gummi, nicht aus Leder.

---

**rug** [RAG] Substantiv                       **der Teppich**

*The rug is on the floor.*
Der Teppich ist auf dem Fußboden.

---

**rule** [RUHL] Substantiv                     **die Regel**

*Why are there so many rules?*
Warum gibt es so viele Regeln?

---

**ruler** [RUHL-er] Substantiv                 **das Lineal**

*My ruler is broken.*
Mein Lineal ist kaputt.

---

**to run** [RAN] Verb                         **laufen**

*Is she running on the playground?*
Läuft sie auf dem Schulhof?

---

## S

**sack, bag** [SAK] Substantiv                 **der Sack, die Tüte**

*The potatoes are in the sack.*
Die Kartoffeln sind im Sack.

---

**sad** [SAD] Adjektiv                                      **traurig**

*I cannot go with you. I am sad.*
Ich kann nicht mit dir gehen. Ich bin traurig.

---

**safe and sound**                          **gesund und munter**
    [SÄF-n-SAUND] Ausdruck

*The child comes home safe and sound.*
Das Kind kommt gesund und munter nach Hause.

---

**salad** [SAL-ed] Substantiv                        **der Salat**

*The potato salad tastes good.*
Der Kartoffelsalat schmeckt gut.

---

**saleswoman** [SEHLS-WU-man] Substantiv    **die Verkäuferin**

**salesman** [SEHLS-män] Substantiv          **der Verkäufer**

*The salesman is showing him a sweater.*
Der Verkäufer zeigt ihm einen Pullover.

---

**salt** [SOHLT] Substantiv                              **das Salz**

*Please pass the salt.*
Das Salz bitte!

---

**same** [SEHM] Adjektiv                              **gleich(e)**

*My girlfriend and I are wearing the same dress.*
Meine Freundin und ich tragen das gleiche Kleid.

**It's all the same to me.**                         **Es ist mir egal.**
  [its OHL tha SEHM tu mie] Ausdruck

---

**sand** [SÄND] Substantiv                              **der Sand**

*The children are playing in the sand.*
Die Kinder spielen im Sand.

---

**sandwich** [SÄND-<u>w</u>itsch] Substantiv        **belegtes Brot,
das Sandwich**

*The sandwich has two pieces of bread.*
Das Sandwich hat zwei Stück Brot.

---

**Saturday** [SAT-er-deh] Substantiv                **der Samstag,
der Sonnabend**

*Let's have a picnic on Saturday.*
Machen wir doch ein Picknick am Samstag.

---

**sausage** [soh-SIDG] Substantiv                    **die Wurst**

*Who will cook the sausage?*
Wer kocht die Wurst?

---

**saucer** [SOH-ser] Substantiv                    **die Untertasse**

*The woman puts the cup on the saucer.*
Die Frau stellt die Tasse auf die Untertasse.

---

**to save, rescue** [SEHW] Verb                       **retten**

*My aunt rescues the cat from the tree.*
Meine Tante rettet die Katze aus dem Baum.

**to save (money)** [SEHW] Verb                       **sparen**

*The boy saves money in the piggy bank.*
Der Junge spart Geld im Sparschweinchen.

---

**to say** [SEH] Verb                      **sagen**

*The neighbor always says, "Good morning."*
Der Nachbar sagt immer "Guten Morgen."

**school** [SKUHL] Substantiv       **die Schule**

*We don't have school on Saturdays.*
Wir haben samstags keine Schule.

**science (natural)**       **die Naturwissenschaft**
    [SEI-enz] Substantiv

**scientist**           **der Naturwissenschaftler,**
    [SEI-en-tist] Substantiv   **die Naturwissenschaftlerin**

*Gregor Mendel was a famous scientist.*
Gregor Mendel war ein berühmter
Naturwissenschaftler.

**scissors** [SIS-ers] Substantiv, pl.     **die Schere**

*I cut the paper with scissors.*
Ich schneide das Papier mit der Schere.

**to scold** [SKOHLD] Verb         **schimpfen**

*My mother scolds me when I am late.*
Meine Mutter schimpft, wenn ich
verspätet bin.

**scream, shout** [SKRIEM] Verb      **schreien**

*Mom shouts, "Come quickly!"*
Mutti schreit, "Komm doch schnell!"

**sea** [SIE] Substantiv           **das Meer**

*I like looking at the sea.*
Ich sehe das Meer gern.

**seamstress** [SIEM-stress] Substantiv      **die Schneiderin**

*The seamstress owns the shop.*
Die Schneiderin besitzt den Laden.

---

**season** [SIE-sen] Substantiv      **die Jahreszeit**

*Which season do you like best?*
Welche Jahreszeit hast du am liebsten?

---

**seat, place** [SIET] Substantiv      **der Platz**

*Is this seat free?*
Ist dieser Platz frei?

---

**second** [SEK-end] Adjektiv      **zweite**

*What is the second day of the week?*
Wie heißt der zweite Tag der Woche?

---

**secret** [SIE-kret] Substantiv      **das Geheimnis**

*Tell me the secret.*
Sag mir doch das Geheimnis!

---

**secretary** [SEK-re-ter-ie] Substantiv      **die Sekretärin**
                                   **der Sekretär**

*The secretary distributes the mail.*
Der Sekretär verteilt die Post.

---

**to see** [SIE] Verb      **sehen**

*I see the helicopter in the sky.*
Ich sehe den Hubschrauber im Himmel.

**to see again** [SIE a-GEN] Ausdruck      **wiedersehen**

*I am going to see the film again next week.*
Ich sehe den Film nächste Woche wieder.

**See you soon!** [SIE ju soon] Ausdruck      **Bis bald!**

---

**seesaw** [SIE-soh] Substantiv                    **die Wippe**

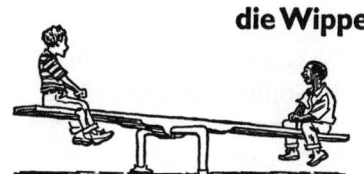

*The boys are on the seesaw.*
Die Jungen sind auf der Wippe.

---

**to sell** [SEL] Verb                                   **verkaufen**

*She sells toys in this store.*
Sie verkauft Spielzeug in diesem Geschäft.

---

**to send** [SEND] Verb                                  **schicken**

*I am sending my parents a letter.*
Ich schicke meinen Eltern einen Brief.

---

**sentence** [SEN-tenz] Substantiv                       **der Satz**

*I am writing a sentence in my notebook.*
Ich schreibe einen Satz in mein Heft.

---

**September** [sep-TEM-ber] Substantiv          **der September**

*September has thirty days.*
Der September hat dreißig Tage.

---

**serious** [SIER-ie-es] Adjektiv                          **ernst**

*There is a serious film at the movies.*
Es gibt einen ernsten Film im Kino.

---

**to serve** [SURW] Verb                                **servieren**

*They are serving the cake to the children first.*
Sie servieren den Kindern den Kuchen zuerst.

---

**to set** [SET] Verb                                          **untergehen**

*The sun sets in the late afternoon.*
Die Sonne geht am späten Nachmittag unter.

**to set the table**                                   **den Tisch decken**
    [SET tha TEH-bl] Ausdruck

*The children are setting the table.*
Die Kinder decken den Tisch.

**setting, a place setting at the table**                    **der Platz**
    [SET-ting] Substantiv

*There are eight settings at the table.*
Da sind acht Plätze am Tisch.

**seven** [SEW-en] Adjektiv                                      **sieben**

*It is already seven thirty in the evening.*
Es ist schon sieben Uhr dreißig abends.

**seventeen** [sev-en-TIEN] Adjektiv                            **siebzehn**

*Nine plus eight is seventeen.*
Neun und acht macht siebzehn.

**seventy** [SEW-en-tie] Adjektiv                               **siebzig**

*Leo's grandfather is seventy years old.*
Leos Großvater ist siebzig Jahre alt.

**several** [SEW-rel] Adjektiv                                  **mehrere**

*There are several cars on the road.*
Es gibt mehrere Autos auf der Straße.

**to sew** [SOW] Verb                                            **nähen**
**sewing needle** [SOW-ing nie-dl] Substantiv         **die Nähnadel**

*The pupils are learning to sew with a sewing needle.*
Die Schüler lernen mit einer Nähnadel zu nähen.

**shadow** [SCHÄD-ow] Substantiv                     **der Schatten**

*My shadow dances with me.*
Mein Schatten tanzt mit mir.

---

**to shake** [SCHEHK] Verb                           **schütteln**

*Mary shakes her head, "No!"*
Maria schüttelt den Kopf, "Nein!"

---

**to shake hands**                                   **Hände schütteln**
    [tu SCHEHK händs] Ausdruck

*The guests shake hands before going home.*
Die Gäste schütteln die Hände zum Abschied.

---

**to share** [SCHEHR] Verb                           **teilen**

*Let us share the dessert.*
Lass uns doch den Nachtisch teilen!

---

**she** [SCHIE] Pronomen                              **sie**

*She is my cousin.*
Sie ist meine Kusine.

---

**sheep, lamb** [SCHIEP] Substantiv        **das Schaf, das Lamm**

*The sheep is in the field.*
Das Schaf ist auf dem Feld.

---

**sheet of paper**                           **das Stück Papier**
    [SCHIET af PEH-per] Ausdruck

*He is giving each one a sheet of paper.*
Er gibt jedem ein Stück Papier.

---

**shell** [SCHEL] Substantiv      **die Muschel**

*I am looking for shells on the shore.*
Ich suche Muscheln am Strand.

**ship** [SCHIP] Substantiv      **das Schiff**

*The family travels by ship.*
Die Familie reist auf dem Schiff.

**shirt** [SCHÜRT] Substantiv      **das Hemd**

*He needs a clean shirt.*
Er braucht ein sauberes Hemd.

**shoe** [SCHUH] Substantiv      **der Schuh**

*I don't like these shoes.*
Ich habe diese Schuhe gar nicht gern.

**shop** [SHOP] Substantiv      **das Geschäft**

*Do all the shops close at six in the evening?*
Schließen alle Geschäfte um sechs Uhr abends?

**to shop** [SHOP] Verb      **einkaufen**

*My parents shop Wednesdays.*
Meine Eltern kaufen mittwochs ein.

**shore** [SHOHR] Substantiv      **der Strand**

*We like to walk on the shore.*
Wir spazieren gern am Strand.

**short** [SHOHRT] Adjektiv                                   **kurz**

*One ruler is short, the other is long.*
Ein Lineal ist kurz, das andere ist lang.

**short (height)** [SHOHRT] Adjektiv                          **klein**

*The tree on the left is short; the tree on the right is tall.*
Der Baum links ist klein; der Baum rechts ist groß.

---

**shoulder** [SHOHL-der] Substantiv                          **die Schulter**

*The ball hits Claudia's shoulder.*
Der Ball trifft Claudias Schulter.

---

**to shout** [SCHAUT] Verb                                   **schreien**

*Mom schouts, "Come quickly!"*
Mutti schreit, "Komm schnell!"

---

**shovel** [SCHOW-el] Substantiv                             **die Schaufel**

*The shovel is in the pail.*
Die Schaufel ist im Eimer.

---

**to show** [SCHOW] Verb                                      **zeigen**

*Anna is showing me her computer.*
Anna zeigt mir ihren Computer.

---

**to shower** [SCHAU-er] Verb                                **duschen**

*The child is showering now.*
Das Kind duscht jetzt.

---

**sick** [SIK] Adjektiv                                       **krank**

*The boy is sick.*
Der Junge ist krank.

---

**sidewalk** [SEID-wohk] Substantiv                          **der Bürgersteig**

*The children are playing on the sidewalk.*
Die Kinder spielen auf dem Bürgersteig.

---

**silent (quiet)** [SEIL-ent] Adjektiv                              **ruhig**

*The class is silent at the beginning and loud at
the end.*
Die Klasse ist ruhig am Anfang und laut am Ende.

---

**silly** [SIL-ie] Adjektiv                                        **albern**

*This puppy is silly.*
Dieses Hündchen ist albern.

---

**silver** [SIL-wer] Substantiv                                **das Silber**

*The ring is made of silver.*
Der Ring ist aus Silber.

---

**similar (alike)** [SIM-il-er] Adjektiv                          **ähnlich**

*The dogs look alike.*
Die Hunde sehen ähnlich aus.

---

**to sing** [SING] Verb                                           **singen**

*Which song would you rather sing?*
Welches Lied singst du lieber?

---

**sink** [SINK] Substantiv                              **das Waschbecken**

*The sink in the bathroom is large.*
Das Waschbecken im Bad ist groß.

---

**sister** [SIS-ter] Substantiv                           **die Schwester**

*My aunt is my mother's sister.*
Meine Tante ist die Schwester meiner Mutter.

**to sit** [SIT] Verb **sitzen**

*We are sitting around the table.*
Wir sitzen um den Tisch.

**to sit down** [SIT DAUN] Ausdruck **sich setzen**

*My grandmother sits down on the sofa.*
Meine Großmutter setzt sich auf das Sofa.

**Please be seated!** **Bitte nehmen Sie Platz!**
[plees bie SIET-ed] Ausdruck

---

**six** [SIKS] Adjektiv **sechs**

*There are six eggs in the refrigerator.*
Es gibt sechs Eier im Kühlschrank.

---

**sixteen** [SIKS-tien] Adjektiv **sechzehn**

*She is sixteen years old.*
Sie ist sechzehn Jahre alt.

---

**sixty** [SIKS-tie] Adjektiv **sechzig**

*An hour has sixty minutes.*
Eine Stunde hat sechzig Minuten.

---

**size** [SEIS] Substantiv **die Größe**

*In the store they ask, "What is your size?"*
Im Geschäft fragt man, "Welche Größe haben Sie?"

---

**skates (ice)** [SKEHTS] Substantiv **die Schlittschuhe**

**skates (roller)** **die Rollschuhe**
[SKEHTS] Substantiv

**to ice skate** [EIS skeht] Ausdruck **Schlittschuh laufen**

**to roller skate** [ROL-er skeht] Ausdruck **Rollschuh laufen**

*Let's go roller skating!*
Gehen wir doch Rollschuh laufen!

---

**skin** [SKIN] Substantiv         **die Haut**

*Too much sun burns your skin.*
Zu viel Sonne verbrennt die Haut.

---

**skirt** [SKÜRT] Substantiv         **der Rock**

*Elfrieda's skirt is new.*
Elfriedas Rock ist neu.

---

**sky** [SKEI]         **der Himmel**

*The sky is blue today.*
Der Himmel ist blau heute.

---

**skyscraper**         **der Wolkenkratzer**
    [SKEI-skreh-per] Substantiv

*New York City has many skyscrapers.*
Die Stadt New York hat viele Wolkenkratzer.

---

**sled** [SLED]         **der Schlitten**

*The sled is fun.*
Der Schlitten macht Spaß.

---

**to sleep** [SLIEP] Verb         **schlafen**

*Are you sleeping? I would like to talk to you.*
Schläfst du? I möchte mit dir sprechen.

**to be sleepy** [SLIEP-ie] Ausdruck         **schläfrig sein**

*Cats are always sleepy.*
Katzen sind immer schläfrig.

---

**to slip** [SLIP] Verb         **rutschen**

*The child slips on the rug.*
Das Kind rutscht auf dem Teppich

**slowly** [SLOW-lie] Adverb        **langsam**

*The turtle walks slowly.*
Die Schildkröte geht langsam.

**small** [SMAUL] Adjektiv        **klein**

*Our house is small.*
Unser Haus ist klein.

**to smell** [SMEL] Verb        **riechen**

*Beate smells the flowers.*
Beate riecht die Blumen.

**to smile** [SMEIL] Verb        **lächeln**

*The baby smiles when it sees a dog.*
Das Baby lächelt, wenn es einen Hund sieht.

**to smoke** [SMOWK] Verb        **rauchen**

*Our family does not smoke.*
Unsere Familie raucht nicht.

**No smoking!** [NOW SMOWK-ing]        **Rauchen verboten!**

**snack** [SNÄK] Substantiv        **etwas zum Naschen**

*Is there a snack for us?*
Gibt es etwas zum Naschen für uns?

**snake** [SNEHK] Substantiv        **die Schlange**

*I am afraid of snakes.*
Ich habe Angst vor Schlangen.

**to sneeze** [SNIES] Verb **niesen**

*I'm sneezing because it is cold.*
Ich niese, denn es ist kalt.

---

**snow** [SNOW] Substantiv **der Schnee**

*I like to play in the snow.*
Ich spiele gern im Schnee.

**It is snowing.** [it is SNOW-ing] Ausdruck **Es schneit.**

*A storm is coming. It is snowing already.*
Ein Sturm kommt. Es schneit schon.

---

**snowman** [SNOW-män] Substantiv **der Schneemann**

*The snowman is wearing a hat.*
Der Schneemann trägt einen Hut.

---

**so** [SO] Adverb **so**

*The baby is eating so slowly.*
Das Baby isst so langsam.

**Isn't that so?** [IS-nt that so] Ausdruck **Nicht wahr?**
**Isn't that true?**

**so much** [SO MATSCH] Ausdruck **so viel**

**so many** [SO MEN-ie] Ausdruck **so viele**

---

**soap** [SOWP] Substantiv **die Seife**

*I wash my hands with soap.*
Ich wasche mir die Hände mit Seife.

---

**soccer** [sok-er] Substantiv     **das Fußballspiel**

*I like soccer.*
Ich liebe das Fußballspiel.

---

**sock** [sok] Substantiv     **die Socke**

*I would like to buy a pair of socks.*
Ich möchte ein Paar Socken kaufen.

---

**soda** [soh-da] Substantiv     **der Softdrink**

*I'll have a soda, please.*
Ich nehme einen Softdrink, bitte.

---

**sofa** [soh-fah] Substantiv     **das Sofa**

*The sofa is comfortable.*
Das Sofa ist bequem.

---

**soft** [soft] Adjektiv     **weich**

*The armchair is soft.*
Der Sessel ist weich.

**softly, quietly** [soft-lie] Adverb     **leise**

*The radio is playing softly.*
Das Radio spielt leise.

---

**soldier** [sohl-dger] Substantiv     **der Soldat**

*The soldier walks to the train.*
Der Soldat geht zum Zug.

---

**somebody, someone**     **jemand**
      [sam-bad-ie, sam-wan] Pronomen

*Somebody is in the restaurant.*
Jemand ist im Restaurant.

---

**something** [SAM-thing] Pronomen　　　　**etwas**

*Is there something to eat?*
Gibt es etwas zu essen?

---

**sometimes** [SAM-teims] Adverb　　　　**manchmal**

*Sometimes I sing in the kitchen.*
Manchmal singe ich in der Küche.

---

**son** [SAN] Substantiv　　　　　　　**der Sohn**

*I know his son.*
Ich kenne seinen Sohn.

---

**song** [SONG] Substantiv　　　　　　**das Lied**

*Which song do you like best?*
Welches Lied hast du am liebsten?

---

**soon** [SUHN] Adverb　　　　　　　　**bald**

*The mail will come soon.*
Die Post kommt bald.

**See you soon!** [sie ju SUHN] Ausdruck　　**Bis bald!**

---

**what sort of** [WAHT sort af] Ausdruck　**was für eine(e)**

*What sort of apple is that?*
Was für ein Apfel ist denn das?

---

**soup** [SUP] Substantiv　　　　　　**die Suppe**

*My sister serves soup to my brother.*
Meine Schwester serviert meinem Bruder die Suppe.

---

**south** [SAUTH] Substantiv　　　　**der Süden**

*Munich is in the south of Germany.*
München ist im Süden Deutschlands.

**space** [SPEHS] Substantiv            **der Weltraum**

**spaceship** [SPEHS-schip] Substantiv     **das Raumschiff**

**space station** [SPEHS steh-schn]     **die Raumstation**

*Astronauts work in space in a spacestation.*
Astronauten arbeiten im Weltraum in einer Raumstation.

---

**Spanish** [SPÄN-isch] Adjektiv            **spanisch**

*The Spanish Riding School is in Vienna.*
Die Spanische Reitschule ist in Wien.

---

**to speak** [SPIEK] Verb                **sprechen**

*He'll speak with you now, Eric.*
Er spricht jetzt mit dir, Erik.

---

**to spend (time)** [SPEND] Verb        **verbringen**

*I will spend all day in the library.*
Ich verbringe den ganzen Tag in der Bibliothek.

**to spend (money)** [SPEND] Verb       **ausgeben**

*He does not spend a lot of money.*
Er gibt nicht viel Geld aus.

---

**spider** [SPEI-der] Substantiv           **die Spinne**

*Who is afraid of spiders?*
Wer hat Angst vor Spinnen?

---

**to spill** [SPIL] Verb               **verschütten**

*The baby spills the milk.*
Das Baby verschüttet die Milch.

---

**spoon** [SPUHN] Substantiv　　　　　　　　**der Löffel**

*I don't have a spoon.*
Ich habe keinen Löffel.

---

**sport** [SPOHRT] Substantiv　　　　　　　　**der Sport**

*Baseball is an American sport.*
Baseball ist ein amerikanischer Sport.

---

**spot, stain** [SPAT] Substantiv　　　　　　**der Flecken**

*There is a spot on the rug.*
Es gibt einen Flecken auf dem Teppich.

---

**spotted** [SPAT-ed] Adjektiv　　　　　　　**gefleckt(e)**

*There is the spotted dog.*
Dort ist der gefleckte Hund.

---

**spring** [SPRING] Substantiv　　　　　　　**der Frühling**

*One sees a lot of flowers in the spring.*
Man sieht viele Blumen im Frühling.

---

**square** [SKWEHR] Adjektiv　　　　　　　　**viereckig**

*The table is square.*
Der Tisch ist viereckig.

---

**stairs** [STEHRS] Substantiv　　　　　　　**die Treppe**

**staircase** [STEHR-kehs]

*I am now going down the stairs.*
Jetzt gehe ich die Treppe hinunter.

---

**stamp, postage stamp**　　　　　　　　**die Briefmarke**
　　[STÄMP] Substantiv

*Liechtenstein has beautiful stamps.*
Liechtenstein hat schöne Briefmarken.

---

**to stand** [STÄND] Verb **stehen**

*He is standing in front of the hotel.*
Er steht vor dem Hotel.

**to stand up, to get up** [STÄND AP] Ausdruck **aufstehen**

*Please get up, Johnny, it is late!*
Bitte steh auf, Hans, es ist spät!

---

**star** [STAHR] Substantiv **der Stern**

*How many stars are there in the sky?*
Wie viele Sterne gibt es im Himmel?

---

**state** [STEHT] Substantiv **der Staat**

*Here is a map of the United States of America.*
Das ist eine Karte von den Vereinigten Staaten von Amerika.

---

**station (train)** [STEH-schen] Substantiv **der Bahnhof**

*The train stops only at the station.*
Der Zug hält nur im Bahnhof.

---

**to stay** [STEH] Verb **bleiben**

*We will stay for ten days at Grandmother's house.*
Wir bleiben zehn Tage bei der Großmutter.

---

**to steal** [STIEL] Verb **stehlen**

*The mouse steals the cheese.*
Die Maus stiehlt den Käse.

---

**steamship, ship** [STIEM-schip] Substantiv **der Dampfer**

*This ship crosses the Atlantic Ocean.*
Dieser Dampfer überquert den Atlantischen Ozean.

---

**step** [STEP] Substantiv **der Schritt**

*The children take three steps forward.*
Die Kinder gehen drei Schritte vorwärts.

---

**stereo system**          **die Stereoanlage**
    [STIER-ie-oh CYC- tem] Substantiv

*We have a stereo system.*
Wir haben eine Stereoanlage.

---

**stick** [STIK] Substantiv          **der Stock**

*The policeman carries a stick.*
Der Polizist trägt einen Stock.

---

**still, yet** [STIL] Adverb          **noch**

*Yes, it is eight o'clock and I am still at home.*
Ja, es ist acht Uhr und ich bin noch zu Hause.

---

**to sting, bite** [STING] Verb          **stechen**

*Mosquitoes bite me often.*
Mücken stechen mich oft.

---

**stocking** [STAK-ing] Substantiv          **der Strumpf**
**pantyhose** [PÄN-tie hohs]          **die Strumpfhose**

*Where can I buy stockings, please?*
Wo kann ich denn Strümpfe kaufen, bitte?

---

**stomach** [STOM-äk] Substantiv          **der Magen**

*George has a stomachache.*
Georg hat Magenschmerzen.

---

**stone** [STOWN] Substantiv          **der Stein**

*There are many stones on the playground.*
Es gibt viele Steine auf dem Spielplatz.

---

**to stop** [STAP] Verb          **halten**

*The cars stop at the red light.*
Die Autos halten bei Rot.

---

**store, shop** [STOHR] Substantiv     **das Geschäft, der Laden**

*The store is open.*
Das Geschäft ist offen.

---

**storm** [STOHRM] Substantiv                    **der Sturm**

*It is windy in the storm.*
Im Sturm ist es windig.

---

**story** [STOHR-ie] Substantiv     **die Geschichte**

*The teacher is reading the children a story.*
Der Lehrer liest den Kindern eine Geschichte vor.

---

**stove** [STOHW] Substantiv                    **der Herd**

*The stove is dangerous for small children.*
Der Herd ist gefährlich für kleine Kinder.

---

**strange** [STREHNDG] Adjektiv                    **komisch**

*The weather is strange this summer, cool and rainy.*
Das Wetter ist komisch diesen Sommer, kühl und
regnerisch.

---

**stranger** [STREHN-dger] Substantiv          **der Fremde**
                                               **die Fremde**

*Who is the woman? She is a stranger.*
Wer ist denn die Frau? Sie ist eine Fremde.

---

**strawberry** [STROH-ber-ie] Substantiv     **die Erdbeere**

*There are strawberries for dessert.*
Es gibt Erdbeeren zum Nachtisch.

---

**street** [STRIET] Substantiv                                   **die Straße**

*It is dangerous to play in the street.*
Es ist gefährlich, auf der Straße zu spielen.

**street cleaner**                                      **der Straßenkehrer**
       [STRIET-klien-er] Substantiv     **die Straßenkehrerin**

*There are men and women street cleaners.*
Es gibt Straßenkehrer und Straßenkehrerinnen.

---

**string** [STRING] Substantiv                                   **die Schnur**

*A string is on the floor.*
Eine Schnur liegt auf dem Fußboden.

---

**string beans** [STRING-biens] Substantiv, pl.     **grüne Bohnen**

*The string beans are ready to be picked.*
Die grünen Bohnen sind reif zum Pflücken.

---

**strong** [STROHNG] Adjektiv                                       **kräftig**

*The soccer player is strong.*
Der Fußballspieler ist kräftig.

---

**student (university)** [STUD-nt] Substantiv        **der Student**
                                                                     **die Studentin**

*My sister is a student at a university in Berlin.*
Meine Schwester ist Studentin an einer Universität in Berlin.

---

**student, pupil (school)**                               **der Schüler**
       [STUD-nt] Substantiv                               **die Schülerin**

*I am still a pupil in grade school.*
Ich bin noch ein Schüler in der Grundschule.

---

**to study** [STAD-ie] Verb                                         **lernen**

*We are studying together for the test.*
Wir lernen zusammen für den Test.

---

**to study** [STAD-ie] Verb                     **studieren**
*He is studying law.*
Er studiert Jura.

---

**stupid** [STU-pid] Adjektiv                   **dumm**
*The fox is not a stupid animal.*
Der Fuchs ist kein dummes Tier.

---

**subway** [SAB-weh] Substantiv    **die Untergrundbahn,**
                                          **die U-Bahn**
**by subway** Ausdruck              **mit der U-Bahn**
*The nurse takes the subway.*
Die Krankenschwester fährt mit der U-Bahn.

---

**suddenly** [SAD-en-lie] Adverb                **plötzlich**
*Suddenly the lights go out.*
Plötzlich sind die Lichter aus.

---

**sugar** [SCHUG-er] Substantiv                 **der Zucker**
*He takes sugar with the tea.*
Er nimmt Zucker mit dem Tee.

---

**suit** [SUT] Substanativ       **der Anzug, das Kostüm**
*He wears a suit when he works at the office.*
Er trägt einen Anzug, wenn er im Büro arbeitet.

*Anna's suits for work are practical.*
Annas Kostüme für die Arbeit sind praktisch.

---

**suitcase** [SUT-kehs] Substantiv              **der Koffer**
*She is carrying a suitcase.*
Sie trägt einen Koffer.

---

**summer** [SAM-er] Substantiv                  **der Sommer**
*Do you prefer summer or winter?*
Was hast du lieber, Sommer oder Winter?

---

**summer vacation**                              **die Sommerferien**
    [SAM-er weh-KEH-shen] Ausdruck

*Our summer vacation begins soon.*
Unsere Sommerferien beginnen bald.

---

**sun** [SAN] Substantiv                              **die Sonne**

*What time does the sun rise?*
Wann geht die Sonne auf?

**The sun is shining.** Ausdruck          **Die Sonne scheint.**

**It is sunny.** Ausdruck                      **Es ist sonnig.**

---

**supermarket, market**          **der Supermarkt, der Markt**
    [SUP-er MAHRK-et] Substantiv

*I'm going to the supermarket with my girlfriend.*
Ich gehe mit meiner Freundin zum Supermarkt.

---

**sure** [SCHUHR] Adverb                              **sicher**

*Today is Tuesday. Are you sure?*
Heute ist Dienstag. Bist du sicher?

---

**surprise** [su-PREIS] Substantiv          **die Überraschung**

*She likes the surprise.*
Sie hat die Überraschung gern.

**surprising** [su-PREIS-ing] Adjektiv          **überraschend**

*The news is not surprising.*
Die Nachricht ist nicht überraschend.

---

**sweater** [SWED-er] Substantiv         **der Pullover, der Pulli**

*I am wearing a sweater because it is cool.*
Ich trage einen Pullover, denn es ist kühl.

---

**sweet** [SWIET] Adjektiv                      **süß**

*Some cherries are sweet.*
Manche Kirschen sind süß.

---

**to swim** [SWIM] Verb                   **schwimmen**

*I swim in the summer.*
Ich schwimme im Sommer.

---

**swimming pool, pool**           **das Schwimmbad**
     [SWIM-ing PUHL] Substantiv

*We are swimming in the pool.*
Wir schwimmen im Schwimmbad.

---

**swing** [SWING] Substantiv              **die Schaukel**

*The little girl is on the swing*
Das kleine Mädchen ist auf der Schaukel.

---

**switch** [SWITSCH] Substantiv          **der Schalter**

*He turns the light switch on right away.*
Er knipst den Schalter sofort an.

---

**Switzerland** [SWIZ-er-länd] Substantiv     **die Schweiz**

*They speak four languages in Switzerland.*
Man spricht vier Sprachen in der Schweiz.

---

## T

**table** [TEH-bl] Substantiv         **der Tisch**

*The paintbox is on the table.*
Der Malkasten ist auf dem Tisch.

**tablecloth** [TEH-bl-kloth] Substantiv     **die Tischdecke**

**to set the table**     **den Tisch decken**
    [tu set tha TEH-bl] Ausdruck

*George likes to set the table for the family.*
Georg deckt den Tisch für die Familie gern.

---

**tail** [TEHL] Substantiv     **der Schwanz**

*My dog wags his tail when I come home.*
Mein Hund wedelt den Schwanz, wenn ich
nach Hause komme.

---

**tailor** [TEH-ler] Substantiv     **der Schneider**

*My neighbor is a tailor.*
Mein Nachbar ist Schneider.

---

**to take** [TEHK] Verb     **nehmen**

*It is raining and she takes along an umbrella.*
Es regnet und sie nimmt einen Regenschirm mit.

---

**to take a bath** [tu tehk ä BÄTH] Ausdruck     **baden**

*She takes a bath early in the morning.*
Sie badet früh am Morgen.

---

**to take off** [tu tehk off] Ausdruck     **ausziehen**

*We take our shoes off at the door.*
Wir ziehen unsere Schuhe an der Tür aus.

---

**to take a trip**      **eine Reise machen**
[tu tehk ä TRIP] Ausdruck

*In the spring we will take a trip to Asia.*
Im Frühling machen wir eine Reise nach Asien.

**to take a walk**      **spazieren gehen**
[tu tehk ä WOHK] Ausdruck

*Here everyone takes a walk on Sunday evenings.*
Hier gehen alle sonntagabends spazieren.

**tale**      **die Geschichte**
see **story**

**to talk, speak** [TOHK] Verb      **sprechen**

*My little brother talks softly.*
Mein kleiner Bruder spricht leise.

**tall** [TOHL] Adjektiv      **groß**

*The giraffe is tall.*
Die Giraffe ist groß.

**tape recorder**      **der Kassettenrekorder**
[TEHP re-KOHR-der] Substantiv

*The teacher uses a tape recorder in class.*
Der Lehrer benutzt einen Kassettenrekorder im Unterricht.

**taxi** [TÄK-sie] Substantiv      **das Taxi**

*My sister drives a taxi.*
Meine Schwester fährt ein Taxi.

**tea** [TIE] Substantiv      **der Tee**

*My aunt always drinks tea.*
Meine Tante trinkt immer Tee.

**to teach** [TIETSCH] Verb                        **unterrichten**

*She likes teaching German.*
Sie unterrichtet Deutsch gern.

---

**teacher** [TIE-tscher] Substantiv              **der Lehrer**
**die Lehrerin**

*Where is our music teacher?*
Wo ist denn unser Musiklehrer?

---

**team** [TIEM] Substantiv                     **die Mannschaft**

*We all play on the same team.*
Wir spielen alle in einer Mannschaft.

---

**tear** [TIER] Substantiv                        **die Träne**

*It hurts so much that there are tears in his eyes.*
Es tut so sehr weh, dass er Tränen in den Augen hat.

---

**telephone** [TEL-e-fohn] Substantiv            **das Telefon**

*Our telephone rings often.*
Unser Telefon klingelt oft.

---

**television set (TV)**                           **der Fernseher**
[TEL-eh-wisch-en set] Substantiv

*My brother and I like to watch television.*
Mein Bruder und ich sehen gern fern.

**television antenna**                      **die Fernsehantenne**
[an-TEN-a] Substantiv

*The TV antenna is not broken.*
Die Fernsehantenne ist nicht kaputt.

---

**to tell** [TEL] Verb                                **erzählen**

*The babysitter is telling us a fairy tale.*
Der Babysitter erzählt uns ein Märchen.

---

**ten** [TEN] Adjektiv                                **zehn**

*I have ten fingers and ten toes.*
Ich habe zehn Finger und zehn Zehen.

---

**tent** [TENT] Substantiv                            **das Zelt**

*When we go camping I sleep in a tent.*
Wenn wir campen, schlafe ich in einem Zelt.

---

**test** [TEST] Substantiv              **die Prüfung, der Test**

*I like tests when I understand everything.*
Ich habe Prüfungen gern, wenn ich alles verstehe.

---

**Thank you!** [THÄNK ju] Ausdruck                    **Danke!**

**Thanks a lot!** [THÄNKS a lat] Ausdruck        **Vielen Dank!**

---

**that** [THÄT] Pronomen                              **das**

*That is certainly a surprise.*
Das ist sicher eine Überraschung.

---

**That's fun!** [THÄTS fan] Ausdruck         **Das macht Spaß!**

**That's too bad!** [THÄTS tu bäd] Ausdruck   **Das ist schade!**

---

**the** [THA] Artikel                            **der, die, das**

*The children are hungry already.*
Die Kinder sind schon hungrig.

---

**theater** [THIE-eh-ter] Substantiv             **das Theater**

*This play is in the new theater.*
Dieses Stück ist im neuen Theater.

---

**their** [THEHR] Adjektiv **ihr(e)**

*The girls are pulling their sleds.*
Die Mädchen ziehen ihre Schlitten.

---

**them** [THEM] Pronomen **sie**

*Here are the wood blocks. I give them to the child.*
Hier sind die Holzklotze. Ich gebe sie dem Kind.

**to them** [THEM] Pronomen **ihnen**

*I give (to) them a menu.*
Ich gebe ihnen eine Speisekarte.

---

**then** [THEN] Adverb **dann**

*I get up, then I eat breakfast.*
Ich stehe auf, dann frühstücke ich.

---

**there** [THEHR] Adverb **dort**

*The hammer is lying there.*
Der Hammer liegt dort.

**over there** [o-wer THEHR] Ausdruck **dort drüben**

*That's my father over there.*
Das ist mein Vater dort drüben.

---

**there is, there are** [thehr IS, thehr AHR] Ausdruck **es gibt**

*Is there a coat for me?*
Gibt es einen Mantel für mich?

---

**they** [THEH] Pronomen **sie**

*They are going to the movies.*
Sie gehen ins Kino.

---

**thick** [THIK] Adjektiv **dick**

*The grapefruit has a thick skin.*
Die Pampelmuse hat eine dicke Schale.

---

**thief** [THIEF] Substantiv                                **der Dieb**
*They are looking for the thief everywhere.*
Man sucht den Dieb überall.

**thin** [THIN] Adjektiv                                     **dünn**
*The little boy is thin.*
Der kleine Junge ist dünn.

**thing** [THING] Substantiv                                **die Sache**
*They sell all sorts of things here.*
Man verkauft allerhand Sachen hier.

**to think** [THINK] Verb                                   **denken**
*She thinks that she understands the assignment.*
Sie denkt, dass sie die Aufgabe versteht.

**to be thirsty** [THIRS-tie] Ausdruck                      **Durst haben**
*The horse is thirsty.*
Das Pferd hat Durst.

**thirteen** [thir-TIEN] Adjektiv                           **dreizehn**
*She has thirteen books in her backpack.*
Sie hat dreizehn Bücher im Rucksack.

**thirty** [THIR-tie] Adjektiv                              **dreißig**
*It is already ten thirty.*
Es ist schon zehn Uhr dreißig.

**this** [THISS] Adjektiv                               **dieser, dieses**
**these** [THIES]                                           **diese**
*I will buy this shirt, but not these pants.*
Ich kaufe dieses Hemd, aber nicht diese Hosen.

**this** [THISS] Pronomen                                   **das**
*This is my son.*
Das ist mein Sohn.

**thousand** [THAU-send] Adjektiv      **tausend**

*I would like to have a thousand dollars.*
Ich möchte tausend Dollar haben.

---

**three** [THRIE] Adjektiv      **drei**

*There are three glasses on the table.*
Es sind drei Gläser auf dem Tisch.

---

**throat** [THROWT] Substantiv      **der Hals**

*Do you have a sore throat?*
Hast du Halsschmerzen?

---

**through** [THRU] Präposition      **durch**

*The bear is walking through the forest.*
Der Bär geht durch den Wald.

---

**to throw** [THROW] Verb      **werfen**

*She is throwing the ball.*
Sie wirft den Ball.

---

**thunder** [THAN-der] Substantiv      **der Donner**

*The thunder comes after the lightning.*
Der Donner kommt nach dem Blitz.

---

**Thursday** [THÜRS-deh] Substantiv      **der Donnerstag**

*On Thursday I have my German lesson.*
Am Donnerstag habe ich meinen Deutschunterricht.

---

**ticket** [TIK-it] Substantiv      **die Karte**

*I would like to buy a ticket.*
Ich möchte eine Karte kaufen.

---

**tie** [TEI] Substantiv      **der Schlips, die Krawatte**

*I can tie my tie.*
Ich kann meinen Schlips binden.

---

**tiger** [TEI-ger] Substantiv                             **der Tiger**
*A tiger can jump very far.*
Ein Tiger kann sehr weit springen.

---

**tight** [TEIT] Adjektiv                                        **eng**
*This coat is too tight for me.*
Dieser Mantel ist zu eng für mich.

---

**time** [TEIM] Substantiv                                   **die Uhr**

**What time is it?** Ausdruck              **Wie viel Uhr ist es?**

**It is dinner time.** Ausdruck    **Es ist Zeit für Abendessen.**

**to have a good time**                    **sich gut unterhalten**
          [häv a gud TEIM] Ausdruck
*I am having a good time.*
Ich unterhalte mich gut.

---

**tip** [TIP] Substantiv                                **das Trinkgeld**
*The woman gives the waiter a tip.*
Die Frau gibt dem Kellner ein Trinkgeld.

---

**tired** [TIE-erd] Adjektiv                                   **müde**
*After a game of tennis I am tired.*
Nach einem Tennisspiel bin ich müde.

---

**to** [TU] Präposition                                        **nach**
*They are traveling to Brazil.*
Sie reisen nach Brasilien.

**to the** [TU] Präposition                 **zum, zur, zu den**
*She is going to the airport.*
Sie fährt zum Flughafen.

---

**toast** [TOHST] Substantiv                             **der Toast**
*The toast is still hot.*
Der Toast ist noch heiß.

---

**today** [tu-DEH] Adverb                                     **heute**
*Today is October fourth.*
Heute ist der vierte Oktober.

**toe** [TOW] Substantiv                                      **der Zeh**
*The baby touches its toes.*
Das Baby fasst seine Zehen an.

**together** [tu-GETH-er] Adverb                              **zusammen**
*Let's go to school together.*
Lass uns doch zusammen zur Schule gehen!

**tomato** [te-MEH-to] Substantiv                             **die Tomate**
*The tomato is red when it is ripe.*
Die Tomate ist rot, wenn sie reif ist.

**tomorrow** [te-MAR-ow] Adverb                               **morgen**
*Tomorrow I am flying to Australia.*
Morgen fliege ich nach Australien.

**tongue** [TANG] Substantiv                                  **die Zunge**
*Hot soup burns my tongue.*
Heiße Suppe verbrennt meine Zunge.

**too (also)** [TU] Adverb                                    **auch**
*I want some candy, too.*
Ich möchte auch Bonbons.

**Too bad!** [tu BÄD] Ausdruck                                **Schade!**

**too much** [tu MATSCH] Ausdruck                             **zu viel**
*I have too much to do today.*
Ich habe heute zu viel zu tun.

**too many** [tu MEN-ie] Adjektiv                             **zu viele**
*There are too many people in the elevator.*
Es gibt zu viele Leute im Lift.

**tooth** [TUHTH] Substantiv                                **der Zahn**

*I clean my teeth daily.*
Ich putze meine Zähne täglich.

---

**to have a toothache**        **Zahnschmerzen haben**
    [häv a TUHTH-ehk] Ausdruck

*You go to the dentist when you have a toothache.*
Man geht zum Zahnarzt, wenn man Zahnschmerzen hat.

---

**toothbrush** [TUHTH-brasch] Substantiv        **die Zahnbürste**

**toothpaste** [TUHTH-pehst] Substantiv        **die Zahnpaste**

---

**top** [TAP] Substantiv                                **der Kreisel**

*A top is a toy.*
Ein Kreisel ist ein Spielzeug.

---

**to touch** [TATSCH] Verb                                **anfassen**

*Do not touch the flowers, Alf!*
Fass die Blumen nicht an, Alf!

---

**toward** [TOHRD] Präposition                        **in Richtung**

*Let's go toward the hospital.*
Gehen wir doch in Richtung Krankenhaus.

---

**towel** [TAU-el] Substantiv                        **das Handtuch**

*This towel is very soft.*
Dieses Handtuch ist sehr weich!

---

**tower** [TAU-er] Substantiv                        **der Turm**

*The tower is from the Middle Ages.*
Der Turm stammt aus dem Mittelalter.

---

**toy** [TEU] Substantiv                                **das Spielzeug**

*What kind of toys do you have?*
Was für Spielzeug hast du?

---

**traffic** [TRÄF-ik] Substantiv                        **der Verkehr**

*The traffic stops for the red light.*
Der Verkehr hält bei Rot.

---

**traffic light**
     see **light**

---

**train** [TREHN] Substantiv                              **der Zug**

*Trains are comfortable and not too expensive.*
Züge sind bequem und nicht zu teuer.

---

**to travel** [TRÄV-el] Verb                                  **reisen**

*We will travel by car today.*
Wir reisen heute mit dem Auto.

---

**to take a trip** [TEHK a TRIP] Ausdruck     **eine Reise machen**

*I am taking the trip alone.*
Ich mache die Reise alleine.

---

**traveler** [TRÄV-el-er] Substantiv                  **der Reisende**
                                                                **die Reisende**
                                                               **die Reisenden**

*The traveler carries her computer.*
Die Reisende trägt ihren Computer.

---

**tree** [TRIE] Substantiv                                   **der Baum**

*We are sitting under a tree.*
Wir sitzen unter einem Baum.

---

**trip** [TRIP] Substantiv                   **die Reise**

**to take a trip**             **eine Reise machen**
     [tehk a TRIP] Ausdruck

*We are taking a trip on the Rhine.*
Wir machen eine Reise auf dem Rhein.

---

**truck** [TRAK] Substantiv           **der Lastwagen**

*The truck is carrying vegetables.*
Der Lastwagen liefert Gemüse.

---

**true** [TRUH] Adverb                     **wahr**

*Is it true that cats and dogs fight?*
Ist es wahr, dass Katzen und Hunde streiten?

**Isn't that true?** [is-nt thät TRUH] Ausdruck    **Nicht wahr?**

*The capital of Austria is Vienna, isn't that true?*
Die Hauptstadt Österreichs ist Wien, nicht wahr?

---

**trunk (of car)** [TRANK] Substantiv     **der Kofferraum**

*The baggage is in the trunk.*
Das Gepäck ist im Kofferraum.

---

**to try** [TREI] Verb                    **versuchen**

*I am trying the new cake recipe.*
Ich versuche das neue Kuchenrezept.

---

**Tuesday** [TUS-dä] Substantiv        **der Dienstag**

*Tuesday is my day off.*
Am Dienstag habe ich frei.

---

**turkey** [TÜR-kie] Substantiv      **die Pute, der Truthahn**

*Do you like to eat turkey?*
Isst du Pute gern?

---

**to turn** [TÜRN] Verb      **drehen**

*I turn the picture to me.*
Ich drehe das Bild zu mir.

---

**to turn off** [tu türn OFF] Ausdruck      **ausschalten**

*He always turns the light off when he goes out.*
Er schaltet das Licht immer aus, wenn er ausgeht.

---

**turnpike** [TÜRN-peik] Substantiv      **die Autobahn**
        see **expressway**

---

**turtle** [TÜR-tel] Substantiv      **die Schildkröte**

*The turtle likes the sun.*
Die Schildkröte hat die Sonne gern.

---

**twelve** [TWELV] Adjektiv      **zwölf**

*A year has twelve months.*
Ein Jahr hat zwölf Monate.

---

**twenty** [TWEN-tie] Adjektiv      **zwanzig**

*We have only twenty glasses.*
Wir haben nur zwanzig Gläser.

---

**twice** [TWEISS] Adverb      **zweimal**

*Please say the word twice.*
Sag das Wort zweimal, bitte.

---

**two** [TU] Adjektiv               **zwei**

*He has two dogs.*
Er hat zwei Hunde.

---

**typewriter** [TEIP-rei-ter] Substantiv   **die Schreibmaschine**

**electric typewriter**     **die elektrische Schreibmaschine**
    [i-LEK-trik TEIP-rei-ter]
    see **word processor**

---

**typist** [TEIP-ist] Substantiv        **die Schreibkraft**

*The typist uses a computer with a word processor.*
Die Schreibkraft benutzt einen Computer mit
Textverarbeitungssystem.

---

## U

**ugly** [AG-lie] Adjektiv              **hässlich**

*I don't like this hat; it's ugly.*
Ich mag diesen Hut nicht; er ist hässlich.

---

**umbrella** [am-BREL-a] Substantiv     **der Regenschirm**

*That's a pretty umbrella.*
Das ist aber ein schöner Regenschirm.

---

**uncle** [AN-kel] Substantiv            **der Onkel**

*My uncle is my mother's brother.*
Mein Onkel ist der Bruder meiner Mutter.

---

**under** [AN-der] Präposition           **unter**

*Potatoes grow under the ground.*
Kartoffeln wachsen unter der Erde.

**to understand** [an-der-STÄND] Verb                    **verstehen**

*He understands the question but has no answer.*
Er versteht die Frage, aber hat keine Antwort.

---

**unhappy** [an-HÄP-ie] Adjektiv                         **unglücklich**

*She is unhappy because she may not play ball.*
Sie ist unglücklich, denn sie darf nicht Ball spielen.

---

**united** [ju-NEIT-ed] Adjektiv                     **vereinigt, vereint**

**the United States of America**          **die Vereinigten Staaten**
    Ausdruck                                       **von Amerika**

**the United Nations** Ausdruck          **die Vereinten Nationen**

**the United Kingdom** Ausdruck               **Großbritannien**

---

**university** [ju-ni-WER-ci-tie] Substantiv        **die Universität**

*The university is not far from the center of the city.*
Die Universität ist nicht weit vom Stadtzentrum.

---

**until** [an-TIL] Präposition                                   **bis**

*He works until six o'clock in the evening.*
Er arbeitet bis sechs Uhr abends.

---

**unusual** [an-JUH-schu-al] Adjektiv                   **ungewöhnlich**

*The story has an unusual ending.*
Die Geschichte hat ein ungewöhnliches Ende.

---

**upstairs** [ap-STEHRS] Adverb                              **oben**

---

**us, to us** [AS, tu AS] Pronomen                            **uns**

*She sees us at once.*
Sie sieht uns sofort.

*He gives (to) us candy.*
Er gibt uns Bonbons.

---

**to use** [JUHS] Verb                **benutzen**

*They use the bus often.*
Sie benutzen den Bus oft.

**useful** [JUSS-ful] Adjektiv           **nützlich**

*Some insects are useful.*
Manche Insekten sind nützlich.

**V**

**vacation** [wa-KEH-schen] Substantiv     **der Urlaub**

*Where are you going on your family vacation?*
Wohin geht ihr in eurem Familienurlaub?

**school vacation**                **die Schulferien**
         [SKUHL wa-KEH-schen] Ausdruck

*What are you doing during the school vacation?*
Was machst du in den Schulferien?

**to vaccinate** [WÄK-cin-eht] Verb         **impfen**

*The doctor vaccinates the child.*
Der Arzt impft das Kind.

**vacuum cleaner**             **der Staubsauger**
         [WÄK-jum KLIE-ner] Substantiv

*The vacuum cleaner is very practical.*
Der Staubsauger ist sehr praktisch.

**valley** [WÄL-ie] Substantiv             **das Tal**

*The lake is in a valley.*
Der See ist in einem Tal.

**vanilla** [we-NIL-a] Substantiv         **die Vanille**

*There is no vanilla ice cream today.*
Es gibt kein Vanilleeis heute.

**vegetable** [WEDG-te-bl] Substantiv        **das Gemüse**

*Red cabbage is a vegetable.*
Rotkraut ist ein Gemüse.

**very** [WER-ie] Adverb                      **sehr**

*The palace is very large.*
Das Schloss ist sehr groß.

**village** [WIL-idg] Substantiv            **das Dorf**

*Many tourists come to this village.*
Viele Touristen kommen in dieses Dorf.

**violet** [WEI-o-let] Adjektiv                **violett**

**violin** [WEI-o-lin] Substantiv     **die Violine, die Geige**

*The violin is on the piano.*
Die Violine liegt auf dem Klavier.

**to visit** [WIS-it] Verb                **besuchen**

*My family visits our grandparents often.*
Meine Familie besucht unsere Großeltern oft.

**voice** [WOIS] Substantiv            **die Stimme**

*My aunt's voice is pleasant.*
Die Stimme meiner Tante ist angenehm.

**top of one's voice**          **aus vollem Halse**

**in a low voice**            **mit leiser Stimme**

**in a loud voice**          **mit lauter Stimme**

## W

**to wag** [wÄG] Verb       **wedeln**

*The dog wags his tail when he is happy.*
Der Hund wedelt mit seinem Schwanz, wenn er froh ist.

**waist** [WEHST] Substantiv       **die Taille**

*They measure my waist for the new belt.*
Man misst meine Taille für den neuen Gürtel.

**to wait for** [WEHT vor] Ausdruck       **warten auf**

*She is waiting for her father.*
Sie wartet auf ihren Vater.

**waiter** [WEH-ter] Substantiv       **der Kellner**

**waitress** [WEH-tress] Substantiv       **die Kellnerin**

*The waiter brings the menu.*
Der Kellner bringt die Speisekarte.

**to wake (someone)** [WEHK] Verb       **aufwecken**

*The alarm rings and wakes me up.*
Der Wecker klingelt und weckt mich auf.

**to walk** [WOHK] Verb       **gehen**

*She always walks fast.*
Sie geht immer schnell.

**to go for a walk**       **spazieren gehen**
     [tu GOH vor a WOHK] Ausdruck

*They are going for a walk in the park.*
Sie gehen im Park spazieren.

**Walkman®** [WOHK-män] Substantiv       **der Walkman**

*Where is your Walkman®?*
Wo ist dein Walkman?

**wall** [WOHL] Substantiv                                 **die Mauer**

*The Berlin Wall is no longer a border.*
Die Berliner Mauer ist keine Grenze mehr.

---

**to want to** [WAHNT] Verb                                  **wollen**

*The nurse wants to help the child.*
Die Krankenschwester will dem Kind helfen.

---

**to want, to wish** [WAHNT] Verb                          **möchte**

*I want the roast beef, please.*
Ich möchte das Roastbeef, bitte.

---

**war** [WOHR] Substantiv                                   **der Krieg**

*My uncle is a soldier in the war.*
Mein Onkel ist Soldat im Krieg.

---

**warm** [WOHRM] Adjektiv                                     **warm**

*The meal is still warm.*
Das Essen ist noch warm.

**I am warm.** Ausdruck                                   **Mir ist warm.**

**It is warm.** Ausdruck                                   **Es ist warm.**

---

**to wash** [WOHSCH] Verb                                   **waschen**

*She is washing the car.*
Sie wäscht das Auto.

**washing machine**                          **die Waschmaschine**
     [WOHSCH-ing ma-SHIEN] Substantiv

---

**watch** [WATSCH] Substantiv       **die Armbanduhr**

*What a shame, my watch does not work.*
Schade, meine Armbanduhr geht nicht.

---

**to watch, to see** [WATSCH] Verb       **sehen**

*We see the helicopter in the sky.*
Wir sehen den Hubschrauber in der Luft.

---

**to watch over** [watsch OW-er] Verb    **sich kümmern um**
      see **to care about**

---

**water** [WAH-ter] Substantiv       **das Wasser**

*There is water in the sink.*
Da ist Wasser im Waschbecken.

**to water** [WAH-ter] Verb       **gießen**

*Margaret waters the plants.*
Margaret gießt die Blumen.

---

**watermelon**       **die Wassermelone**
      [WAH-ter-mel-en] Substantiv

*The girl is carrying a watermelon.*
Das Mädchen trägt eine Wassermelone.

---

**wave** [WEHV] Substantiv       **die Welle**

*We see the waves at the ocean.*
Wir sehen die Wellen am Ozean.

---

**way**
      see **path**

---

**we** [WIE] Pronomen       **wir**

*We often drive to the country.*
Wir fahren oft aufs Land.

---

**weak** [WIEK] Adjektiv　　　　　　　　　　**schwach**

*The boy is weak because he is sick.*
Der Junge ist schwach, denn er ist krank.

---

**wealthy, rich** [WEL-thie] Adjektiv　　　　　**reich**

*That is a wealthy country.*
Das ist ein reiches Land.

---

**to wear** [WEHR] Verb　　　　　　　　　　**tragen**

*She is wearing my hat.*
Sie trägt meinen Hut.

---

**weather** [WETH-er] Substantiv　　　　**das Wetter**

*How is the weather? The sun is shining.*
Wie ist denn das Wetter? Die Sonne scheint.

*The weather is bad.*
Das Wetter ist schlecht.

---

**Wednesday** [WENS-deh] Substantiv　　**der Mittwoch**

*On Wednesday I will go to the library.*
Am Mittwoch gehe ich zur Bibliothek.

---

**week** [WIEK] Substantiv　　　　　　　**die Woche**

*A month has four weeks.*
Ein Monat hat vier Wochen.

---

**to weep** [WIEP] Verb　　　　　　　　　**weinen**
　　　　see **to cry**

---

**You're welcome!** [JUR WEL-kom]  Ausdruck　　**Bitte!**
**You're very welcome!**　　　**Bitte sehr! Bitte schön!**
　　　[JUR WERIE WEL-kom] Ausdruck

*I say, "Thank you" and the other person says, "You're welcome."*
Ich sage, "Danke" und die andere Person sagt, "Bitte"!

**well** [WEL] Adverb           **gut**

*She understands me well.*
Sie versteht mich gut.

**Well!** [WEL] Interjektion       **Na, so etwas!**

**to behave well** Ausdruck     **sich gut benehmen**

*The children are behaving well.*
Die Kinder benehmen sich gut.

**Well done!** [WEL dann] Ausdruck     **Gut gemacht!**

---

**the west** [WEST] Substantiv      **der Westen**

*When I go from Dresden to Cologne, I go toward the west.*
Wenn ich von Dresden nach Köln fahre, fahre ich nach Westen.

---

**wet** [WET] Adjektiv           **nass**

*My hair is wet when I swim.*
Mein Haar ist nass, wenn ich schwimme.

---

**What was that?** [WHAT was that] Ausdruck    **Wie bitte?**

*What was that please? Repeat it!*
Wie bitte? Noch einmal, ja!

---

**What's the matter?**       **Was ist denn los?**
     [WHATS tha MÄ-ter] Ausdruck

---

**wheat** [WIET] Substantiv      **der Weizen**

*I see wheat in the fields.*
Ich sehe Weizen auf den Feldern.

---

**wheel** [WIEL] Substantiv       **das Rad**

*My cousin fixes the wheel of my bicycle.*
Meine Kusine repariert das Rad meines Fahrrads.

---

**when** [WEN] Adverb      **wann**

*When are they coming?*
Wann kommen sie?

**when** [WEN] Konjunktion      **wenn**

*I read a book when it rains.*
I lese ein Buch, wenn es regnet.

**where** [WEHR] Adverb      **wo**

*Where is the entrance?*
Wo ist der Eingang?

**whether, if** [WETH-er] Konjunktion      **ob**

*He asks if the shop is open.*
Er fragt, ob das Geschäft offen ist.

**which** [WITSCH] Adjektiv      **welcher, welche, welches**

*Which book are we reading?*
Welches Buch lesen wir?

**in a little while** [in ä LIT-l WEIL] Ausdruck      **bald**

*We will eat in a little while.*
Wir essen bald.

**to whistle** [WISS-el] Verb      **pfeifen**

*She whistles because she is happy.*
Sie pfeift, denn sie ist froh.

**white** [WEIT] Adjektiv      **weiß**

*His shoes are white.*
Seine Schuhe sind weiß.

**who** [HU] Pronomen      **wer**

*Who is that guest?*
Wer ist der Gast?

**whole** [HOHL] Adjektiv                     **ganz**

*Of course, I would like to eat the whole cake.*
Natürlich möchte ich den ganzen Kuchen essen.

---

**whom** [HUM] Pronomen                       **wen**

*Whom do you know here?*
Wen kennst du hier?

---

**(to) whom** [HUM] Pronomen                  **wem**

*To whom are you giving the present?*
Wem gibst du das Geschenk?

---

**why** [wei] Adverb                          **warum**

*Why is he late?*
Warum ist er denn verspätet?

---

**wide** [WEID] Adjektiv                       **breit**

*This is a wide road.*
Das ist eine breite Straße.

---

**wife** [WEIF] Substantiv       **die Frau, die Ehefrau**

*What is the name of the doctor's wife?*
Wie heißt die Frau des Arztes?

---

**wild** [WEILD] Adjektiv                      **wild**

*The gamekeeper catches the wild bear.*
Der Förster fängt den wilden Bären.

---

**to win** [WIN] Verb                         **gewinnen**

*Mark wins the game of chess.*
Markus gewinnt das Schachspiel.

---

**wind** [WIND] Substantiv                    **der Wind**

*In the storm the wind is louder than the thunder.*
Im Sturm ist der Wind lauter als der Donner.

---

**window** [WIN-dow] Substantiv                  **das Fenster**

*Our dog likes to look out the window.*
Unser Hund sieht gern aus dem Fenster.

---

**wine** [WEIN] Substantiv                          **der Wein**

*The waiter brings the wine.*
Der Kellner bringt den Wein.

---

**wing** [WING] Substantiv                          **der Flügel**

*A bird has two wings.*
Ein Vogel hat zwei Flügel.

---

**winter** [WIN-ter] Substantiv                    **der Winter**

*Winter comes after fall.*
Der Winter kommt nach dem Herbst.

---

**wise** [WEIS] Adjektiv                                **weise**

*My grandfather is wise.*
Mein Großvater ist weise.

---

**wish** [WISCH] Substantiv                        **der Wunsch**

*Do you have a wish for your birthday?*
Hast du einen Wunsch für deinen Geburtstag?

---

**with** [WITH] Präposition                            **mit**

*I eat with my family.*
Ich esse mit meiner Familie.

---

**without** [w̲ith-AUT] Präposition                    **ohne**

*She often travels without her family.*
Sie reist oft ohne ihre Familie.

---

**wolf** [W̲ULF] Substantiv                    **der Wolf**

*Red Riding Hood is not afraid of the wolf.*
Rotkäppchen hat keine Angst vor dem Wolf.

---

**woman** [W̲UM-en] Substantiv                    **die Frau**

*The woman is going to work.*
Die Frau geht zur Arbeit.

---

**wonderful** [W̲AN-der-voll] Adjektiv                    **wunderbar**

*It is a wonderful party.*
Es ist eine wunderbare Party.

---

**wood** [W̲UD] Substantiv                    **das Holz**

*The beautiful floor is made of wood.*
Der schöne Fußboden ist aus Holz.

---

**woods, forest** [W̲UDS] Substantiv                    **der Wald**

*The forest is full of trees.*
Der Wald ist voll mit Bäumen.

---

**wool** [W̲UL] Substantiv                    **die Wolle**

*My socks are made of wool.*
Meine Socken sind aus Wolle.

---

**word** [W̲ÜRD] Substantiv         **das Wort**

*How do you spell the word "dictionary?"*
Wie schreibt man das Wort "Wörterbuch?"

**word processor**       **das Textverarbeitungssystem**
    [W̲URD pra-sess-er] Substantiv

*I use the word processor often.*
Ich benutze das Textverarbeitungssystem oft.

**work** [W̲ÜRK] Substantiv         **die Arbeit**
*The work is hard.*
Die Arbiet ist schwer.

**to work (person)** [W̲ÜRK] Verb     **arbeiten**

*This man works in his home.*
Dieser Mann arbeitet in seinem Haus.

**to work (machine)** [W̲ÜRK] Verb     **funktionieren**

*Does the refrigerator work well?*
Funktioniert der Kühlschrank gut?

**world** [W̲URLD] Substantiv         **die Welt**

*How many nations are there in the world?*
Wie viele Nationen gibt es in der Welt?

**worm** [W̲URM] Substantiv         der Wurm

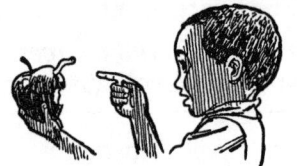

*There is a worm in my apple.*
Da ist ein Wurm in meinem Apfel.

**to write** [REIT] Verb                                        **schreiben**

*They write letters on the Internet.*
Sie schreiben Briefe im Internet.

---

**to be wrong** [RAUNG] Ausdruck                                **sich irren**

*She is wrong. We have the answer.*
Sie irrt sich. Wir haben die Antwort.

---

**X**

**to X-ray** [EKS-reh] Verb                                     **röntgen**

*The doctor X-rays the child's foot.*
Der Arzt röntgt den Fuß des Kindes.

---

**Y**

**year** [JIER] Substantiv                                      **das Jahr**

*There are fifty-two weeks in a year.*
Es gibt zweiundfünfzig Wochen in einem Jahr.

---

**yellow** [JEL-ow] Adjektiv                                    **gelb**

*A lemon is yellow or green.*
Eine Zitrone ist gelb oder grün.

---

**yes** [JES] Adverb                                            **ja**

*Do the children want some candy? Yes, of course.*
Möchten die Kinder Bonbons? Ja, natürlich.

---

**yesterday** [JES-ter-deh] Adverb                              **gestern**

*Today is Wednesday; yesterday was Tuesday.*
Heute ist Mittwoch; gestern war Dienstag.

---

**you** [JU] Pronomen                                         **du, ihr, Sie**

*Do you have a telephone, Anna?*
Hast du ein Telefon, Anna?

*Are you coming, Sebastian and Fred?*
Kommt ihr, Sebastian und Fritz?

*Do you speak German, Mr. Barker?*
Sprechen Sie Deutsch, Herr Barker?

**you** [JU] Pronomen                                         **dich, euch, Sie**

*I see you, Anna!*
Ich sehe dich, Anna!

**to you** [JU] Pronomen                                      **dir, euch, Ihnen**

*I will give you the answer, Anna.*
Ich gebe dir die Antwort, Anna.

---

**young** [JANG] Adjektiv                                     **jung**

*The puppy is young; it is only six weeks old.*
Das Hündchen ist jung, es ist nur sechs Wochen alt.

---

**your** [JUHR] Adjektiv                                      **dein, euer, Ihr**

*Is this your cat, Anna?*
Ist das deine Katze, Anna?

---

**You're welcome!** [JUHR WEL-kum] Ausdruck                   **Bitte!**

**You're very welcome!**                                      **Bitte sehr!**
      [juhr WER-ie WEL-kum] Ausdruck

---

## Z

**zebra** [SIE-bra] Substantiv                              **das Zebra**

*A zebra has black and white stripes.*
Ein Zebra hat schwarze und weiße Streifen.

---

**zero** [SIER-o] Substantiv                                **die Null**

*The number ten has a one and a zero.*
Die Zahl zehn hat eine Eins und eine Null.

---

**zoo** [SUH] Substantiv     **der Zoo, der zoologische Garten**

*What time does the zoo open?*
Wann öffnet der Zoo?

---

## DAYS OF THE WEEK
### Die Tage der Woche

| English<br>Englisch | Deutsch<br>German |
|---|---|
| Monday | Montag |
| Tuesday | Dienstag |
| Wednesday | Miittwoch |
| Thursday | Donnerstag |
| Friday | Freitag |
| Saturday | Samstag, Sonnabend |
| Sunday | Sonntag |

## MONTHS OF THE YEAR
### Die Monate des Jahres

| English<br>Englisch | Deutsch<br>German |
|---|---|
| January | Januar |
| February | Februar |
| March | März |
| April | April |
| May | Mai |
| June | Juni |
| July | Juli |
| August | August |
| September | September |
| October | Oktober |
| November | November |
| December | Dezember |

## PERSONAL NAMES
### *Eigennamen*

#### Boys/*für Jungen*

| English Englisch | Deutsch German |
|---|---|
| Alex(ander) | Alexander |
| Andrew | Andreas |
| Chris(tian) | Christian |
| Dan(iel) | Daniel |
| Dominic | Dominik |
| Eric | Erich |
| Felix | Felix |
| Florian | Florian |
| Frank | Franz |
| John | Johannes |
| Jonas | Jonas |
| Julian | Julian |
| Kevin | Kevin |
| Lucus | Lukas |
| Marcel | Marcel |
| Marvin | Marvin |
| Max(imillian) | Maximillian |
| Michael | Michael |
| Paul | Paul |
| Philip | Philipp |
| Sebastian | Sebastian |
| Simon | Simon |
| Thomas | Thomas |
| Tobias | Tobias |

| Girls/für Mädchen | |
|---|---|
| English<br>Englisch | Deutsch<br>German |
| Ann | Anna |
| Carol(ine) | Carolin |
| Christina | Christina |
| Francesca | Franziska |
| Jennifer | Jennifer |
| Jessica | Jessica |
| Joan(na) | Johanna |
| Julia | Julia |
| Katherine | Katharina |
| Laura | Laura |
| Leah | Lea |
| Lena | Lena |
| Lisa | Lisa |
| Louise | Luisa |
| Mary | Maria |
| Martha | Marta |
| Melanie | Melanie |
| Michelle | Michelle |
| Nicole | Nicole |
| Paula | Paula |
| Sarah | Sarah |
| Theresa | Theresia |
| Sophie | Sophia |
| Vanessa | Vanessa |

## NUMBERS 1–100
### Die Zahlen 1–100

| English Englisch | Deutsch German |
| --- | --- |
| one | eins |
| two | zwei |
| three | drei |
| four | vier |
| five | fünf |
| six | sechs |
| seven | sieben |
| eight | acht |
| nine | neun |
| ten | zehn |
| eleven | elf |
| twelve | zwölf |
| thirteen | dreizehn |
| fourteen | vierzehn |
| fifteen | fünfzehn |
| sixteen | sechzehn |
| seventeen | siebzehn |
| eighteen | achtzehn |
| nineteen | neunzehn |
| twenty | zwanzig |
| twenty-one | einundzwanzig |
| twenty-two | zweiundzwanzig |
| twenty-three | dreiundzwanzig |
| twenty-four | vierundzwanzig |
| twenty-five | fünfundzwanzig |
| twenty-six | sechsundzwanzig |
| twenty-seven | siebenundzwanzig |

| | |
|---|---|
| twenty-eight | achtundzwanzig |
| twenty-nine | neununddzwanzig |
| thirty | dreißig |
| forty | vierzig |
| fifty | fünfzig |
| sixty | sechzig |
| seventy | siebzig |
| eighty | achtzig |
| ninety | neunzig |
| one hundred | (ein) hundert |

## AMERICAN-GERMAN CONVERSION TABLES
### WEIGHTS AND MEASURES*
#### Maße und Gewichte

| English<br>Englisch | Deutsch<br>German |
| --- | --- |
| 0.39 inches | 1 Zentimeter |
| 0.62 miles | 1 Kilometer |
| 6.21 miles | 10 Kilometer |
| 0.035 ounces | 1 Gramm |
| 2.20 pounds | 1 Kilogramm |
| 1 inch | 2,54 Zentimeter |
| 1 foot | 30,5 Zentimeter |
| 1 yard | 91,4 Zentimeter |
| 1 mile | 1,61 Kilometer |
| 1 ounce | 28,3 Gramm |
| 1 pound | 453,6 Gramm |

*Approximate.

## PARTS OF SPEECH
*Die Redeteile*

| English<br>Englisch | Deutsch<br>German |
| --- | --- |
| adjective | Adjektiv |
| adverb | Adverb |
| article | Artikel |
| conjunction | Konjunktion |
| idiomatic expression | Ausdruck |
| interjection | Interjektion |
| noun | Substantiv |
| feminine (fem.) | Feminin (Fem.) |
| masculine (masc.) | Maskulin (Mask.) |
| neuter (neut.) | Neutrum (Neut.) |
| preposition | Präposition |
| pronoun | Pronomen |
| verb | Verb |

# German Verb Supplement

*Beispiele Deutscher Verben*

| | Present, Future | Conversational Past, Perfect | Simple Past, Narrative |
|---|---|---|---|
| **haben**  to have | | | |
| ich | habe | habe gehabt | hatte |
| du | hast | hast gehabt | hattest |
| er, sie, es | hat | hat gehabt | hatte |
| wir, sie, Sie | haben | haben gehabt | hatten |
| ihr | habt | habt gehabt | hattet |
| **sein**  to be | | | |
| ich | bin | bin gewesen | war |
| du | bist | bist gewesen | warst |
| er, sie, es | ist | ist gewesen | war |
| wir, sie, Sie | sind | sind gewesen | waren |
| ihr | seid | seid gewesen | wart |
| **kaufen**  to buy | | | |
| ich | kaufe | habe gekauft | kaufte |
| du | kaufst | hast gekauft | kauftest |
| er, sie, es | kauft | hat gekauft | kaufte |
| wir, sie, Sie | kaufen | haben gekauft | kauften |
| ihr | kauft | habt gekauft | kauftet |
| **fahren**  to ride, to go | | | |
| ich | fahre | bin gefahren | fuhr |
| du | fährst | bist gefahren | fuhrst |
| er, sie, es | fährt | ist gefahren | fuhr |
| wir, sie, Sie | fahren | sind gefahren | fuhren |
| ihr | fahrt | seid gefahren | fuhrt |

386

**sehen** to see

| ich | sehe | habe gesehen | sah |
|---|---|---|---|
| du | siehst | hast gesehen | sahst |
| er, sie, es | sieht | hat gesehen | sah |
| wir, sie, Sie | sehen | haben gesehen | sahen |
| ihr | seht | habt gesehen | saht |

**kennenlernen** to get to know

| ich | lerne kennen | habe kennengelernt | lernte kennen |
|---|---|---|---|
| du | lernst kennen | hast kennengelernt | lerntest kennen |
| er, sie, es | lernt kennen | hat kennengelernt | lernte kennen |
| wir, sie, Sie | lernen kennen | haben kennengelernt | lernten kennen |
| ihr | lernt kennen | habt kennengelernt | lerntet kennen |

**sich erkälten** to catch cold

| ich | erkälte mich | habe mich erkältet | erkältete mich |
|---|---|---|---|
| du | erkältest dich | hast dich erkältet | erkältetest dich |
| er, sie, es | erkältet sich | hat sich erkältet | erkältete sich |
| wir | erkälten uns | haben uns erkältet | erkälteten uns |
| ihr | erkältet euch | habt euch erkältet | erkältetet euch |
| sie, Sie | erkälten sich | haben sich erkältet | erkälteten sich |

## Modal Verbs

Usually used with another verb: see dictionary listings with examples

**wollen** to want to

| ich, er, sie, es | will | wir, sie Sie wollen |
|---|---|---|
| du | willst | ihr wollt |

**sollen** should

| ich, er, sie, es | soll | wir, sie, Sie sollen |
|---|---|---|
| du | sollst | ihr sollt |

**dürfen** to be permitted, sie, Sie

| ich, er, sie, es | darf | wir, may dürfen |
| du | darfst | ihr dürft |

**können** to be able to

| ich, er, sie, es | kann | wir, sie, Sie können |
| du | kannst | ihr könnt |

**müssen** to have to, must

| ich, er, sie, es | muss | wir, sie, Sie müssen |
| du | musst | ihr müsst |

---

Note: For beginners the present is like the future, with only the addition of "tomorrow" (*morgen*), "later" (*später*) or similar phrases. The conversational past (perfect) is used in everyday speech about the past. The simple or narrative past is for narrating something.

The verbs directly above (modals) are the most useful of all. Use them with any other verb in its infinitive form (-*en*/-*n*). In addition, there are only four forms!

**German Spoken Here**